THE NATURE CONNECTION

AN OUTDOOR WORKBOOK
for Kids, Families, and Classrooms

Clare Walker Leslie

Illustrations by the author

Storey Publishing

DEDICATED TO THE INHABITANTS OF THE NATURAL WORLD who lured me back outdoors. The book is the culmination of 40 years of exploring, drawing, writing, teaching, raising kids, and sharing a love of nature with all around me. I wish to thank my family for endless, joyful hours being outdoors together. I thank all those who have patiently taken me out and taught me over the years. I thank those wise scientists who reviewed this manuscript. And I thank everyone at Storey Publishing who believe in what I teach and also believe in the importance of connecting people with nature. To my editors, Deborah Balmuth and Lisa Hiley, with the deepest gratitude – it has been a great pleasure and a huge amount of work!

The mission of Storey Publishing is to serve our customers by publishing practical information that encourages personal independence in harmony with the environment.

Edited by Deborah Balmuth and Lisa H. Hiley
Art direction and book design by Jessica Armstrong

Front cover photographs by CSquared Studios/Getty Images: black-eyed Susan; ©iStockPhoto.com: Aleksej Sergejev (leaf), Ivan Ivanov (rock), Mr_Jamsey (cardinal), Tomasz Zachariasz (grasshopper, ants), WieslawFila (acorn); Mars Vilaubi: hand; © Rolf Nussbaumer/Nature Picture Library: butterfly
Back cover photographs by © Joel Sartore/National Geographic Stock: salamander; © 2009 Veer/Corbis: top left, middle left and right; Anna Leslie: author
Illustrations by the author

Indexed by Nancy D. Wood

Storey Publishing is committed to making environmentally responsible manufacturing decisions. This book was printed in the United States on paper made from sustainably harvested fiber.

Storey Publishing
210 MASS MoCA Way
North Adams, MA 01247
www.storey.com

Printed in the United States by Versa Press
10 9 8 7 6 5 4 3 2

Contents

A Note to Kids from Clare

One of the best things a student ever said to me was, "I used to think there was nothing in my backyard, but now I know it's a jungle out there!" I love teaching kids about nature because they are so enthusiastic once they start realizing what a wonderful world is right around them, even if they don't know much about it and even if it is "just" a schoolyard, vacant lot, or back hayfield.

I came to my study of nature knowing nothing. I was a musician and a painter. I spent my days indoors, not roaming about outside. But then I met some people who took me out and showed me amazing dune landscapes and soaring seabirds and fox tracks in the sand. I was hooked.

It's that easy. You can get hooked too. I've written this book to help take you outside, as my friends did for me.

I am self-taught, and you can be too. Everything in this book has come from my own observations, questions, and research. I've spent endless hours drawing and roaming outdoors. My notes and drawings fill 43 journals about nature through the seasons, both where I live and where I travel. I've written a number of books about observing nature, and I love sharing my passion with kids like you.

WHY STUDY NATURE?

When I ask students why we should study nature, they have many wonderful answers, though some of them wonder, "Can't we live without it?" Sometimes we forget we are part of the family of living creatures. We are all connected, and if you look around, you will find relatives who are not just two- or four-legged, but eight-legged or no-legged or even many-legged!

COMMON PLANTAIN

Cardinals, skunks, spiders, centipedes, and snakes all share the air, soil, water, and space called the Web of Life. With all the changes happening to our global ecosystem, it is increasingly important that we learn about nature right near us, so that we understand better what is happening in our own neighborhoods as well as far away from us.

The word "nature" comes from the Latin word *nasci* meaning "to be born." This makes sense, as nature includes everything in the world that is living (and also many things that aren't!). So the study of nature is the study of the world surrounding you and your place in that world. You don't need to know anything about insects, flowers, reptiles, or the weather to begin exploring nature out your doorstep. You don't even need to know what you're looking for!

Hawk chasing pigeons over downtown N. Adams 2/5/10 8:30 a.m.

You do need a little bit of time, the desire to watch things, the ability to notice things, and some patience. Then you need to come back inside and ask questions, read books, do research, and find people to help you find out why and how and what if? You will find many people who share your joy of nature.

I never go out knowing what I am going to find.
The interest is in finding what I didn't know I was going to find.

— **HENRY DAVID THOREAU**

Someone who studies nature is called a "naturalist." You are already a naturalist if you are curious about rocks, trees, birds, ants, weather, or clouds and you want to find out more about what interests you. Becoming a naturalist is all about paying attention, noticing, being curious, and being willing to spend some time outdoors. You may get wet, cold, tired, and bug bitten, but you will also be happy and engaged and learning about your world.

SOME FAMOUS NATURALISTS TO LEARN MORE ABOUT:

* GALILEO (seventeenth century astronomer)

* JOHN JAMES AUDUBON (famous for his paintings and descriptions of American birds)
* HENRY DAVID THOREAU (wrote *Walden*, about living a simple life in nature)
* BEATRIX POTTER (a keen observer of rabbits, fox, mice)

* CHARLES DARWIN (developed the theory of evolution)
* RACHEL CARSON (her book *Silent Spring* helped launch the modern environmental movement)
* EDWARD WILSON (a biologist who probably knows more about ants than anyone in the world)

* JANE GOODALL (knows more about chimpanzees than anyone in the world; founder of Roots and Shoots)
* WANGARI MAATHAI (founder of the Green Belt Movement and winner of the 2004 Nobel Peace Prize)

WHAT'S THIS BOOK ALL ABOUT, ANYWAY?

This book is your place to keep a record of your home — not your actual house or apartment, but the world where you live, which includes all the nature around you. You will learn how to do this over a period of time, to notice and record both the small and large changes going on right in front of you, month after month and season after season.

Scientists use their observations over time to understand how the world works and predict how it might be changing. This is called *phenology* and you can do it too. There are ideas throughout this book that will help you learn more about using phenology right in your own yard, neighborhood, and environment.

This book is my guide to help launch you on the most wonderful adventure I can think of. And it is only just beyond your doorstep. Draw and write directly in this book or just take a few sheets of paper along to record your observations and stick them in the book afterward. Take it with you when you go on a hike. Enjoy using it by yourself, with friends, with your class, with your family, with your pet guinea pig or dog.

Most importantly, go outside and use all your senses to ask questions about, learn about, and appreciate this amazing world that exists all around us! For your first adventure, go outside and figure out why this is true:

"Nature needs us and we need nature."

Happy Exploring!

Clare Walker Leslie

PART ONE

How to Be a Naturalist

Finding Nature Wherever You Are

HOW WE RELATE TO NATURE has a lot to do with where we live, what season it is, and what the weather is like on a given day. No matter where we are, the seasons of the year are always changing, as they have been since the dawn of time. Even in war-torn countries, areas of drought or flood, or places that seem to be made entirely of concrete, the cycle of the natural year is always slowly moving.

These days it's possible to know a lot about nature in far-off places around the world, but sometimes we don't know very much about nature right around us. Here is your chance to become a naturalist, an explorer, a nature detective. If you watch carefully and record your observations, you might discover something that no one else has noticed! Here are lots of ways to study and enjoy nature, no matter what the season or the weather. Use this book to record your notes and drawings (or photos).

It is a wholesome and necessary thing
for us to turn again to the earth and in the contemplation
of her beauties to know of wonder and humility.

—RACHEL CARSON

Pack Your Outdoor Adventure Kit

All you really need for any nature expedition is curiosity, but make sure your clothing, including shoes, fits the weather. Take a snack and a reusable water bottle if you like. You can also take the following:

Observing and Recording

Scientists around the world are studying, testing, and observing many aspects of how our world's climate and environment are changing. But what you may not know is that much knowledge comes from the careful observations of many other people as well. You too can be part of this great study!

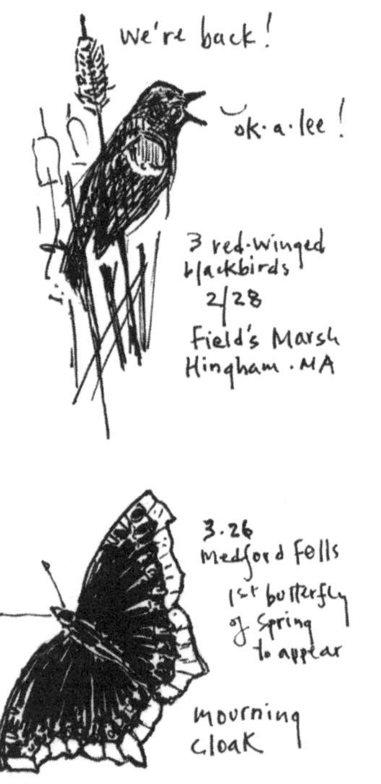

To keep good scientific records or journals, naturalists use the same form to make sure that they don't miss anything that might be changing from day to day. The record sheets used throughout this book are variations of phenology charts that I use in my teaching.

Phenology is the study of the seasonal timing of life cycle events. You are doing phenology when you record the date that a certain plant flowers, an insect hatches, or a migratory bird appears in its nesting grounds.

Factors such as length of day, temperature, and rainfall affect the dates on which these events happen each year. By tracking the timing of seasonal changes, you can see how climate, weather, and temperature are changing the patterns of nature.

Different people like to record information in different ways. I hope you will use this book to learn what works best for you. Experiment with the different forms in the book and then copy the ones that fit your style.

SETTING UP YOUR NATURE JOURNAL NOTES

I've included many different types of journal pages throughout this book. You can use any or all of them, or make up your own to suit your style of study. A good entry includes information on when, where, what, and why. It should also have questions, drawings, and sometimes objects collected from your observations.

Whatever format you chose, here are the suggested points to note and questions to ask:

Describe what you see with as much detail as possible.

* What am I looking at?
* What is it doing?
* How does it move, sound, smell, even feel or taste, if appropriate?

bank swallows are back! over the pond

Think about connections.

* Why is this (animal, plant, rock formation) here?
* What else is living nearby?
* How can it live in this place or how did it come to be here?

x 3/4

raccoon tracks in mud

Consider the big picture.

* What can I learn from it?
* How does it relate to my world?
* What more would I like to learn about this?

earthworm castings in mud

Who Lives Beside You?

Make a list of nature in the area where you live. You can list things you have seen or that you know about. For example, I know we have raccoons but I don't often see them. Be as specific as you can.

If you don't know the name of a bird, plant, or insect, be a detective and try to find out. The animals you see will vary from season to season, and in different places, so always note the date, time, and place on your observation records. Keep adding to your list as you explore and discover more outdoors. Make the list as long as you want. As the seasons change, you'll discover new things.

SAMPLE LIST

- robin
- cardinal
- maple tree (sugar)
- ants
- worms
- ladybug
- coyote
- raccoon
- white-tailed deer
- fox (red)
- skunk
- salamander
- green frogs
- little fish in stream
- hawk (what kind?)
- dandelion
- tulips
- clover
- flock of starlings
- snake (copperhead?)
- crow
- pigeons on roof
- black bear
- herring gull
- pine tree
- hemlock
- oak tree, lots of acorns
- monarch butterfly
- mosquito
- yellow jacket

More Things to Do

* **See how many different things you can list** and have a little competition with your family or friends.
* **See how your list differs** from a cousin or friend who lives far away.
* **Write a report** or use your list as spelling words.

NATURE AROUND ME

WHAT I SAW	WHAT I SAW	WHAT I SAW
1.	13.	25.
2.	14.	26.
3.	15.	27.
4.	16.	28.
5.	17.	29.
6.	18.	30.
7.	19.	31.
8.	20.	32.
9.	21.	33.
10.	22.	34.
11.	23.	35.
12	24.	36.

To print out more pages like this, go to *www.storey.com/thenatureconnection.php.*

Watch Nature for a Week

You can follow in the tradition of the great explorers who kept science journals. If keeping a daily record is too much at first, start by keeping your journal for one week. Just write down a note or two every day about what you see or notice about nature. It doesn't have to be long, just don't miss a day!

SAMPLE LIST

February 16	I went outside and it wasn't very pleasant. It was around 29–33°F out there. It was damp and there was a cold southern wind. The trees look bare and I am waiting for baseball weather.
February 17	More of the same today . . .
February 18	It is about ready to rain or snow or something. You can see the clouds building up. I don't want to go outside.
February 19	There might be a little more rain . . .
February 20	Finally a nice day! Basketball, basketball, basketball! Yippee! There are birds singing and the sun is shining.

More Things to Do

* **Make this a family or class project.** Get a notebook just for nature observing and take turns recording each week. See if you can do this for a whole month — or a whole year! One school I visited gave a bound copy of the year's nature records to parents as a final report for the year.

MY NATURE NOTES

DATE	NOTES

To print out more pages like this, go to *www.storey.com/thenatureconnection.php.*

Nature Is Full of Surprises!

These short poems by the seventeenth century Japanese poet Matsuo Basho beautifully capture one small moment — a nature surprise.

"Red pepper pods!
Add wings to them,
And they are dragonflies."

"On a withered branch
a crow has settled —
autumn nightfall."

Every day, no matter where you live, you can see small, amazing things in nature. You can spot them waiting for the school bus, running into a store, or walking the dog. You can even be surprised in your house, like finding a spider in the shower!

oops! what am I doing here?

Sitting at my desk on a cold, dark,
December afternoon, I look out the window
and see a squirrel staring back at me.

I just smile. I think he smiles back,
shakes his tail, and leaps off the roof.

What fun! I feel refreshed.

Nature can be a healer. If you are having a bad day for some reason, maybe you flunked a test or had a fight with a friend or are just bored to tears on a car trip, look out and find something in nature that takes you away for a moment. These unexpected moments of wonder are free, simple, unexpected, and often happen quickly, so keep your eyes peeled and your senses alert.

NATURE SURPRISES YOU MIGHT FIND

* Late afternoon light on winter trees
* The squeak of snow on a bitterly cold day
* The flash of a red cardinal through green leaves

* The smell of a leaf rubbed between your fingers
* A red-tailed hawk sailing over city streets

* The feel of the warm sun on your face
* Mist rising from a pond
* Sun emerging from behind the clouds
* The sound of the wind on a stormy night

* A skunk waddling across the lawn
* A lacy pattern of ice on a puddle
* Two crows watching as you go into the mall

Enjoying Nature Surprises

What nature surprises have you encountered today? Any birds? A pretty sky? A flower? A tree shape? A special rock? An unusual sound?

SAMPLE LIST

4/12 at 6:30 p.m.	Full moon rising over the river, on the way home
4/13 at 5:15 p.m.	Pink clouds from the kitchen window
4/14 at 7:30 a.m.	A line of ants on the sidewalk while walking Max
4/15 at 7:30 a.m.	Robin singing in the front yard tree next door
4/16 at 7:35 a.m.	Pigeons flying around the parking lot in big swooping circles
4/17 at 1:30 p.m.	Sound of rain on the windows; strong NE wind blowing

More Things to Do

* **Share your favorite nature surprise** with your family at dinner, then go around the table and ask everyone to share a surprise.
* **See if you can spot one nature surprise every day** and keep a list for a whole year, no matter where you are.
* **Exchange nature surprises with a friend** (it's okay to e-mail or text).
* **You can draw your nature surprise or take a photo** if you're quick enough. See how your attention to nature's small ways improves over time. Mine certainly has!

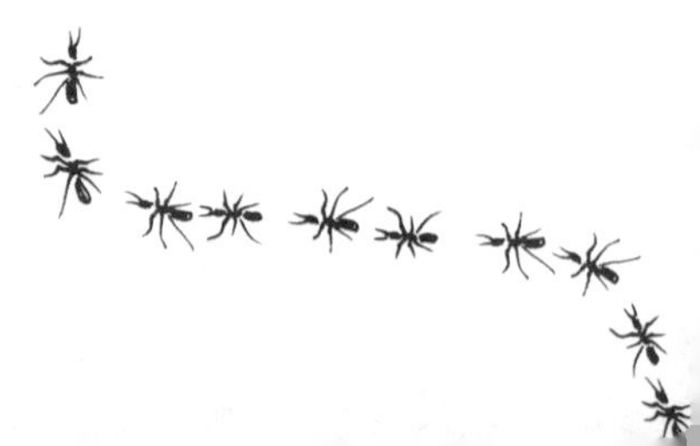

MY NATURE SURPRISE LIST

DATE AND TIME	THE SURPRISE

To print out more pages like this, go to *www.storey.com/thenatureconnection.php.*

Play the Nature Game

I often play a game I call "Where Is Nature?" when I am going for a walk, looking out a window, or on a trip. It's a diversion from the sometimes boring business of shopping, running errands, sitting at a stoplight, and all the everyday things we must do.

It's like "License Plate Bingo" or "I Spy." All these games tune the eyes, help you take notice, and are fun. You can play this game in familiar and unfamiliar places: the desert, mountains, highway, farm country, seacoast, suburbia, city.

This is my list for Cambridge, Massachusetts, November 20, 3:00 p.m., while walking the dog:

1. Dark early; sun will set before 4:30 p.m.
2. Trees mostly bare
3. Colors of this day: browns, dark greens, orange/yellows, gray, lavenders
4. Cold wind from the North, but sky very blue
5. Long afternoon shadows across lawns and buildings
6. Starlings in flocks, chattering high in maples. What are they doing?
7. I hear one, slow cricket, in long grasses!
8. Brown leaves, fallen, everywhere on sidewalks, rustling sounds
9. Some marigolds, chrysanthemums, pansies, roses blooming in protected yards
10. Robins madly eating crab apples and chokecherries

Find ten (or more!) nature things happening right near you and list them here. Record details of time, place, and weather. (If you need a project for school, you could turn this list into an essay, a report, even a poem or short story.)

1. ______

2. ______

3. ______

4. ______

5. ______

6. ______

7. ______

8. ______

9. ______

10. ______

______

Find a Favorite Spot

We should all have a secret spot where we can go to think and be alone. Find a place for yourself that you can visit often. You might find it leaning against a big tree, sitting on a rock near a flowing stream, or lying on a hillside. It doesn't have to be too far away from home, but if you can, and you feel comfortable, go out of sight of any buildings.

Go there whenever you can and spend time just enjoying and watching the outdoors. Bring a book and read, collect some discoveries, climb a tree, draw or take notes if you wish.

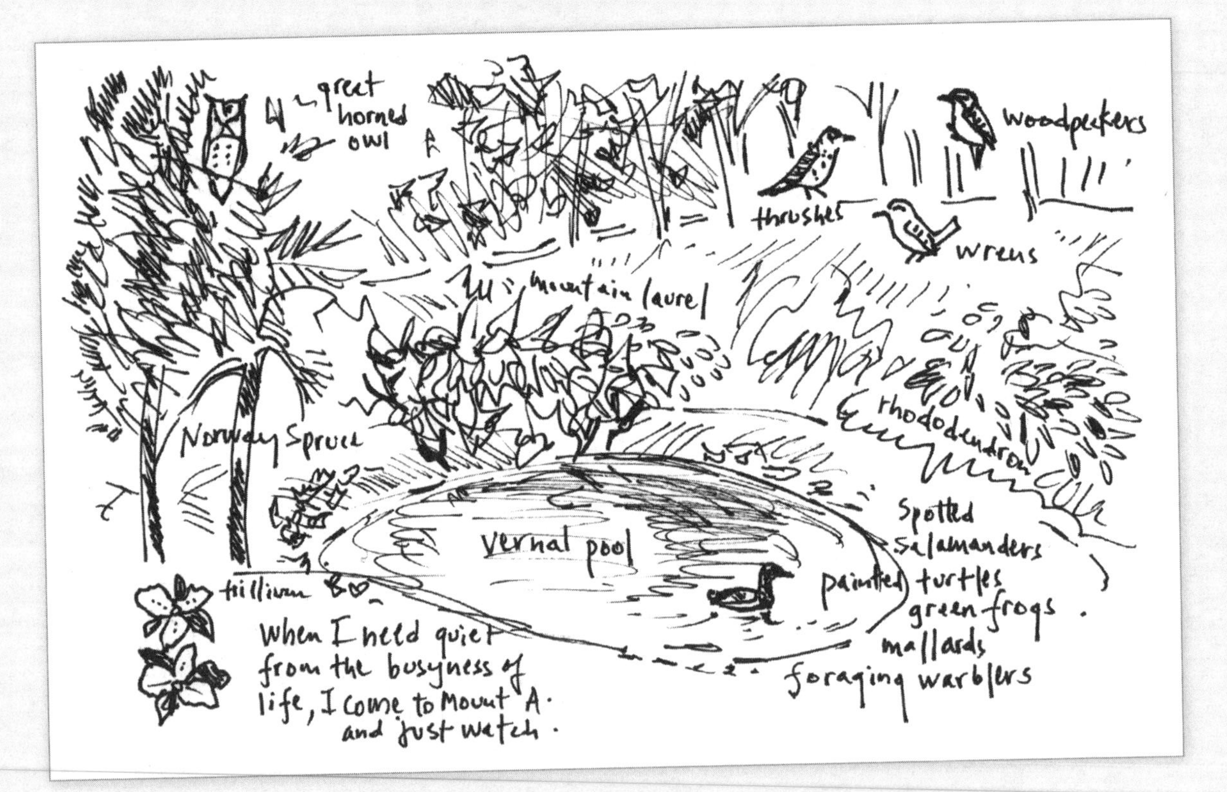

For over 30 years, my favorite spot has been a dell in Mount Auburn Cemetery, which is a wooded and hilly piece of pastoral landscape within our city's limits. There I see coyote, fox, owls, hawks, raccoon, multitudes of birds, and only a few people, just a mile away from my home.

Make a Nature Arrangement

Go on a nature expedition around your neighborhood and collect seeds, leaves, seedpods, fruits, wildflowers, feathers, pine needles, and other little bits of nature. Make sure it's okay to do this where you are. Some places, like national and state parks, are protected so people can't take away bits of them, but your own backyard or neighborhood is a great place to collect things.

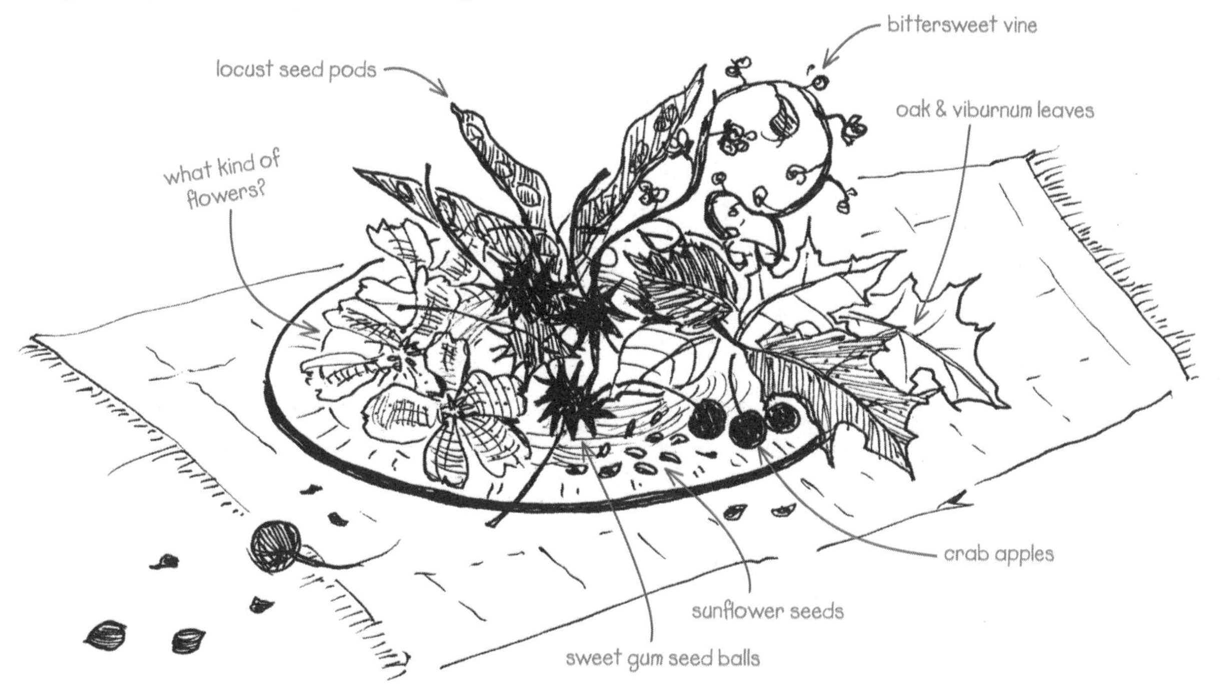

When you get home, make a nature arrangement and put it on a table for your family to enjoy. Have everyone gather around the table so you can tell them what each thing is and where you found it. If you picked up something that you can't identify (like a tree leaf), see if you can find out what kind of tree it came from. (Read about making a naturalist's cabinet on page 216.)

Write a Nature Poem

Go outdoors for 15 minutes and just walk around for a little bit. Don't talk, just watch and listen. See if you can become part of nature around you.

Think about these questions: What is happening around you at this time of day? What is the weather like? What season is it? What do you hear? Where is it coming from? How does being here make you feel? Why? What other wild things live here? What might they be doing? Where do they spend the night?

Now find a place to sit down and write a short poem about this place.

SAMPLE POEM

I hear the leaves blowing
The sky is colored gold
with the sun.
I could sleep here if my
mom would let me.

Some Other Ideas to Write About

* Why do you like being outdoors?
* What do you already know about nature?
* What are you curious about? What would you like to know more about?
* If you could save one thing in the environment, what would it be? Why?
* What's your favorite thing to do outdoors?
* If you could be an animal, what would it be and why?

When I am out in nature, I am happy. I didn't think I would be!

— A STUDENT

Tell a Story about Nature

Taking notes and filling in charts isn't the only way to keep a record of nature. It's important to remember your place in the world and think about what nature means to you. Try this writing activity:

Tell the first story that comes into your head about a time in nature you remember — scary, funny, exciting. Where were you? Were you alone or with friends? How old were you?

Tell the first story that comes into your head.

Interview family and friends and ask them, "What is your very first memory of being outdoors?"

I can think of a time when I was hiking in snowy woods and got lost as it was getting dark. I found I was going in circles, following porcupine tracks. How did I get unlost? By retracing my snowshoe tracks!

To print out more pages like this, go to *www.storey.com/thenatureconnection.php.*

The Colors of the Seasons

Have you ever noticed how the color of the sky, the trees, the earth, and the sun change with the months, weather, even time of day?

What color is the sky in different seasons?

____

Is it a different color in winter?

____

What month of the year is the greenest where you live?

____

The bluest? The orangest? The brownest?

____

Make a color wheel of the seasons. Use paint, colored pencils, or crayons to color in this circle to show the seasons or months as you see the colors of each to be. This is a fun project to do as a group. Put your heads together to think of all the colors that you see in each season.

I find it enough to follow the seasons.

— **HENRY DAVID THOREAU**

MY COLOR WHEEL OF THE SEASONS

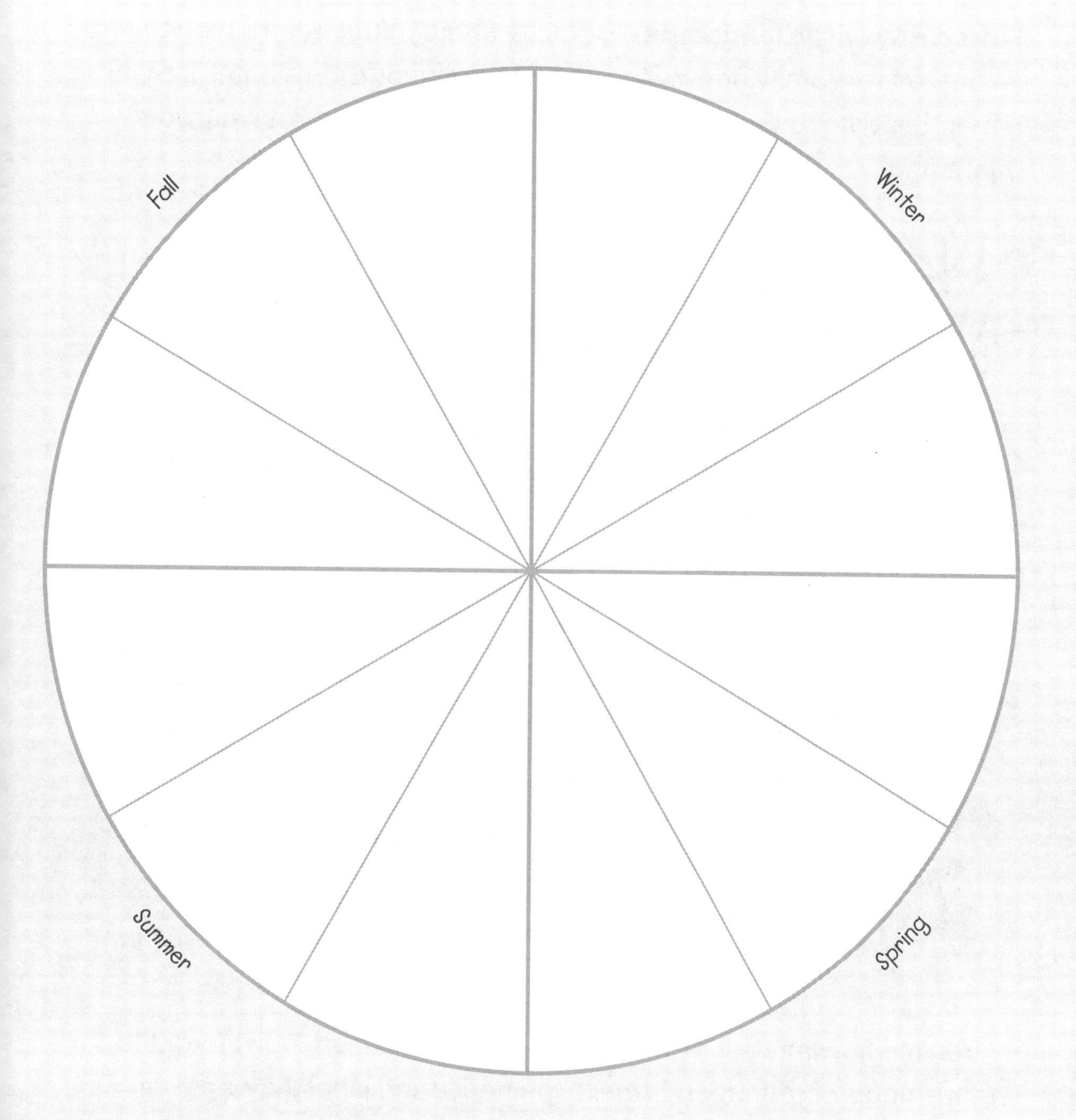

To print out more pages like this, go to *www.storey.com/thenatureconnection.php.*

Take a Closer Look

I often draw little landscapes in places where nature seems hard to find — out a classroom window, along a highway, or outside a hotel. Do you remember *Where's Waldo?* If you look, you'll be surprised at what you might find!

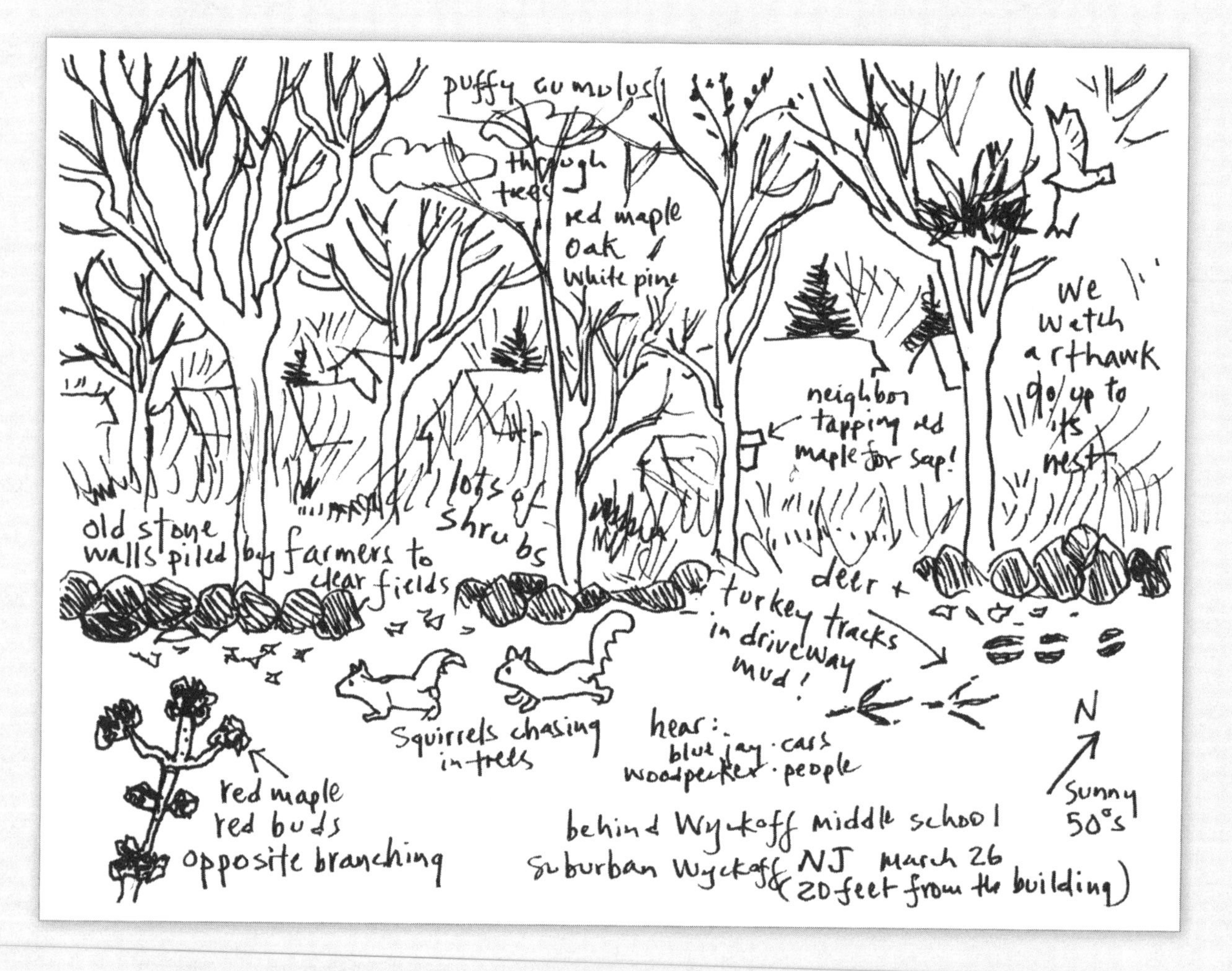

You might want to start with the sky and work down. Don't forget to include notes of sounds and smells you notice and label things as I've done above. See page 190 for how to draw a landscape.

Make your landscape drawing here.

Date: Place: Time:

A Quick Drawing Lesson!

Drawing is an important way of seeing. Before the invention of cameras, it was the only way naturalists could keep visual records of what they saw. The more you practice looking closely at an object, the easier you will find it is to draw. Anyone can learn to draw, but like any skill, it takes time and it helps to know a few techniques. Here is how I teach kids to draw in my classes.

DRAWING ONE — BLIND CONTOUR

Place your pencil or pen on the paper and look at the object you want to draw — a cloud, a leaf, a piece of fruit. Without taking your eyes off the object, start drawing, making one continuous line as you go. Don't look at the paper and don't lift your pencil or pen! Take only one minute!

Here's what my pumpkin looked like when I drew it this way. Your drawing will look goofy —so does mine! But this exercise really gets you looking, which is important.

All artists do this when they are learning to draw.

Some people call these "creepy crawly" or "bug" drawings because of the way the pen or pencil roams over the page.

Put your blind contour drawings here.

Date: Place: Time:

DRAWING TWO — MODIFIED CONTOUR

This time, you can look back and forth from the thing you're drawing to your paper, but still don't lift your pencil. Just keep on drawing the shape *without taking your pencil off the paper* until you're completely finished. This is called a modified contour drawing.

Here's what my PUMPKIN looked like when I drew it this way.

I use modified contours for slow moving animals like FROGS or SALAMANDERS . . .

. . . or a BIRD perched at a feeder.

Put your modified contour drawings here.

Date: Place: Time:

DRAWING THREE — QUICK SKETCH

Now make some quick drawings, using only a few lines to show the basic shape or feeling of what you're seeing. You can improve your sketch into a finished drawing later if you like.

My quick sketches:

5 seconds

20 seconds

Many things in nature move fast, and this is a very useful exercise to practice capturing a bird as it flies by or a leaf blowing in the wind.

10 seconds

10 seconds

Put your quick sketches here.

Date: Place: Time:

DRAWING FOUR — FIELD SKETCHES

When scientists are out in the field, they usually don't have time to make detailed drawings. They may not be able to collect specimens, and while they can take photos, many botanists, geologists, entomologists, and ornithologists also rely on field sketches to illustrate what they observe.

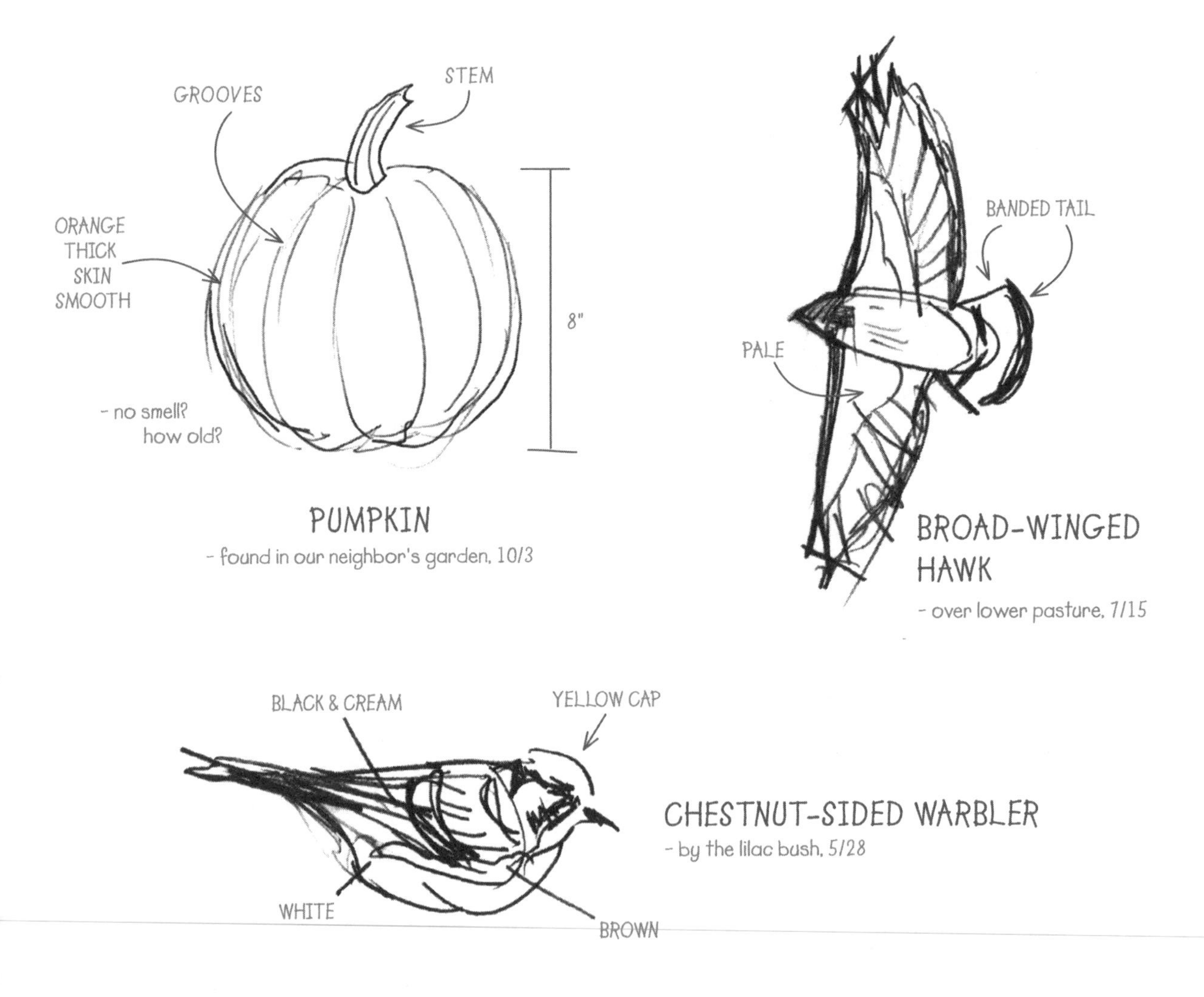

(See pages 44–45 for examples of some field sketches in a journal.)

Put your field sketches here.

Here are some prompts to use:

* size?
* shape?
* color?
* texture?
* smell?
* what is it?
* where is it?
* what is it doing?

Date: Place: Time:

DRAWING FIVE — FINISHED DRAWINGS

These drawings can take from 10 minutes to 10 hours to complete. Learning to draw takes time and technique, and you can find many other books that will teach you more. For now, just have fun and do the best you can. The important thing is to really see and learn about the object you are drawing.

You can also draw from photographs in books or magazines (or take your own), from pictures you find online, from observing animals at a petting farm or zoo, or even from mounted exhibits at a science museum. But always keep your eyes open for spotting nature around you and enjoy being a nature detective wherever you are!

Put your finished drawings here.

Date: Place: Time:

Go on a Field Trip

It's time for a treasure hunt! Find a place outside your house or nearby where you can sit and be totally quiet. Pretend you are invisible, or that you are one of the plants or animals. Shhhhhh!

Down among the cobwebs, at the roots of grass,
Green and creepy quiet, dewy beads of glass,
Little spiders spinning, beetles bumbling through . . .

— NANCY DINGMAN WATSON

After a few minutes of silent watching and listening, start making notes. Think about what month it is and look for clues to the season.

Colors you see.

____

____

____

____

____

____

Can you see:

- Dark green
- Light green
- Pink
- Yellow
- Brown

To print out more pages like this, go to *www.storey.com/thenatureconnection.php.*

An Outdoor Field Expedition

This is an example of my observations from a class with 4th grade students. These notes and drawings were all done outdoors while standing up and moving around.

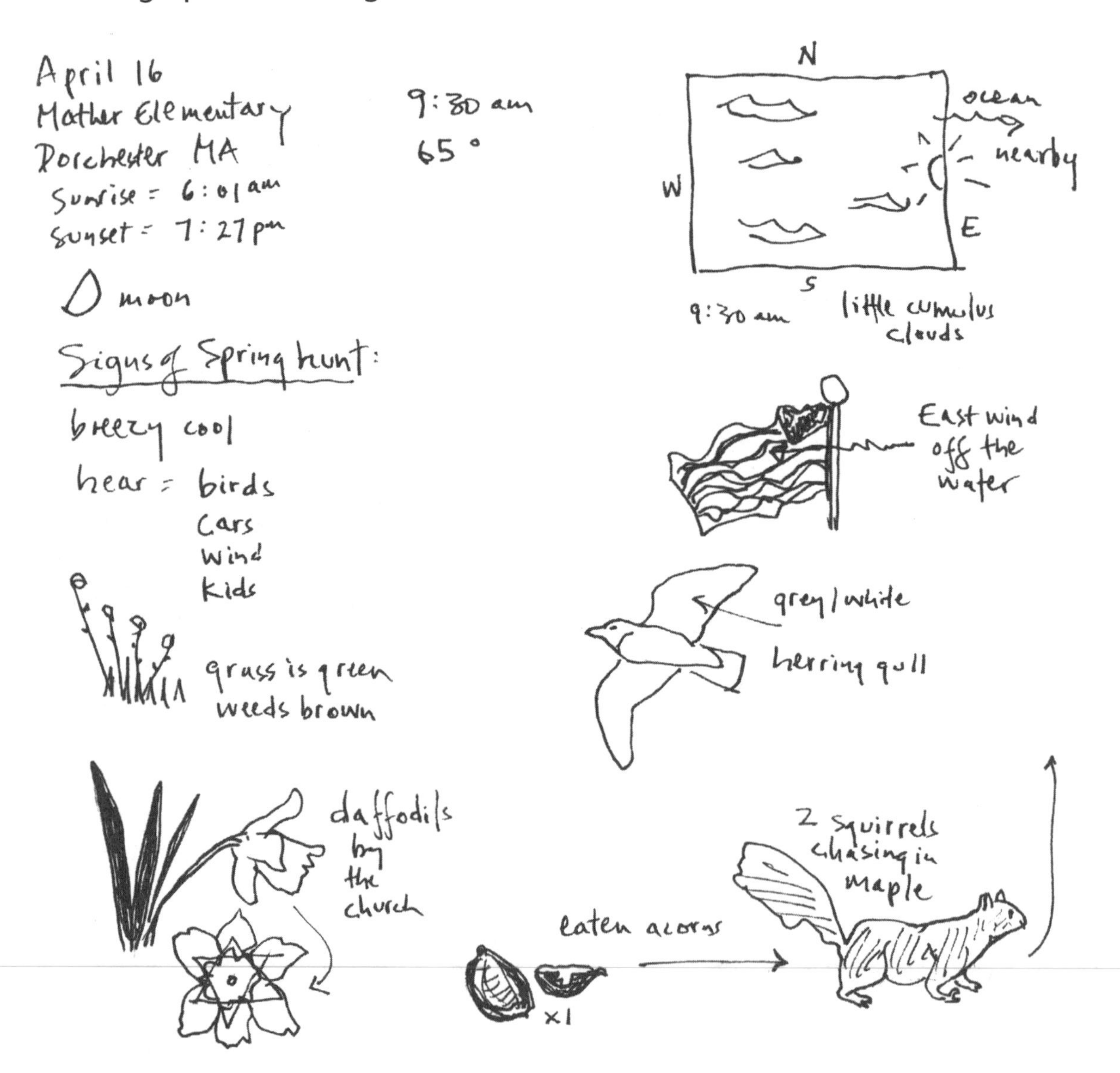

You can see that my drawings are quick and simple. Yours should be too. Don't worry about how well you draw. It's all about how well you look and see!

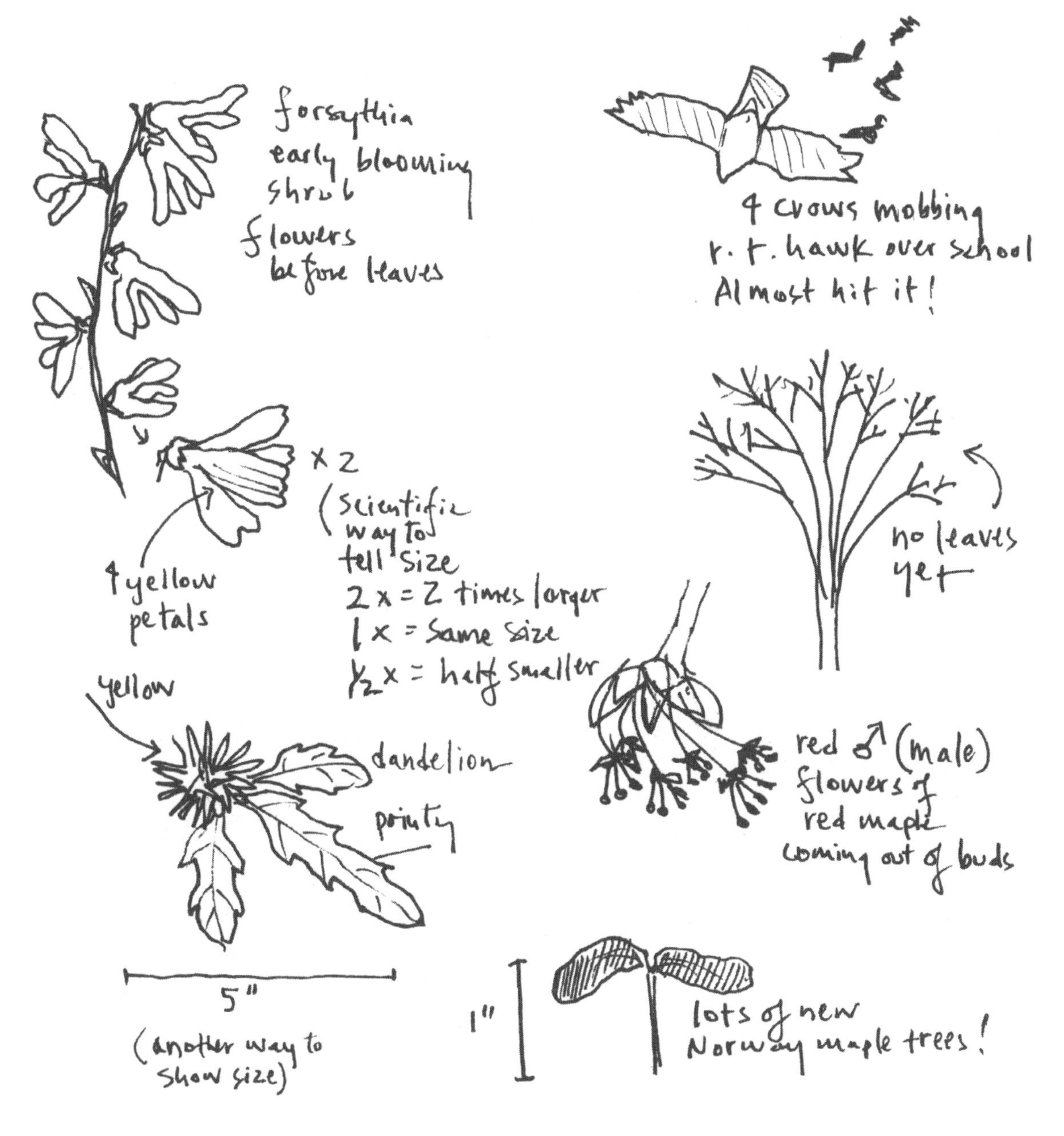

Your Outdoor Field Expedition

You can go on your own field expedition any time of day, in any season, and any kind of weather, by yourself or with family and friends. You can pack a full adventure kit (see page 9) or just grab a notebook and a pencil and take off. (Just make sure someone knows where you're going and when you'll be back.)

Use these pages to record your notes and drawings.

PART TWO

Learning the Sky

Its Cycles and Seasons

THE SKY IS ALWAYS CHANGING, from sunny to cloudy, rainy to snowy, and from night to dawn to dusk. No matter where you are, you can always look up at the sky. Sometimes when I'm in a big city or a place where I don't feel very comfortable, I'll just look up at the clouds floating overhead and think about how those shapes have been seen by people of all eras, from prehistoric times to the great ages of exploration and from the industrial age to modern times.

The sky is a good place to start thinking about nature's endless cycles. No matter what people are doing on and to Earth, our planet continues to move in its orbit around the sun. Day and night come every 24 hours, the moon waxes and wanes over the course of a month, and the seasons come and go, bringing great changes in the weather as the year passes. Even as we learn more about how human activity is affecting the climate, the fundamental cycles remain the same.

Red sky at night, sailors delight —
Red sky at morning, sailors take warning.

— OLD PROVERB

Try This Exercise — Sky Samples

Make a series of boxes. Draw in the sky over your head, wherever you are, over several days or weeks at different times. See how the light, clouds, and colors change. Be sure to write the time of day and the date.

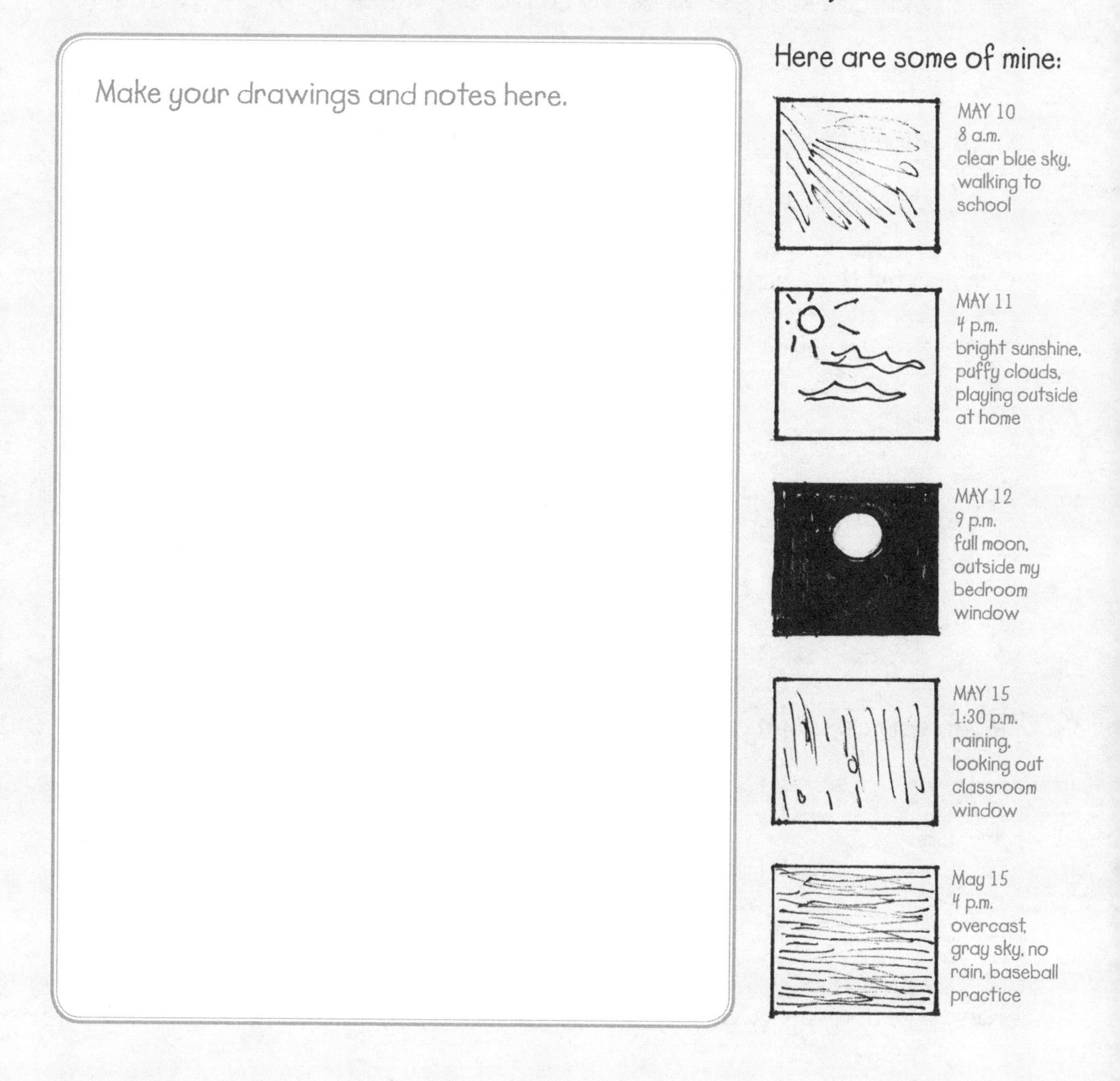

Look! Up in the Sky!

Step outside and look up. What do you see in the sky?

Write what you see here. Birds? An airplane? Clouds? Blowing leaves?

___

What color is the sky? Try to use more adjectives than "blue."

___

Can you tell the weather by what's happening in the sky?

___

___

Can you feel the wind? Which way do you turn to face into it?

___

___

Which way do you turn to find the sun? How high in the sky is it?

___

___

For more ideas on looking at the sky, visit *www.forspaciousskies.com.*

Draw a picture of the sky in this box.

Date: Place: Time:

Learn to Read Clouds

People used to be able to look up at the clouds and know what the weather was going to be. I knew a farmer in Vermont who would sit for long hours on his porch watching the clouds pile up or spread out across his pastures. He could tell when the rain was coming, which meant he needed to get his hay in. He could smell the difference between oncoming rain and the dry air. Can you do that?

There are three basic types of clouds: cirrus, cumulus, and stratus. Cirrus clouds are thin and wispy and spread out high in the sky. Cumulus clouds are the ones that look like giant cotton balls. Stratus clouds form in the lower atmosphere and spread in layers over most or all of the sky. Some clouds are a combination of these types (see my sketches on the next page).

More Things to Do

* **Find a field guide to weather and clouds** in your library or bookstore and learn more about cloud shapes. You can also go online to weather and cloud sites.
* **Record what clouds appear most often** where you live and see if you can figure out how they affect the weather around you: rain, fog, snow, sleet, sun, hail, hurricane, tornado.
* **Learn where the weather fronts** usually come into your area from around the country.
* **Watch the wind and determine its direction.** How does this affect cloud pileup and weather changes?

CLUES IN THE CLOUDS: What's the Weather Going to Be?

FAIR
no clouds means good weather

CIRRUS
high and wispy, "mare's tails" – possible change in weather

CIRROCUMULUS
small ripples, covering sky, "mackerel sky" – usually means fair but cold

ALTOCUMULUS
with planes leaving contrails – fair weather

CUMULONIMBUS
tall, puffy, sometimes dark – possible rain, thunder, lightning

STRATUS
low, thick layers across the sky – fog or mist

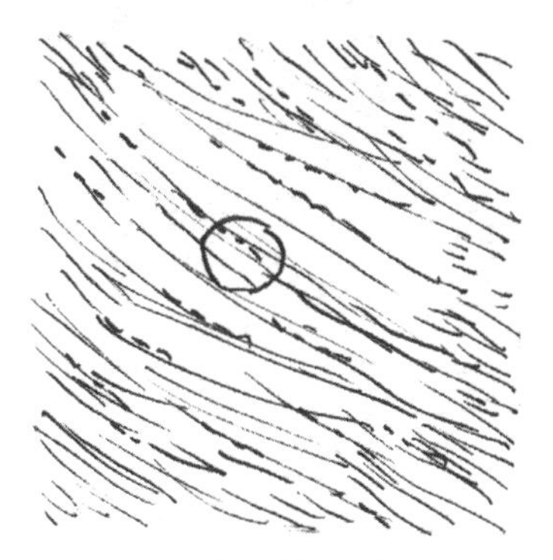

ALTOSTRATUS
high layers across the sky, haze – precipitation coming

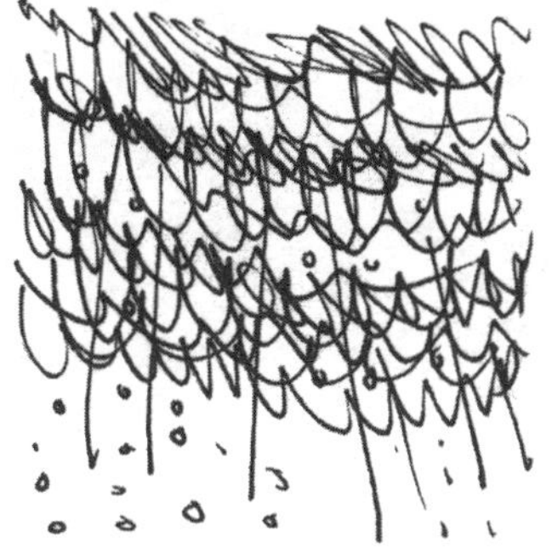

NIMBOSTRATUS
gray, cover the whole sky – rain, sleet, snow is falling!

Can you see clouds at night?

The Sky and the Weather: The Big Picture

The sky tells us a great deal about the weather — after all, that's where the weather comes from, in the form of sun, rain, snow, wind, and more. Sometimes the weather stays the same for days on end, but it can change dramatically in just a few hours. Sometimes it rains in the morning and is sunny in the afternoon.

Studying and predicting the weather is fun, and it has always been an important skill. The weather affects many people such as farmers, fishermen, construction workers, and others who work outdoors. You can use the chart on the next page to monitor changes in the weather over a whole week. Just make copies to keep records for a month or longer.

Someone who studies and reports on the weather is called a meteorologist, even though they don't study meteors (that's an astronomer!). Visit the National Weather Service (*www.nws.noaa.gov*) or the World Meteorological Organization (*www.wmo.int*) to learn more about weather.

Hurricanes are gigantic water and sky combinations

MY WEATHER WATCH WORKSHEET

DATE	TEMPERATURE		WEATHER	ANIMAL/PLANT ACTIVITY	WHAT I DID OUTSIDE
	MAX	MIN			

To print out more pages like this, go to *www.storey.com/thenatureconnection.php.*

Make a Weather Map of Where You Live

I live by the Atlantic Ocean in eastern Massachusetts. The ocean brings in lots of moisture, but it also helps cool the air in the summer. We have four distinct seasons, with hot summers and cold winters. Here's a map that shows how the land where I live is affected by the weather.

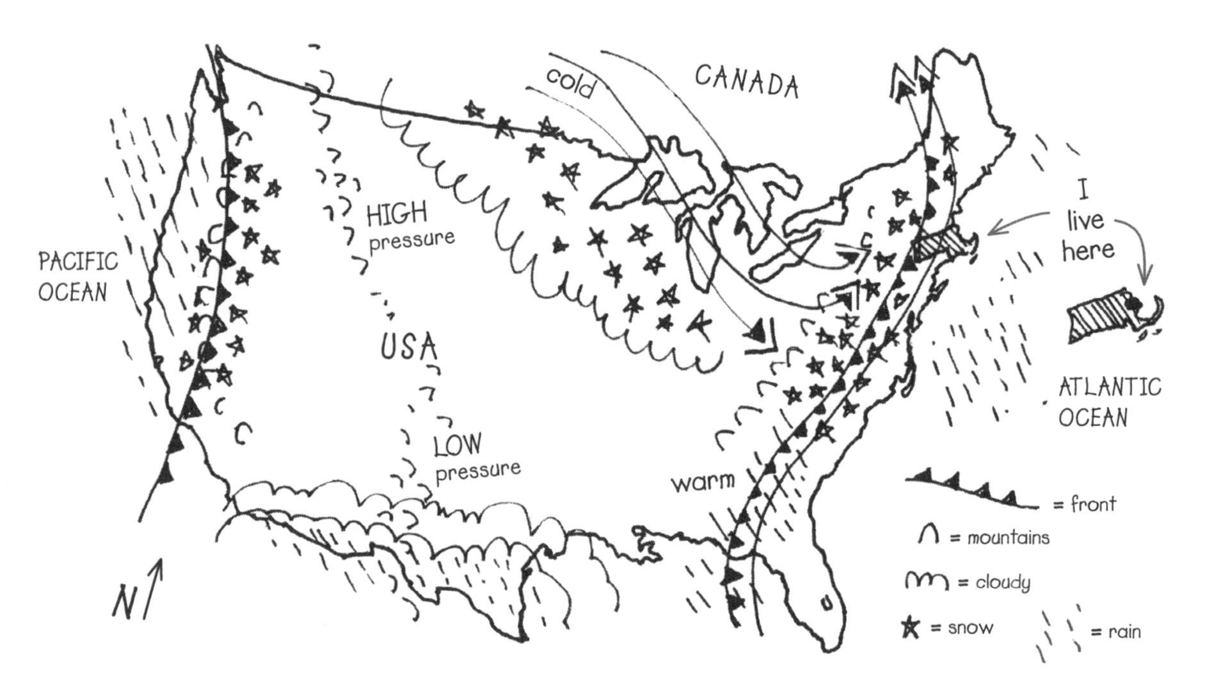

WEATHER FACTS

* The highest temperature ever recorded was 136°F (57.8°C) in Libya in 1922.
* The lowest was ⁻128.6°F (⁻89.2°C) at Vostok Station in the Antarctic in 1983.
* Between February 19, 1971, and February 18, 1972, 102 feet (31.1m) of snow fell on Mount Rainier in Washington State.
* The heaviest hailstone on record weighed 2.25 pounds (1.0kg); it fell in Bangladesh in 1986.

Draw your own weather map of your area. Are you near woodlands, mountains, prairies, lakes, the ocean, or desert? How does the place where you live influence the weather?

Why Is the Sky Blue?

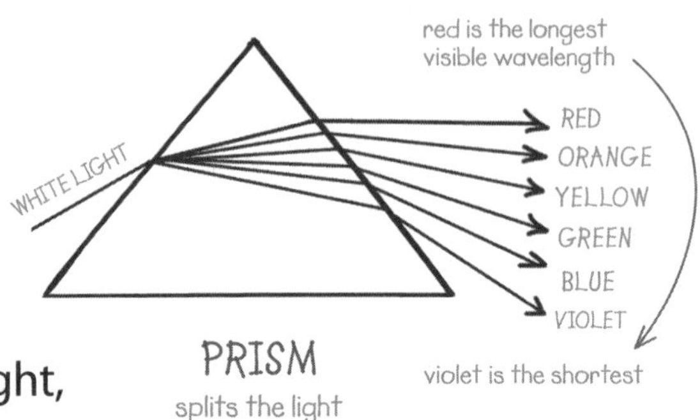

The light coming from the sun is made up of all the colors of the rainbow. We usually see the colors as white because they blend together, but if you put a prism up to the light, it separates the light into different colors.

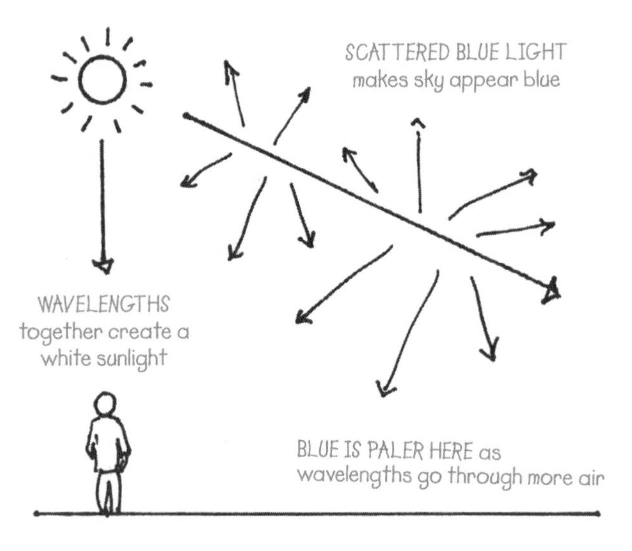

Most of the colors travel in various wavelengths straight through the *atmosphere* (the air surrounding Earth). The blue light, which is made of shorter wavelengths, becomes scattered as it bumps into dust and gas particles. Because the blue light is going in all different directions, rather than coming straight down, the sky looks blue.

WHY IS THE NIGHT SKY BLACK?

At night, no scattered light from the sun reaches your eyes. The absence of sunlight appears as black. Still, there is some light coming from the moon (which reflects light from the sun), the stars (which are actually extremely distant suns giving forth their own light), and the planets (which also reflect light from the sun).

If it's rainy, cloudy, or foggy, of course, you won't be able to see these sky lights. But often, even in the city, you can find the moon, some stars, and a planet or two. (Learn more about the moon on pages 72–79 and about the stars on pages 82–85.)

WHY IS THE SKY RED AT DAWN AND DUSK?

In the morning and evening when the sun is low in the sky, its light must take a longer path through the atmosphere to reach your eyes. Because of this, the red, orange, and yellow colors are scattered by pollutants, dust, and water droplets. The intensity and variety of colors depend on the amount of particulates, including moisture, in the atmosphere. As the sun rises and those colors travel a shorter distance through the atmosphere, the direct light appears white.

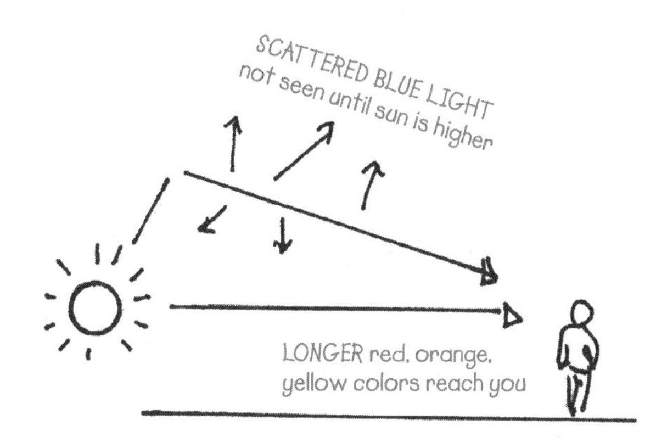

As the sun sets, few greens and blues appear, leaving the reds and yellows remaining. After the sun has set, the sky appears darker and darker blue because you are now seeing only a little bit of blue wavelengths scattering and none of the reds, oranges, and yellows.

WHY DO WE SEE RAINBOWS?

If you are between the sun and the rain droplets in the sky (which may still be falling to the ground), each drop acts like a prism and scatters light back to you. What you see are the different colors of light now separating into layers of color. As the sun shifts, the rainbow disappears.

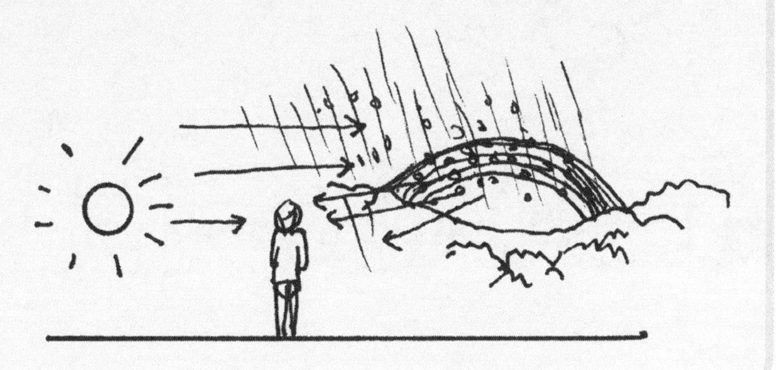

How Does the Sun "Move" through the Sky?

During the day, it sure looks like the sun is moving across the sky. It's not in the same place at 9:00 a.m., noon, 3:00 p.m., or 6:00 p.m., is it? But the sun is not actually moving! It's our planet Earth that is moving, little by little, around the sun in a gigantic, uneven elliptical (oval) orbit.

As it travels around the sun, the earth also turns on its own axis, completing one rotation every 24 hours. As the different areas of the planet face away from or toward the sun, they experience night and day. To make it more complicated, the earth is tilted on its axis 23½ degrees. This tilt gives us our seasons over the course of the year.

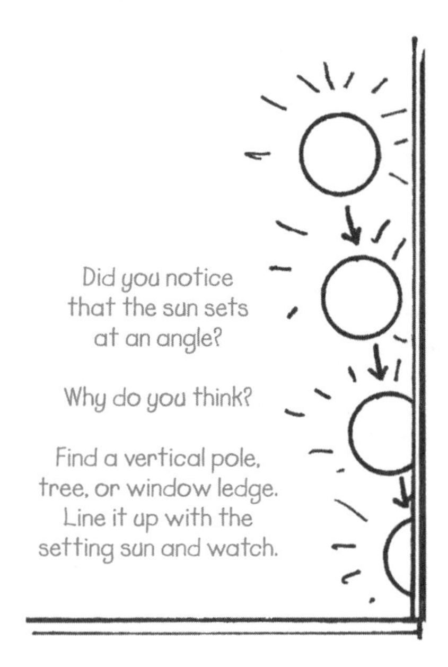

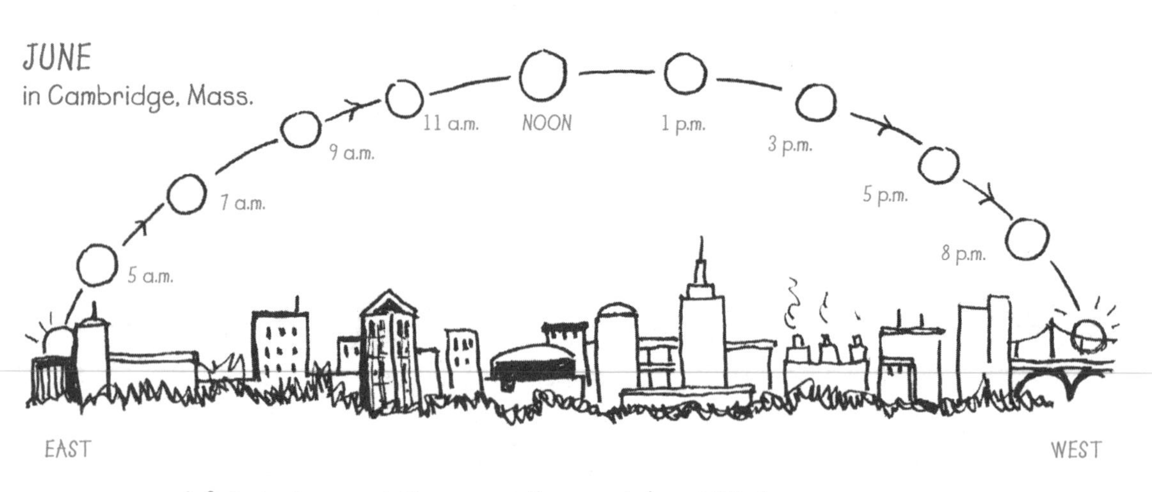

A full circle or orbit around the sun takes 365 days or one year.

REASONS FOR THE SEASONS

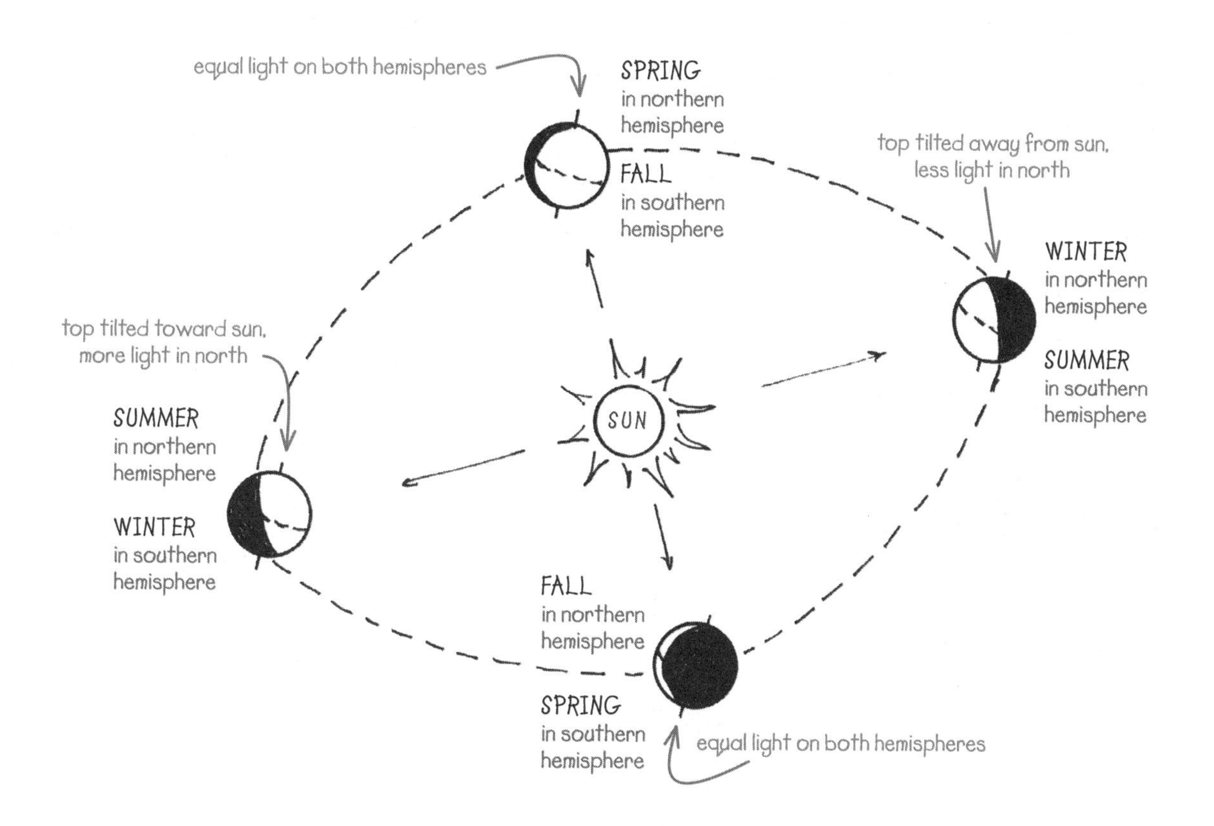

SUN FACTS

* The sun is actually a star – a gigantic ball of burning gas, 93 million miles away. If it were hollow, over one million Earths could fit inside it!
* The temperature at the surface of the sun is 6,000°C (11,000°F).
* Periodically the sun releases great bursts of energy called "solar flares," which can be powerful enough to disrupt satellites. Solar flares interact with the earth's magnetic field to produce auroras, the amazing displays known as the northern and southern lights.

Sunrise, Sunset

Did you know that the times when the sun rises and the sun sets are slightly different every day? And they're different in different locations too. Chart the time of sunrise and sunset where you live every day for one month. You can look up the times for sunrise and sunset where you live, using the Internet, the newspaper, or Farmer's Almanac. Notice how much daylight is lost or gained each day, throughout the month. (You can also do this for a whole year with a friend in another part of the world and then compare your records.)

ABOVE THE ARCTIC CIRCLE

I once spent some time camping above the Arctic Circle in June. We had daylight for 24 hours! That far north, the sun circles above the horizon from early May to late July and never sets.

ARCTIC SUMMER – the sun never sets, May to July

But what do you think it's like in the winter?

You're right – it's always dark, because the sun is circling below the horizon.

ARCTIC WINTER – the sun never rises, November to February

TRACKING THE DAYLIGHT

DATE	TIME OF SUNRISE	TIME OF SUNSET	HOURS OF DAYLIGHT	CHANGE FROM YESTERDAY

To print out more pages like this, go to *www.storey.com/thenatureconnection.php.*

Honoring the Sun

Imagine that you lived long ago, before the discovery of oil and electricity to provide heat and light. You might be frightened as the sun began to come up later and set earlier every day, leaving you in longer and longer times of darkness and cold. You would worry that your family and livestock might not survive the long winter and you would probably pray to the sun gods and light fires to call them back.

When the sun did reappear and bring another season of light, you would celebrate and give thanks. Even though we now have heat and light throughout the winter, modern people are still glad to see the longer days arrive as the season turns to spring and the sun — our source of light and health — is once again higher in the sky.

SKY GODS

Ancient peoples believed that the gods – Zeus or Lug or Thor – controlled what happened overhead. They prayed and offered gifts and sacrifices to the gods in an attempt to influence the forces of the sky.

Many ancient cultures created stone monuments or other markers to "catch" the first light of day. The ritual of following the sun's path through the seasons served as an early form of calendar. This one is Stonehenge, in England, built in stages between 5000 and 3500 years ago to honor the rising of the summer solstice sun.

Fill in the diagram below with activities that connect you to nature during different seasons. Do you like to go sledding or ice fishing, biking or hiking, play sports or sit under a tree, swim or go on picnics?

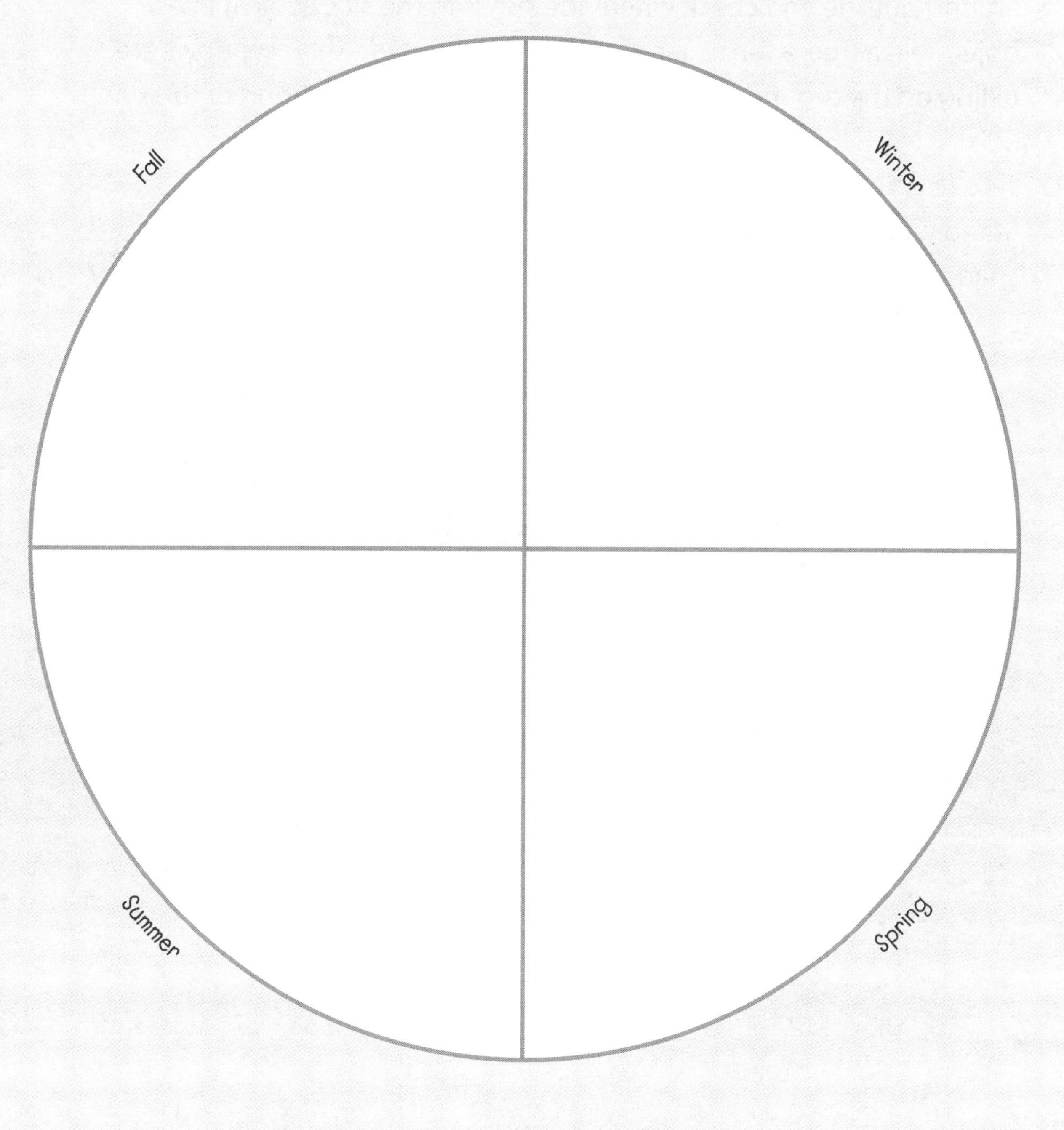

Shadow Fun

An object casts a shadow when it blocks the sun's light. Take a walk around outside and check where the sun is in the sky. Look at a few objects — a tree, a fence, a car — and notice where their shadows are falling on the ground. Note the time of day and the position of the sun.

I do this fun exercise with kids in schoolyards: Stand with your back to the sun and draw your shadow like this.

Notice that shadows are longer when the sun is low in the sky. When do they get shorter? Be sure to write the time and date of your drawings - see how they change over the seasons.

SHADOW GAMES

Remember how Peter Pan was lost without his shadow? Where would you be without yours? Here are some fun things to do with your shadow on a sunny day.

* Play Shadow Tag with your friends by jumping on each other's shadows. If your shadow is jumped on, you're it!
* Make funny shadow shapes with your hands and body. See if you can make your shadow look like an animal.
* If you're near water, watch the reflections on the surface. How are they like shadows? Can you see shadows at the bottom of a pond or stream?

Use this page to draw, paint, or tell a story about shadows.

Can you tell the season or time of day when each of these shadows was drawn?

1. SW

2. E

3. NW

Date: Place: Time:

Do You Like the Night?

Are you afraid of the dark? Lots of people are. What might help you become less afraid? One of the best ways is to go outside with a friend and just listen, look, and relax in a safe place. Walk around as you feel more comfortable (blindfolded walks are fun too). Then write about what it was like.

Many of us live with so many lights that we scarcely notice the difference between night and day. The use of fossil fuels has increased all over the world as more and more people use more and more electricity. But there are still many places in the world where it is very dark when the sun goes down. Search online for an aerial map of the world at night – it is truly illuminating!

Write your thoughts about night here.

After you've spent some time outside at night, use this space to draw what it was like. Make some notes about what you heard and smelled.

Date: Place: Time:

Animals at Night

Many animals move around during both night and day, napping in between. Your own cat or dog probably does this, as do mice, rabbits, deer, foxes, moose, and bears.

Other animals are *diurnal*, meaning they are active during the day and sleep at night. Squirrels, woodchucks, snakes, lizards, and most birds are diurnal. Animals that prefer the nighttime are called *nocturnal*. They include skunks, raccoons, bats, owls, nighthawks, and bobcats.

Some plants are nocturnal too. They open their blossoms when the night-flying pollinators are out and about. Most nocturnal plants have white or light-colored flowers that reflect the light of the moon. Many of them also have strong fragrances to attract those pollinators.

What are some nocturnal animals that live around you? You may not see them often, but you might see signs of them — raccoons sometimes knock over trashcans and skunks dig for grubs in the grass.

BARRED OWLS
hoot & hunt

Draw or paste pictures of nocturnal animals in your area here.

Date: Place: Time:

Why Does the Moon Change Its Shape?

Throughout time, people on Earth have watched the moon wax and wane through its phases. Every time you see the full moon the surface patterns look the same as they did millions of years ago. That is because the moon always keeps the same side facing the earth.

While the moon seems to change its shape every night, its sphere is always half lit by the sun, like the earth. The apparent change in shape results from the moon's position as it revolves around us. We only see the part of the moon's surface area that is reflecting the sun's light back toward us.

The moon makes a complete orbit around the earth every 29 days (see the diagram on the next page). For centuries, people have watched this magical cycle as the moon changes from new to crescent to half to full and back to crescent and new.

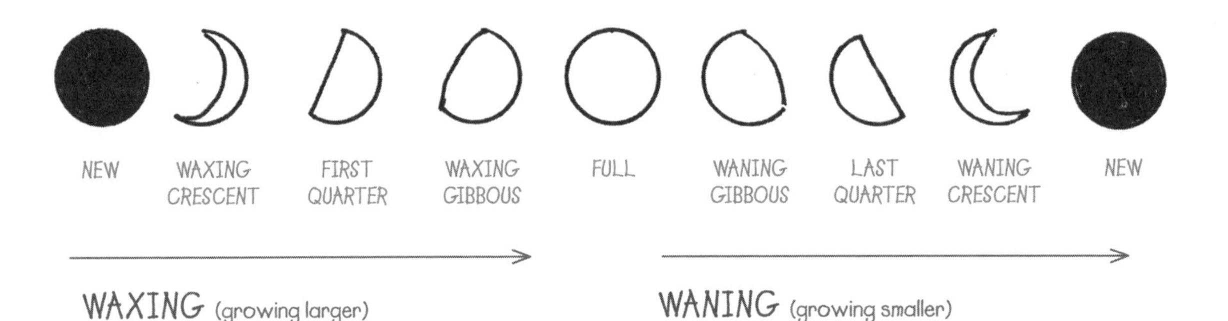

The word "lunatic" (often shortened to "loony") comes from the Latin *lunaticus* meaning "moonstruck." People used to believe that the full moon could make you crazy!

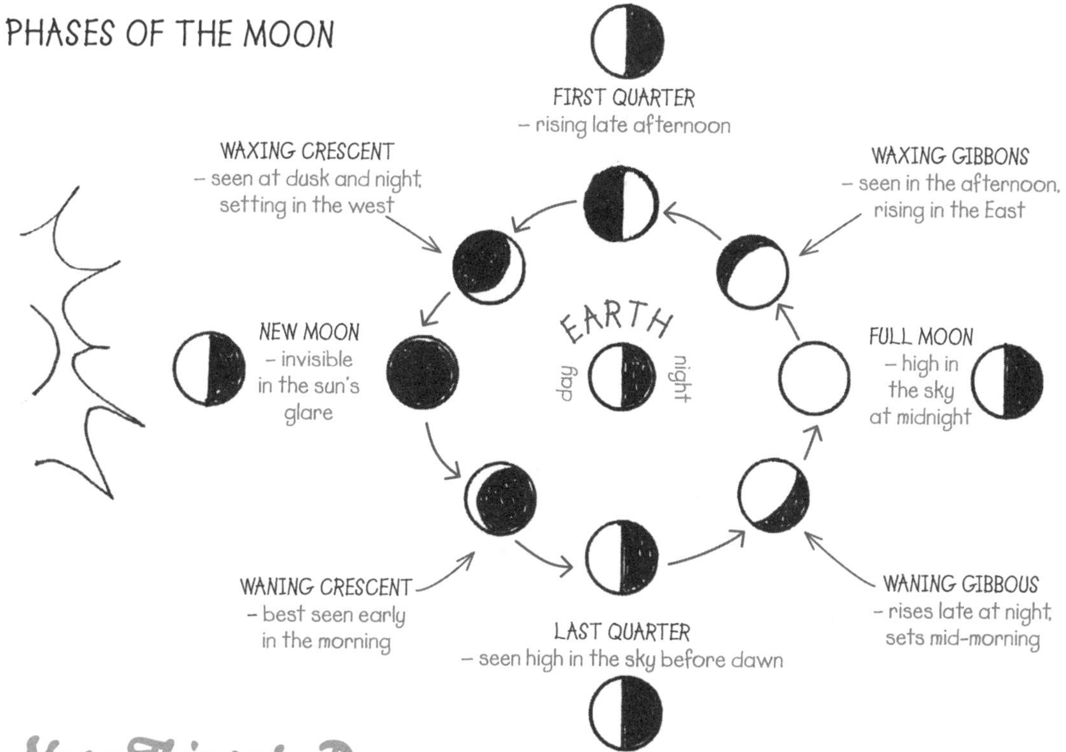

More Things to Do

- **Find stories or myths about the moon** from different cultures. In Greek mythology, the sun god, Apollo, and his twin sister, the moon goddess Artemis, were the children of Zeus, the most important god of all.

- **Do you hear any animals** when there's a full moon? In rural Vermont, we hear coyotes barking and barred owls hooting.

- **Draw or paint** a picture of the moon.

- **Write a poem** about the moon.

- **Some cultures and religions** still follow a 13-month lunar calendar instead of a 12-month solar one. Can you find out more?

Keep a Moon Journal

Find out what phase the moon is currently in for the location where you live and what time it will rise and set. You can use an online resource or an almanac. Write these times down for the next seven days.

Go outside and observe the moon soon after it rises, if the skies are clear and it is not too late. Be sure to look in the day sky as well as the night sky, since sometimes the rising or setting will appear during the daytime.

DAY & TIME	MOON PHASE	RISING TIME	SETTING TIME	WHERE I SAW
Nov. 10 5:30 p.m.		9:14 a.m.	6:19 p.m.	Setting in the west over the school playing field
Nov. 15 4:15 p.m.		12:05 p.m.	11:31 p.m.	Rising in the southeast while I was walking down Mass. Ave.

SOME MOON FACTS

- The moon's surface is actually various shades of gray, but it looks white because of the sun's light reflecting off it.
- The moon travels at 2,000 miles an hour around the earth, completing one full rotation every 29 days.
- Scientists have formulated several theories about the origin of the moon. One is that a huge meteor struck the earth and broke off a piece that fell into the earth's orbit and formed the moon. Do your own research to find out some of the other theories.

MOON JOURNAL

DAY & TIME	MOON PHASE	RISING TIME	SETTING TIME	WHERE I SAW

To print out more pages like this, go to *www.storey.com/thenatureconnection.php.*

Naming the Moons

Some Native American tribes developed names for each full moon that reflected what was happening in their lives at that season. Here are the names the Algonquin tribe of northern New England used:

* **Wolf or Hunger Moon** (January)
* **Snow Moon** (February)
* **Worm or Sap Moon** (March)
* **Grass or Worm Moon** (April)
* **Fish or Full Flower Moon** (May)
* **Hot or Flower Moon** (June)
* **Strawberry or Hay Moon** (July)
* **Thunder or Maize Moon** (August)
* **Corn or Harvest Moon** (September)
* **Corn or Hunter's Moon** (October)
* **Harvest or Beaver Moon** (November)
* **Beaver, Long Night, or Cold Moon** (December)

Why do you think the Algonquin used these names? What can you tell about their lives? Do some research on this tribe or another one that interests you and see what you can find out. You can learn a lot about Native American cultures by reading Joseph Bruchac's books. I especially like *The Thirteen Moons on Turtle's Back*.

You might also try *When the Moon Is Full* by Penny Pollock and my own book *Nature All Year Long*.

It's fun to make up your own names for the full moons based on what happens around your house or school each month. My list would start out "New Year Moon, Cold Moon, Mud Moon . . ."

Write your names here.

January: ______

February: ______

March: ______

April: ______

May: ______

June: ______

July: ______

August: ______

September: ______

October: ______

November: ______

December: ______

The moon is full once every month, but in some years there are actually 13 full moons, because two occur in one calendar month. The phrase "once in a blue moon" refers to something that happens very rarely.

Eclipses: What Is Going On?

Have you ever seen a lunar eclipse? If you didn't know what was happening, you might be scared. The word "eclipse" means "to hide," and that is just what the moon appears to do. If it's a clear night, you can see the earth's shadow move quite quickly across the moon as the moon revolves around us (it takes about 3 or 4 hours). It might seem a little creepy because the moon usually becomes a dark blood color. This is because of the particulates in the earth's atmosphere.

Ancient people took this unusual event as an omen of a glorious or terrible event to come. Now we understand what is happening, but we are still fascinated.

I remember watching the Red Sox and the Cardinals play the final game of the 2004 World Series in St. Louis. A lunar eclipse was happening at the same time, and the sports channel kept showing photos of the moon changing color as the game progressed. The Sox won — what a night!

LUNAR ECLIPSE (nighttime)

The moon must be full for a lunar eclipse. It happens only when the earth is exactly between the sun and the moon, so that the earth blocks the sun's light.

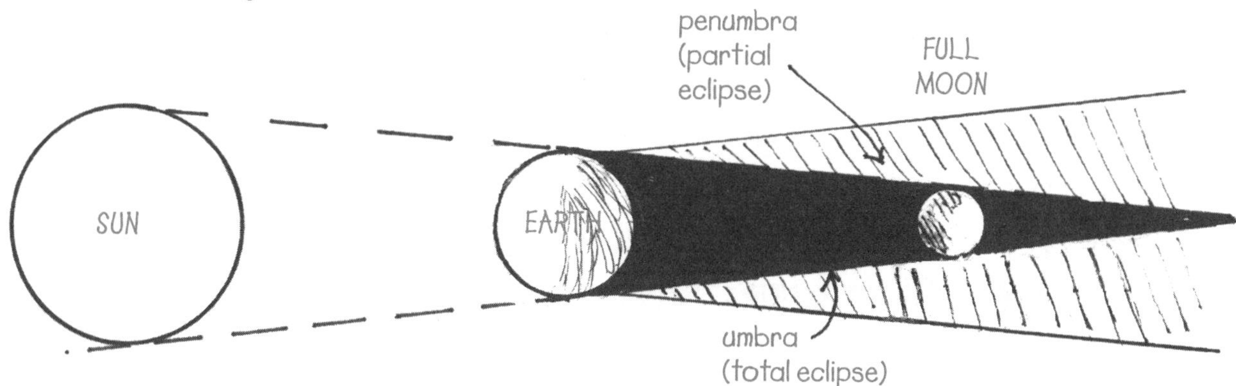

SOLAR ECLIPSE (daytime)

A solar eclipse happens when the moon is between the earth and the sun, preventing the sun's light from reaching part of the earth.

With a partial eclipse (penumbra), which is more common, the light becomes oddly dusky. The air cools off and the birds stop singing and settle down as though it's night.. With a total eclipse (umbra), it can become totally dark in the middle of the day. By the way, "umbra" means "shade or shadow." An umbrella is a little shade!

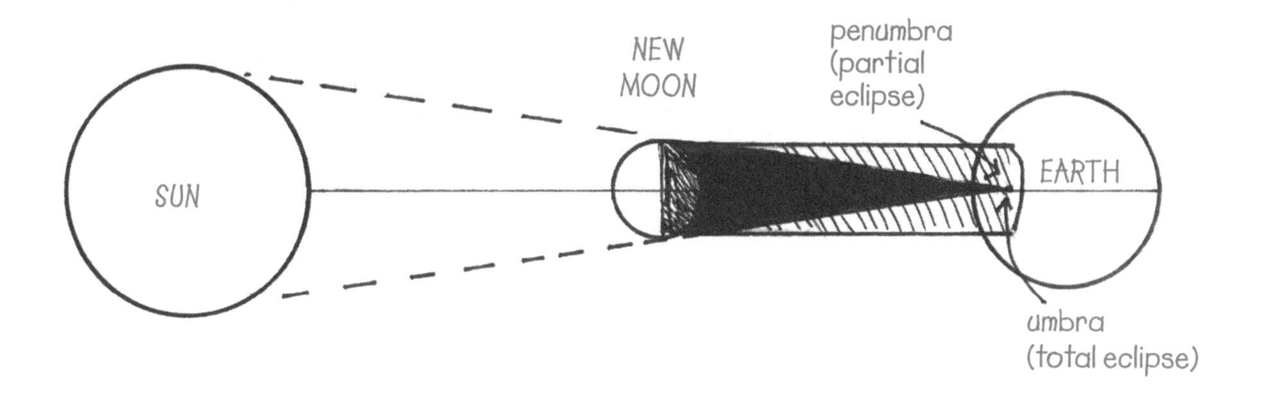

High Tide, Low Tide

If you live near or have ever visited the ocean or a tidal marsh, you have probably noticed that the water level changes over the course of the day as the tide goes in and out. Tides happen all around the world at different rates and depths, and even in large fresh water bodies. Some ancient peoples thought that the water drained in and out of holes at the bottom of the sea or that giant monsters sucked up the water every day.

The real explanation is actually up in the sky — the moon and the sun control the cycle of the tides. Strong gravitational forces between those two bodies and the earth determine when the tides go in and out and how high or low they are.

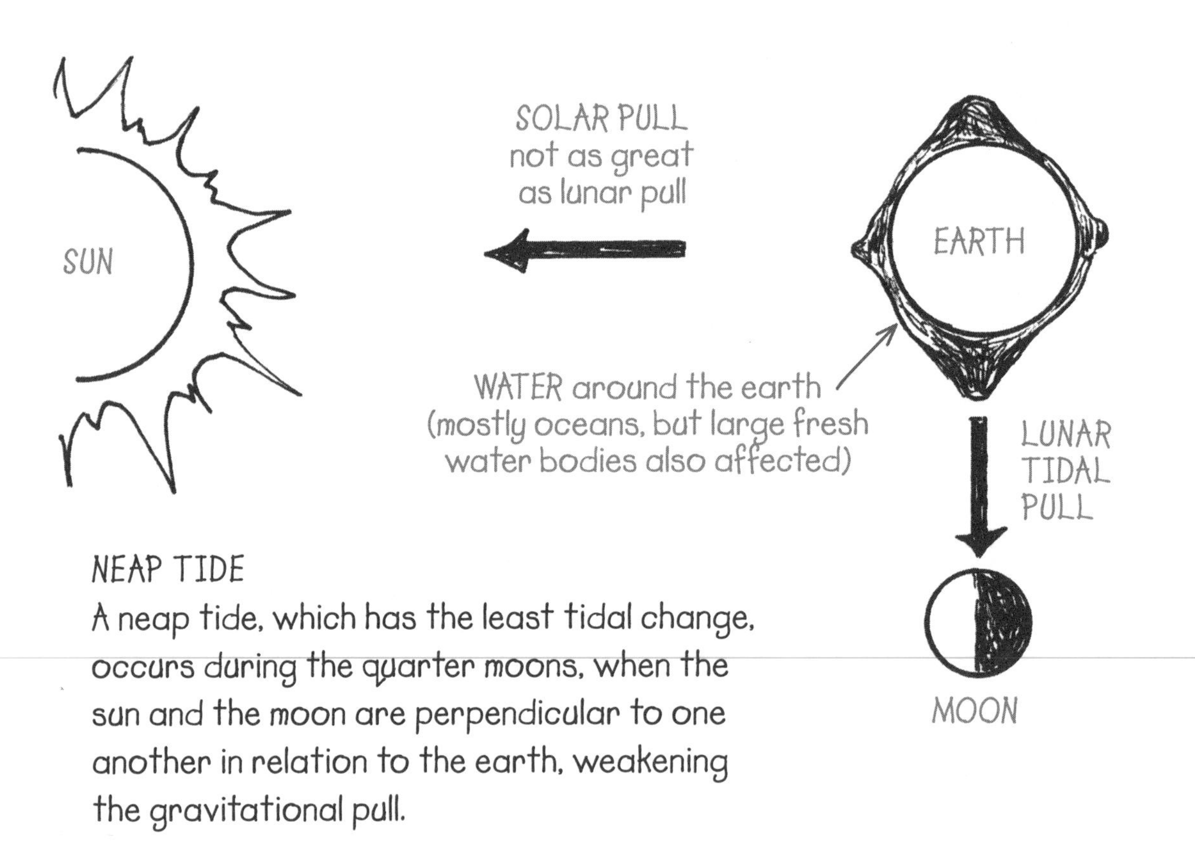

NEAP TIDE
A neap tide, which has the least tidal change, occurs during the quarter moons, when the sun and the moon are perpendicular to one another in relation to the earth, weakening the gravitational pull.

SPRING TIDE

A spring tide has nothing to do with the season, but happens during the full and new moons when the sun and the moon line up and pull together.

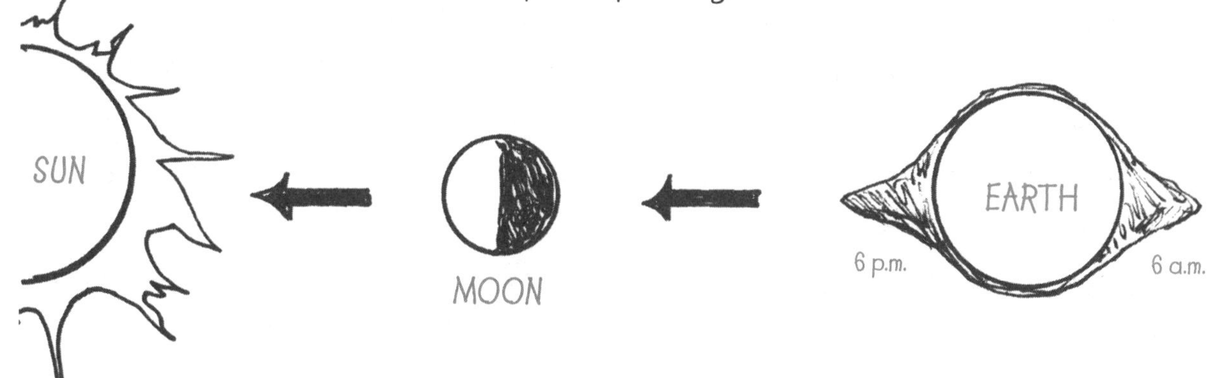

TIDE FACTS

* Tides on the Pacific side of the Panama Canal vary by 12–16 feet, but on the Atlantic side by only 1–2 feet.
* The Bay of Fundy, between Nova Scotia and New Brunswick, has tides as high as 50 feet!
* A proxigean spring tide is an unusually high tide that occurs when the moon is both quite close to the earth and in a new moon phase, which happens only about every 18 months.
* High tides, especially during a storm, can cause flooding on beaches and roads or even wash away houses that are near the water's edge.
* You can learn a lot more about tides at the National Oceanographic and Atmospheric Administration's website (*www.oceanservice.noaa.gov*).

Star Gazing

Nighttime is its own special time, but we don't often think about it once we're indoors. So, get yourself outside and stand in your driveway, on a porch, sidewalk, or in a nearby field or park. Find the darkest spot you can. Look up. What do you see? The moon? Any stars? Planets? The Milky Way?

You might also see a plane, a satellite moving slowly, or perhaps Mars or Venus if you know which direction to look. You might even see a comet or meteor. On brightly lit nights it is harder to see the stars. But even in the city you can find Orion, the Big Dipper, Venus, Mars, and Jupiter.

The Milky Way is the whole galaxy that our sun and solar system are part of. It is made of billions of stars sweeping across the sky like a long scarf.

Use a field guide or a star chart to figure out what is in your part of the sky by season and month.

Don't forget a flashlight so you can read your chart!

Do you know what a horoscope is? Astrologers use the position of the planets and stars to interpret and predict fortunes. The biblical Wise Men who followed a giant star westward to Bethlehem were probably astrologers. Now we think they were seeing an unusually close grouping of the planets Mars, Jupiter, and Saturn.

More Things to Do

* **Learn more about the stars and constellations** from *The Golden Guide to STARS*, or visit your local planetarium and see what the night sky for your season looks like. Look at *www.darksky.org* for some good guidance. Find a good star chart in your local bookstore.
* **Find out if there is a local stargazing group in your area.** There are many amateur astronomers who hold public viewing times.
* **Could you find your way home using the stars?** Sailors, hunters, travelers, and hikers have used the position of the stars to navigate by for centuries when they didn't have a compass or even a map, let alone a GPS. The Inuit of Baffin Island, Canada, hunt by the moon and stars in the long winter months when they have no daylight.
* **Use a star chart or a guide to the stars** to help you locate, by season and time of night, where the planets, constellations, and Milky Way will be.

QUESTIONS FOR BUDDING ASTRONOMERS

(An astronomer studies objects in the sky.)

* What are the northern lights?
* What is the difference between a star and a planet?
* What is the difference between a comet and a meteor?

Learn the Constellations

Constellations are a particular grouping of stars that people made stories about many thousands of years ago to help bring reason to an otherwise confusing and often scary universe. Most of them, like Orion, Pegasus, and Cassiopeia, came from the myths of the Greeks, Romans, and Egyptians. These "shapes in the sky" still appear to us as they did to those ancient stargazers.

Over the course of one night, the visible constellations sweep overhead in an arc, because of the earth's daily rotation. Over the course of a year, seasonal constellations gradually rise and fall in the night sky as the angle of the earth's axis changes relative to the sun. This is the same reason our seasons change.

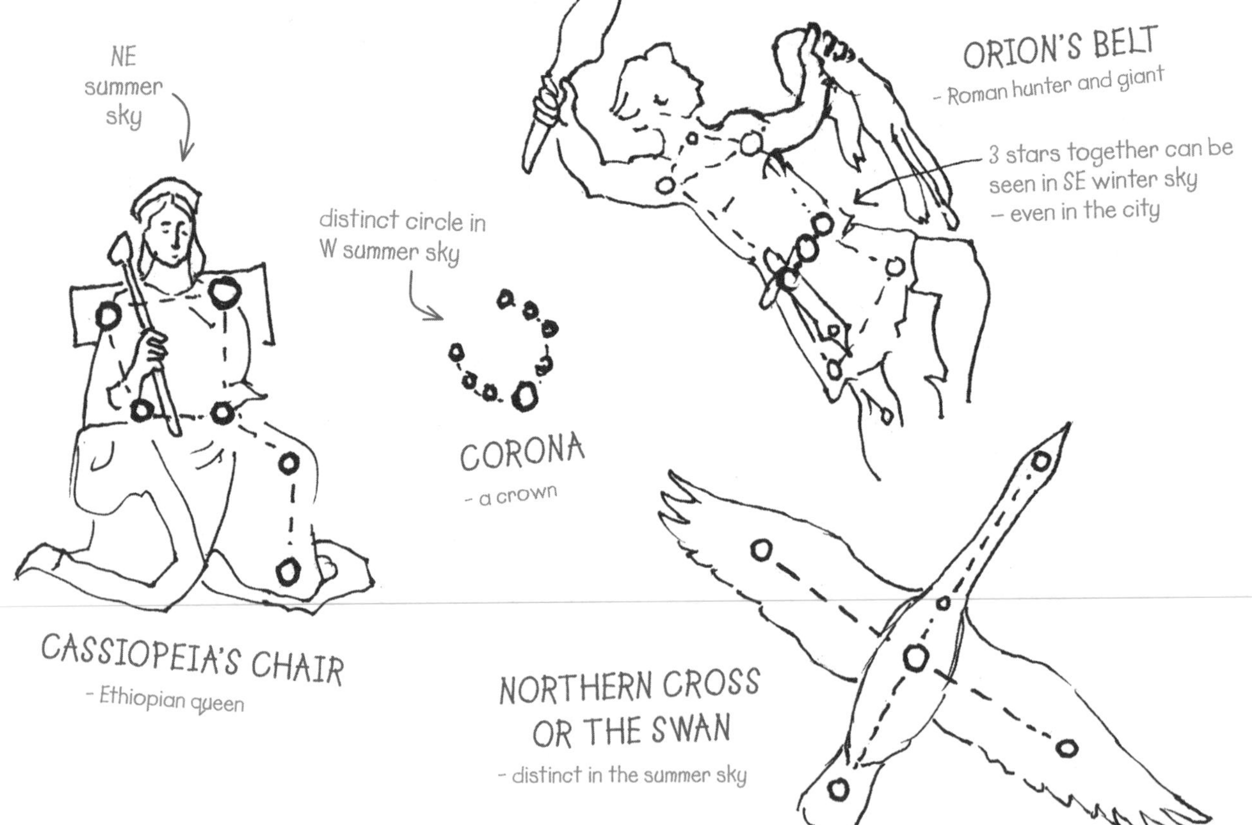

Learn three constellations that you can see. Draw them here, using a star chart for help. Label where in the sky and when you saw them.

In the southern hemisphere, the star patterns and constellations are different.

Date: Place: Time:

Write a Sky Poem

We miss many hours of each day by being indoors, especially at night. The night is as important a part of your 24-hour cycle as is day! Write a poem about the sky, maybe the way it looks from your bedroom window, or when you walk around your neighborhood, play baseball, or lie on your back in your yard.

A poem can be as short as one sentence or as long as you like. It doesn't even have to rhyme, like these:

Blue sky,
Always there.
You comfort me.

Snow, snow, snow, snow!
When will it stop snowing?

Here's a poem I wrote after a long day of teaching in a town far from my home. I went to my hotel to crash but first I looked out the window. It was 4:40 p.m. in November and to the west past the buildings and busy highway, I saw a dramatic sunset, low and far to the southwest. A quick sketch and poem were enough to remember this moment.

Exhaustion leaves me.
Waving bands of orange, red, turquoise
Fly across the sky over streaming commuter traffic.
I stand until dark, watching,
Totally awed by this unasked-for beauty
On the seventh floor of my hotel.

Write your sky poem (or story, if you prefer) here and illustrate it below. You can include heat or cold; rain, sleet, or snow; or dark or light.

Date: Place: Time:

PART THREE

Exploring Nature

A Month-by-Month Guide

NATURALISTS GO OUT TO STUDY THE WORLD all year long and in every kind of weather. There's always something to do and see out in nature, if you just use your senses. This section is divided into months, with plenty of suggestions of things to find, challenges to meet, and stuff to learn about. Most of these activities can be done in any month, so feel free to jump around!

You'll find lots of different ways to record your observations. The various sheets used throughout this book are examples of *phenology* charts. Phenology is the study of the seasonal timing of life cycle events. You are studying phenology when you record the date that a certain plant flowers, an insect hatches, or a migratory bird appears in its nesting grounds. Factors such as length of day, temperature, and rainfall affect the dates on which these events happen each year. By tracking the timing of seasonal changes, you can see how the patterns of nature are changing.

You know that scientists around the world are studying, testing, and observing many aspects of our planet's changing climate and environment. But you may not be aware that much knowledge comes from the careful observations and records of many other people as well. You too can be part of this great study!

Here is one way you can set up your nature journal notes. I start by asking, "What is going on?" Then, walking and drawing, I record my observations as long as I want. You can adapt this to your age, interests, and time available. Or make up your own!

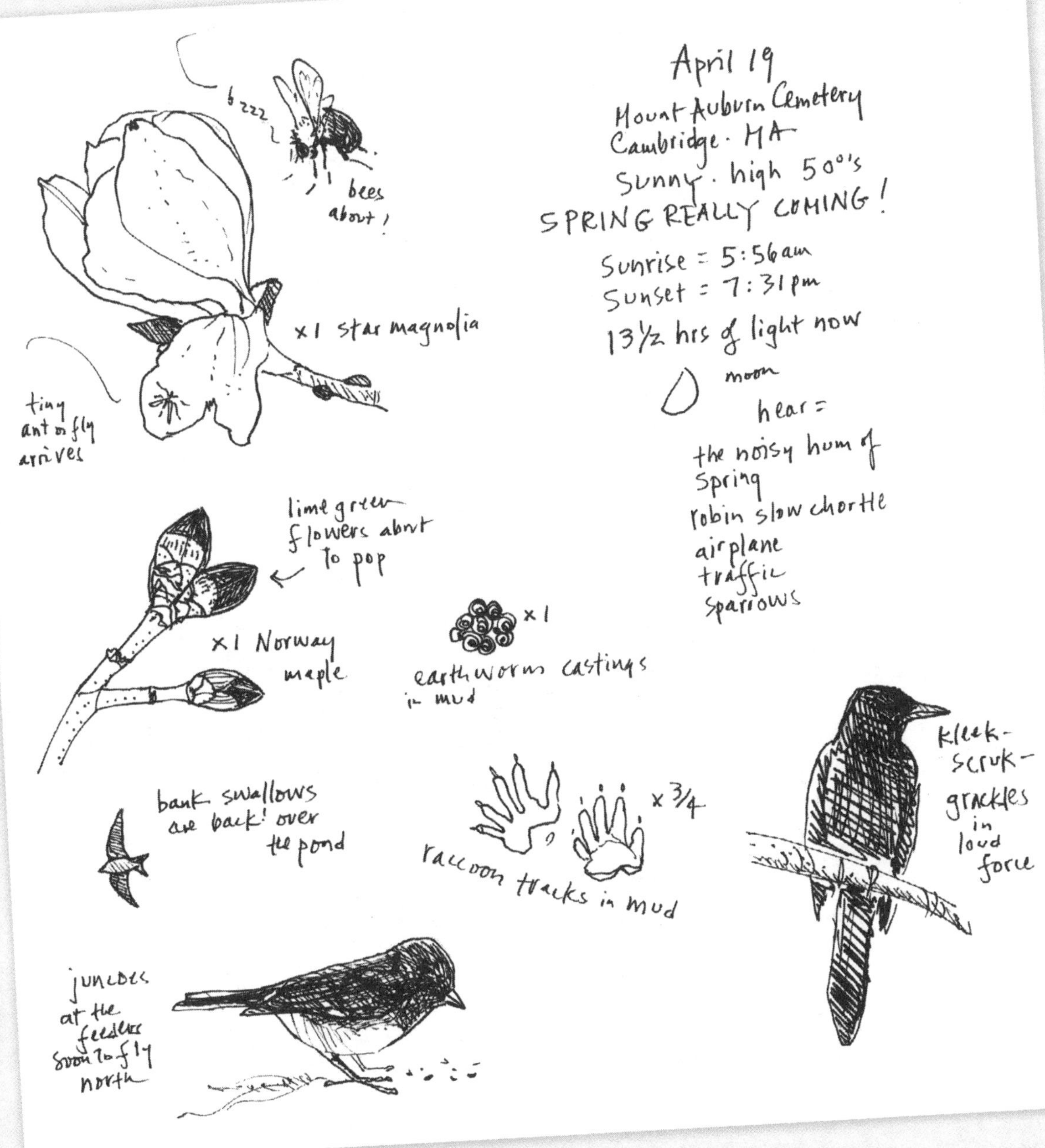

JANUARY

Surviving the Winter

DID YOU KNOW THAT OUR MONTHS OF THE YEAR were named by Roman Emperor Julius Caesar way back in the first century BCE? We still use this calendar, with the addition of leap years, which is based on the cycle of the sun. Other cultures use a calendar calculated on the cycle of the moon instead, or the changes between rainy and dry or growing and harvesting seasons.

This month is named for Janus, the Roman god of doorways, of beginnings, and of the sunrise and sunset. He was depicted as having two faces, which is appropriate for this time of looking back on the previous year while welcoming the new one.

But look at your almanac or sunrise and sunset chart for December and January. You will see that since early December the sun has been setting a bit later every day. Minute by minute, the days are becoming longer. With the Winter Solstice past, both sunrises and sunsets are giving our January days a brighter look.

Adopt the pace of nature:
Her secret is patience.

— RALPH WALDO EMERSON

MY NATURE NOTES

Date:	Time:
Place:	Temperature:
What's the weather like?	
Phase of the moon:	Time of sunrise:
	Time of sunset:
Look out the window or go outdoors, then jot down your observations, draw a picture, or describe a scene.	

To print out more pages like this, go to *www.storey.com/thenatureconnection.php.*

Go on a Nature Quest!

Start each month by taking a good look around. Go for a walk and see what you can find (use all your senses!) that gives a clue to the season. Try it on several different days and see how your answers change.

Can you find...	Describe what you notice.
☐ people ice fishing	
☐ smell of wood smoke	
☐ deer nibbles on bark	

What else can you find?

☐	
☐	
☐	
☐	
☐	
☐	
☐	
☐	
☐	
☐	

Picture of the Month

Choose one or two (or more!) things from your list to draw or photograph here.

Date: Place: Time:

Warm-Blooded Winter Survival

Animals have many different ways to keep warm and find food during the winter. Warm-blooded animals (called *endotherms*), which are mammals and birds, regulate their own body heat by converting food into energy. In cold weather, they must stay active to keep warm, feeding as best they can and finding shelter from the worst weather.

WHAT IS HIBERNATION ALL ABOUT?

Only a few animals truly *hibernate*, meaning that breathing, heart rate, body temperature, and metabolism all slow down tremendously. These animals have an internal alarm clock that tells them when to settle in for winter and when to wake up. They sleep so soundly that they cannot be woken up.

Being in a state of suspended animation allows the animal to use up its energy supply very slowly. That energy supply comes from a thick layer of fat, gained over the summer and fall months.

True hibernators include little brown bats, groundhogs (also called woodchucks), most ground squirrels, and some other small rodents. Bears, chipmunks, skunks, raccoons, and opossums, among others, are called deep sleepers rather than hibernators. They do spend a great deal of time sleeping heavily, but will waken to forage for food on warmer days. Some have caches (stores) of food in their dens.

As our global climate shifts, scientists are watching true hibernators to see if they are coming out of their winter dens earlier than they used to.

OUR FEATHERED FRIENDS

When we go outside, even on a cold winter day, we often see birds of many different species flying around trees or perched on telephone wires or walking on lawns and playing fields. These birds survive because they eat a varied diet of seeds and fruits from shrubs and vines, insects, suet and birdfeeder seed, even trash from Dumpsters and landfills. They keep warm by sheltering from the wind and fluffing up their feathers to trap a layer of warm air next to their skin.

A fun children's book about keeping warm that even older kids will enjoy is *Agatha's Feather Bed: Not Just Another Wild Goose Story*, by Carmen Agra Deedy.

Cold-Blooded Winter Survival

Cold-blooded animals (called *ectotherms*) are fish, reptiles, amphibians, spiders, and insects. They cannot regulate their body heat, so their body temperature is close to that of the air around them. In the summer, they hide out in nooks and crannies if the temperature gets too hot, but on chilly mornings they must seek out the sun to warm up.

In the winter, they must hide out in a protected spot in a state of torpor called *brumation*. This means that their body temperature drops to near freezing and their breathing slows way down. Some frogs and insects actually do freeze, but their bodies produce an antifreeze called *glycerol* that prevents damage to the living cells. (Clever, huh?)

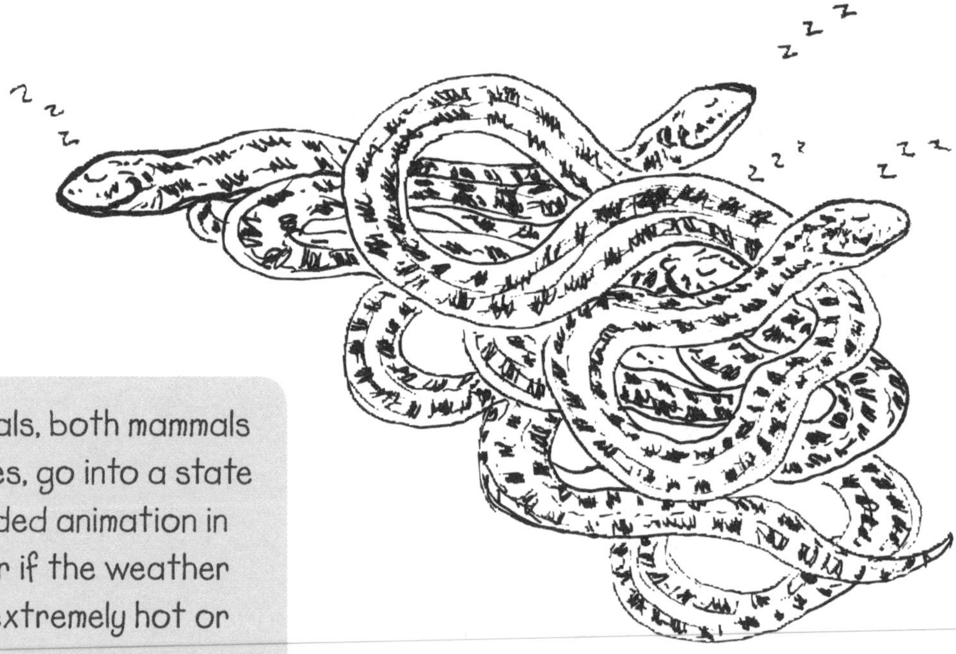

Some animals, both mammals and reptiles, go into a state of suspended animation in the summer if the weather becomes extremely hot or water becomes scarce. This hot-weather survival tactic is called *estivation.*

Many insects such as crickets, dragonflies, mosquitoes, and moths, cannot survive the tough weather. Before they die, they leave eggs or larvae in protected places to hatch in the spring. Other insects, such as flies, ladybugs, and crane flies, do winter over as adults, finding shelter in bark crevices, rolled in leaves, or even in houses and other buildings.

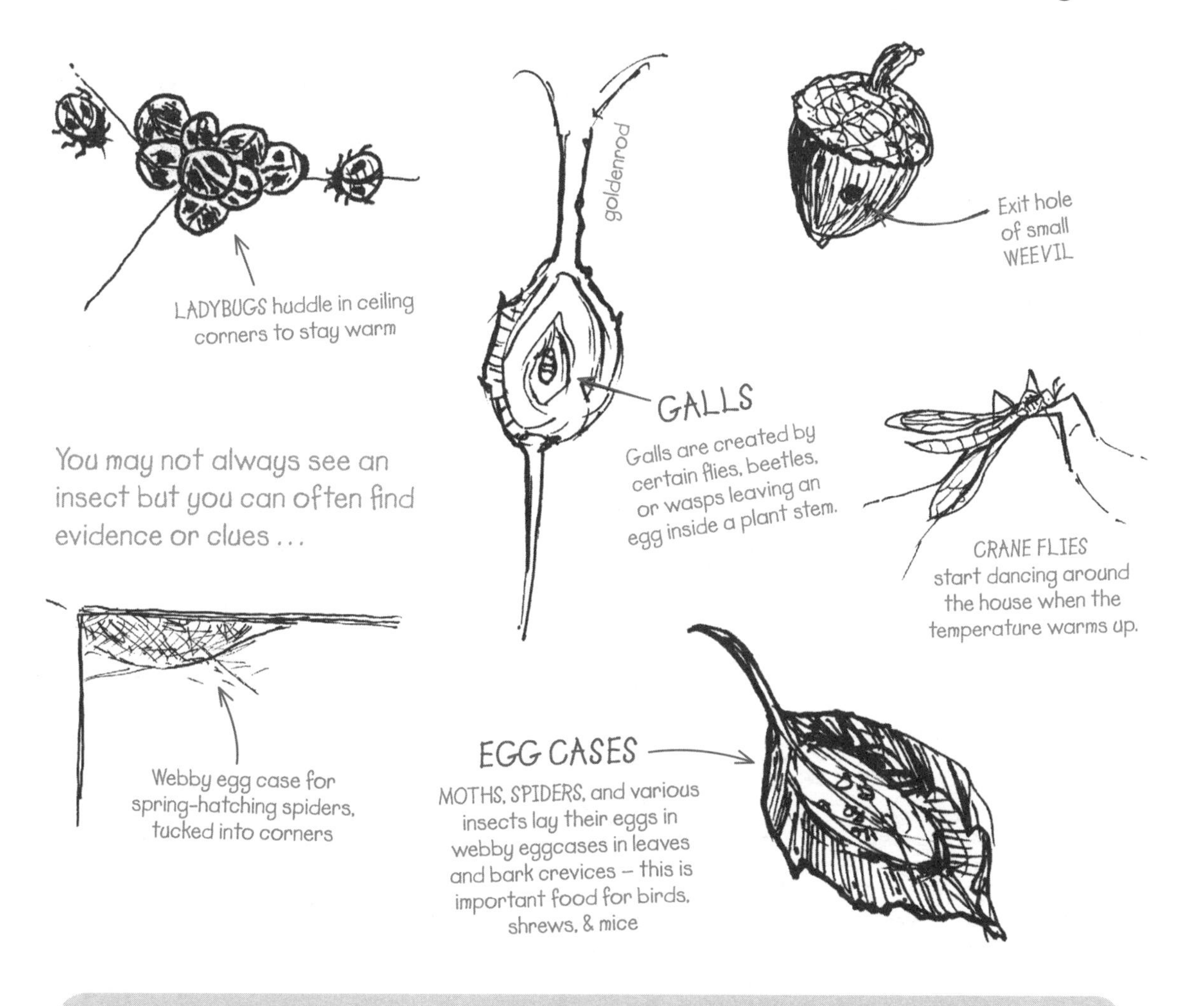

The monarch butterfly is one of the few insects that migrates, traveling thousands of miles on its fragile wings. Learn more at *www.journeynorth.org.*

Bundle up, grab a friend, and find some winter fun!

Here are some things you can do and look for in January. See if you can check them all off by the end of the month.

☐ **Make a list of all the active warm-blooded animals around you** and think about what they are doing to survive the winter. Where do they find shelter? What do they eat?

☐ **Set up a January weather journal** and record the following information every day. Date * Sky Condition and Clouds * Temperature and Time When Taken * Time of Sunrise and Sunset * Moon Phase (See page 91 for a format.)

☐ **Go on a silent walk, either by yourself or with a friend.** No talking — just listen and watch. You can explore nature just along one block if you want. Point out sounds that you hear or interesting things you see.

2:30 p.m.
1/16
lumps caught
on branches

11:30 a.m. 1/4
beautiful shapes of dried weeds

snow falling on my dog's back

5:30 p.m. on 1/20

Take a walk or hike to a place you haven't been to in a while: a local woods, a creek bed, a rocky place, the seashore. How does it look different from summer? When you get home, paint a picture of it and be sure to date it and say where it was.

Look out a window with a paper and pen or pencil. Make a list of all the man-made things you see and of all the natural things. "People" things might include a cement sidewalk, telephone pole, cars, houses, and so on. "Nature" things might include ice on the sidewalk, dead grasses, pine cones on the ground, and rocks with snow on them.

A SNOWMAN is both a people thing and a nature thing!

Bring nature indoors. Make a mural of the animals and plants of your town. Make a clay or papier mâché model of your favorite animal.

Curl up with a good book. You may have already read *Charlotte's Web* by E.B. White, but he also wrote *The Trumpet of the Swan*, a story about a boy who befriends a trumpeter swan who can't trumpet. Parts of it are wonderfully silly but there are lovely descriptions of nature and wildlife. A good nonfiction read is *Urban Roosts* by Barbara Bash, which looks at how birds live in cities.

Drawing What You See: Mammals

You don't have to be a great artist to be a naturalist, but it's fun to be able to draw the things you see. It may seem hard, but if you look closely, most animal bodies can be broken down into simple shapes.

1. Most mammals can be drawn with circles for the hips and shoulders, connected by an oval for the body.

2. Roughly sketch feet, tail, and head to get the right proportions.

3. The fine details of fur and eyes come last and can take time to get right.

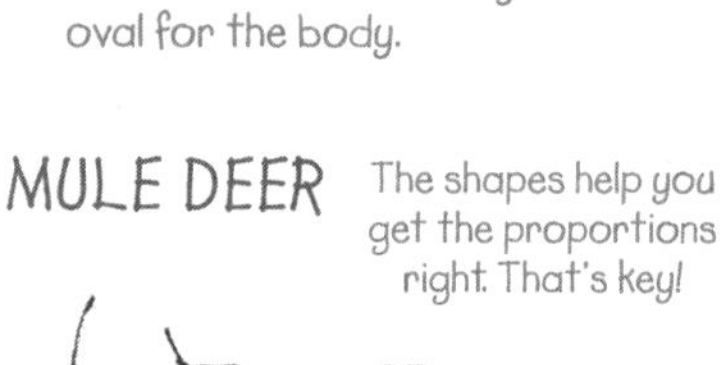

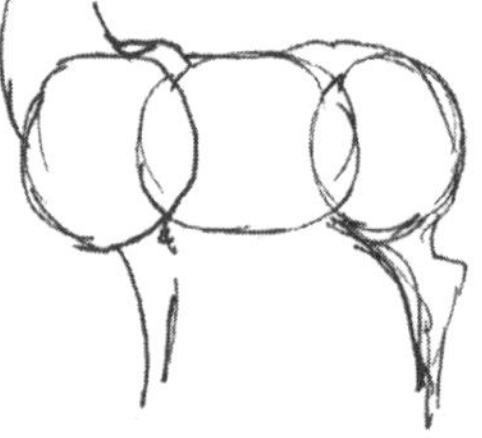

1. Draw the 3 shapes first, working out from there.

2. Cube for a head helps you place ears, eyes, nose.

3. Erase your circles and fill in fur and details.

You can make your drawings as detailed or as sketchy as you like – everyone has an individual style. The important thing is that you observe and record what you see. You can draw from photographs in magazines or books too. (See pages 32–40 for more tips on drawing.)

Draw some wild animals that live around you.

Date: Place: Time:

Snowflake Study

Snowflakes are magical. They seem to appear from nowhere, and they come in an infinite number of shapes. Interestingly, while it's true that no two snowflakes are alike, they are always hexagonal (six-sided).

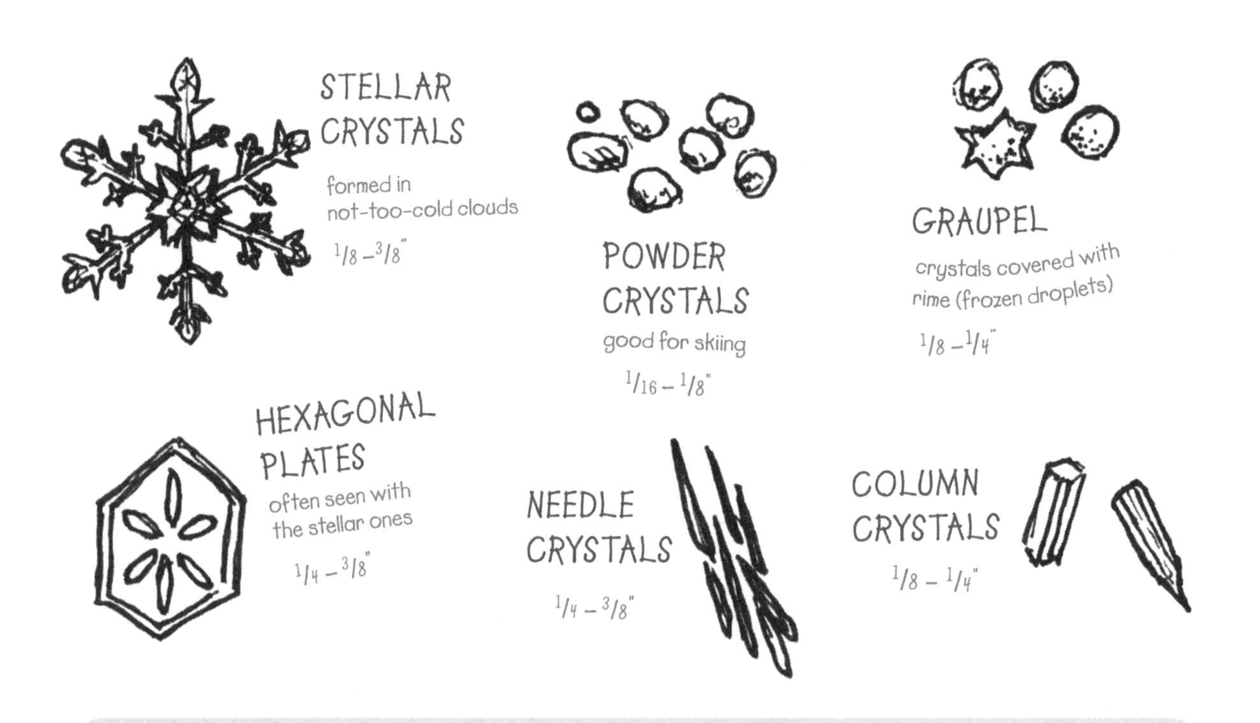

SNOW FACTS

* Snowflakes form in very cold air when water vapor freezes around bits of dust to form solid crystals that fall to the ground.
* Even though snow is cold, it forms an important insulating blanket that protects plants and animals from bitter temperatures and strong winds.
* In many areas, melting snow provides much of the water that the earth will use over the spring and summer. Too much melting snow, however, can cause floods and mud slides.

Catch a few flakes on your mitten or sleeve and draw them here.

Date: Place: Time:

Nature's Little Houseguests

We usually think of nature as being outside our homes, but if you look around, you can probably spot some wildlife indoors. Most houses, especially the basements and attics of older ones, offer plenty of hiding places for mice or even squirrels. Sometimes a snake or a few bats will want to share our space. And you can almost always find a spider in a quiet corner. Look around your house and see what signs of nature you can find!

Insect pests often find their way into our homes: grain and clothes moths, silverfish, houseflies, cockroaches, and earwigs are a few.

A HOUSE MOUSE

We have many mice stories because we live in an old house. (We like to say we rent it from the mice!) Come winter, they move right in. We rarely see them but we know they are there . . .

Who, me?

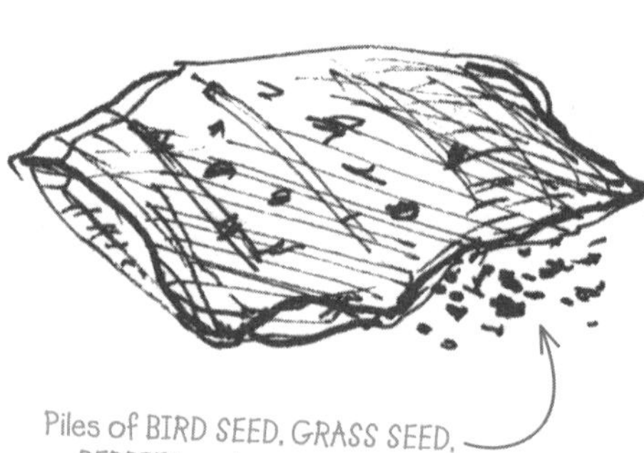

Piles of BIRD SEED, GRASS SEED, BERRIES under our pillows

CHEWED CANDLES

A drawer full of MOUSE NESTS made from our favorite travel brochures.

TELLTALE SCAT (droppings)

Stuart Little by E.B. White is probably the most famous book featuring a mouse as the main character, but some other fun ones are *The Mouse and the Motorcycle*, *Runaway Ralph*, and *Ralph S. Mouse* by Beverly Cleary.

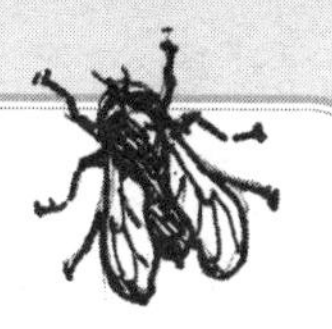

What did you find? Put a drawing or photo here.

Date: Place: Time:

FEBRUARY

Finding the Sun

FOR THE ROMANS, this was a month of purification (*februatus* is the Latin word for purification). For the ancient Celts of northern Europe, February 2 marked the beginning of spring. Early flowers were blooming, the sun was warming the soil, and lambs and calves were being born. The origins of Mardi Gras and Carnival, which are celebrated in a number of countries, come from the early European custom of building bonfires and dancing to celebrate the return of spring.

The increasing daylight at this time of year encourages some wild animals to look for mates so that babies can be born in the spring and grow up over the healthy summer months. You may hear or see great horned owls, foxes, opossums, and raccoons at dusk or later in the evening. Skunks are courting too — sometimes you can even smell them! In warm areas, certain trees begin to bud out at this time, but in many areas it is still winter, with plenty of cold snaps and snow storms still to come.

All living creatures and all plants
derive their life from the Sun. If it were not for the Sun,
there would be darkness and nothing could grow.
The earth would be without life.

— OKUTE, A TETON SIOUX

MY NATURE NOTES

Date:	Time:
Place:	Temperature:
What's the weather like?	
Phase of the moon:	Time of sunrise:
	Time of sunset:
Look out the window or go outdoors, then jot down your observations, draw a picture, or describe a scene.	

To print out more pages like this, go to *www.storey.com/thenatureconnection.php.*

Go on a Nature Quest!

Start each month by taking a good look around. Go for a walk and see what you can find (use all your senses!) that gives a clue to the season. Try it on several different days and see how your answers change.

Can you find...	Describe what you notice.
☐ squirrels playing chase	
☐ birds facing the sun	
☐ cold wind on your cheek	

What else can you find?

☐	
☐	
☐	
☐	
☐	
☐	
☐	
☐	
☐	
☐	

Picture of the Month

Choose one or two (or more!) things from your list to draw or photograph here.

Date: Place: Time:

The Groundhog and Its Shadow

In European countries of old, February 2 was the first day of spring. People would look for badgers and snakes to see if they came out of their holes to find their shadows. If they didn't see a shadow, winter was over, but if they did, another six weeks of winter was predicted. (Six more weeks of winter brings us to around March 21, which now marks the beginning of spring, shadows or not!)

This tradition came to North America with German settlers, who watched for badgers or hedgehogs to come out of their burrows in the spring. Not finding those animals in the areas of Pennsylvania where many Germans built communities, they chose the groundhog, also called a woodchuck or whistle pig.

But the question is, since groundhogs hibernate, how can they wake up in February to check out their shadows? The answer is, they don't. It's just a fun idea that doesn't have much to do with actual nature any more.

Hedgehogs are not native to North America – they come from Europe, Asia, Africa, and New Zealand. The American badger is found in central Canada, the western and central United States, and northern Mexico. Just not in Pennsylvania!

Celebrate Groundhog Day by drawing or photographing a sign of early spring where you live – perhaps longer daylight, melting ice, early green shoots.

Date: Place: Time:

Spotting Animal Tracks

This is a good month to look for tracks after a snow or in the mud as the ground warms up. Look around your backyard, sidewalk, school yard or a local park or woods to see if you can find marks left by people, birds, dogs, cats, squirrels, skunks, deer, rabbits, or even a coyote or fox.

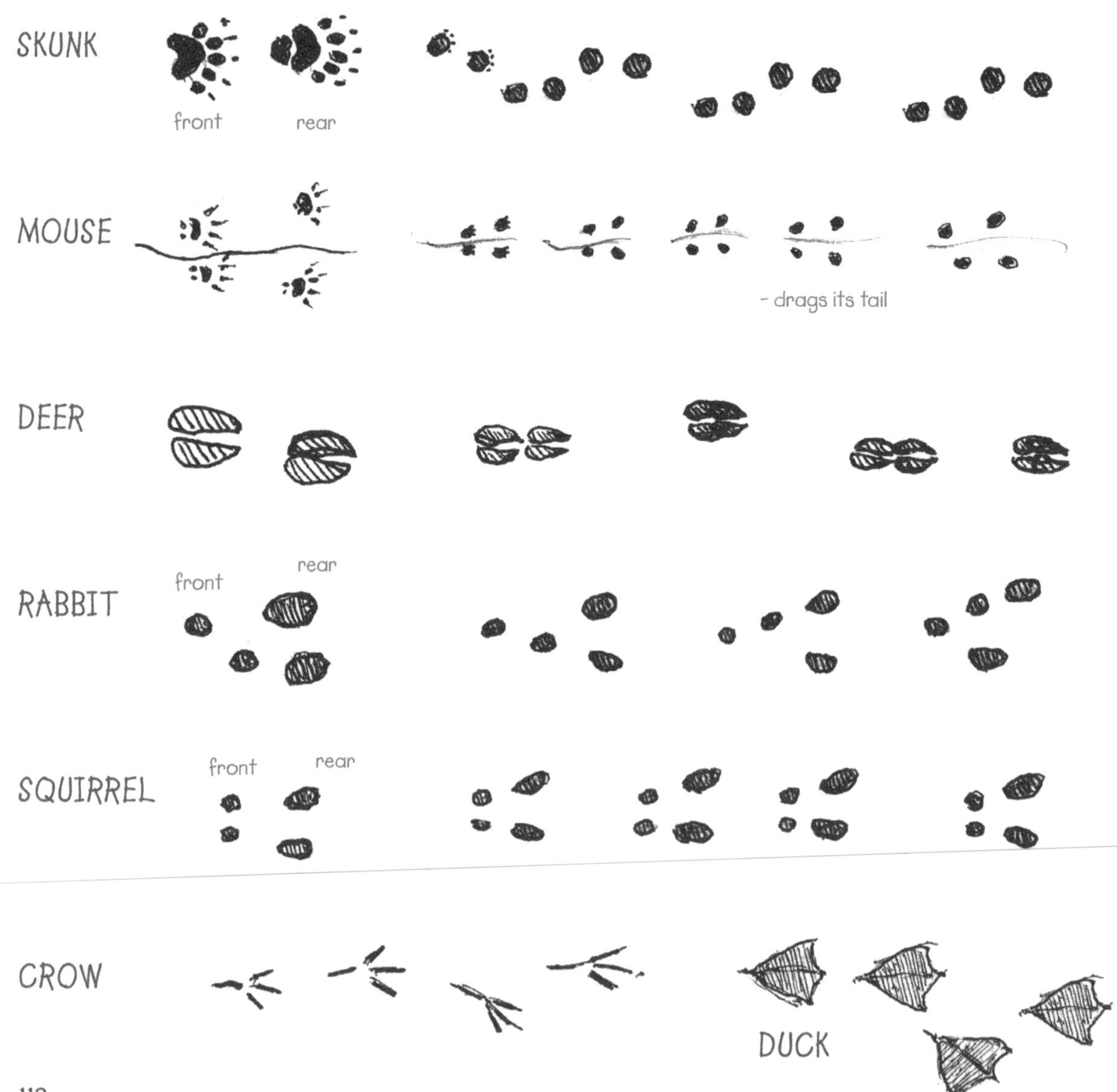

Draw the tracks you find here.

Date: Place: Time:

Outside or inside, winter weather brings lots to do.

Here are some things you can do and look for in February. See if you can check them all off by the end of the month.

☐ **Pretend you live in another hemisphere.** What is winter like on the other side of the world from you? What would you be doing now? If you live in the tropics or in the desert, how is the weather different from other climates this time of year?

☐ **Think about how people keep warm in winter.** What kind of clothes do we wear? What do we do to our houses? When you're playing outside, run, jump, hop, hug someone else. Which keeps you warmest? If you were an animal, what would you need to survive?

☐ **This is a good month for hiking or skiing.** You don't have to be bugged by bugs. You won't get hot. You can see through the woods. Hot food after tastes really good!

☐ **If you're on vacation or if you live where it is warm,** take a hike and look for different birds, plants, insects, reptiles, or amphibians that have adapted to live in a warm place.

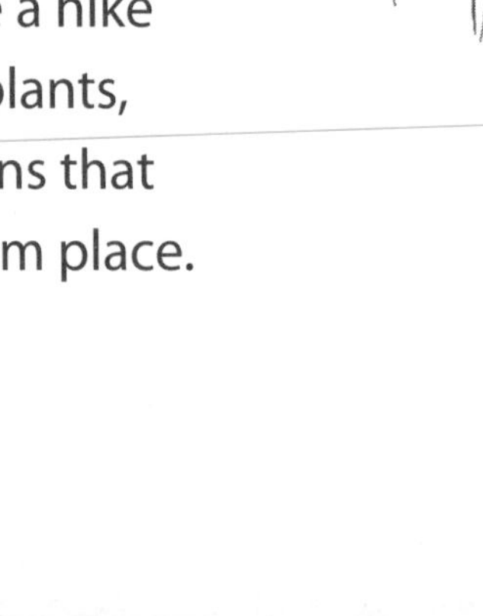

☐ **If you live in a place where there's plenty of snow, play some snow games.** Grab a sled or a tube and find a hill to slide down. Pretend you're at the beach and bury yourself in snow.

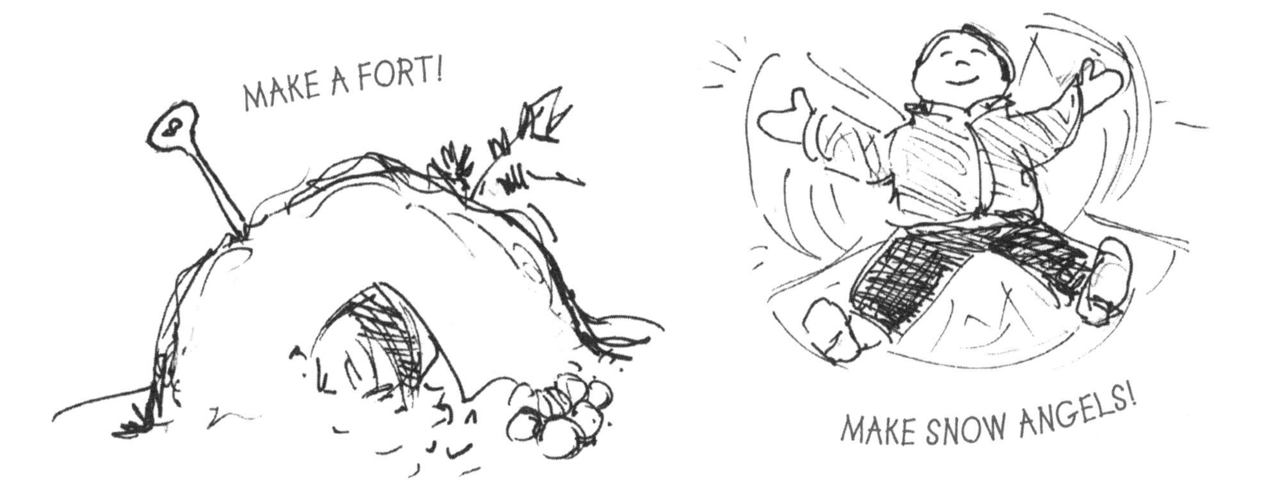

☐ **Track the phases of the moon for a month.** If it is a cloudy night, just draw the clouds. (See pages 72–75 for more ideas.)

☐ **See if a local nature center offers a winter workshop in tracking.** Some good tracking books to check out are *A Field Guide to Animal Tracks* by Olaus Murie and *A Guide to Nature in Winter* by Don Stokes.

☐ **Get cozy with a good book.** Try *Owl Moon* by Jane Yolen, *Cross-Country Cat* by Mary Calhoun, or *The Wind in the Willows* by Kenneth Grahame.

Looking at Trees *(and shrubs!)*

February is a good time to study trees and shrubs. Trees have one main trunk and can get very big, while shrubs have two or more trunks and are usually smaller. See if you can find buds forming, even this early, or leaves, seeds, and fruits still hanging on. Here are some tips for drawing trees.

1. START AT THE TREE TRUNK base and draw up. Split the branches, getting evenly thinner out to the twig tips.

2. JUST KEEP SPLITTING EVENLY – like a highway. Watch the outer shape. Look at individual shapes of birch – maple – oak – sycamore.

3. FILL IN DETAILS of leaves, shadows, bark. Label what kind of tree it is.

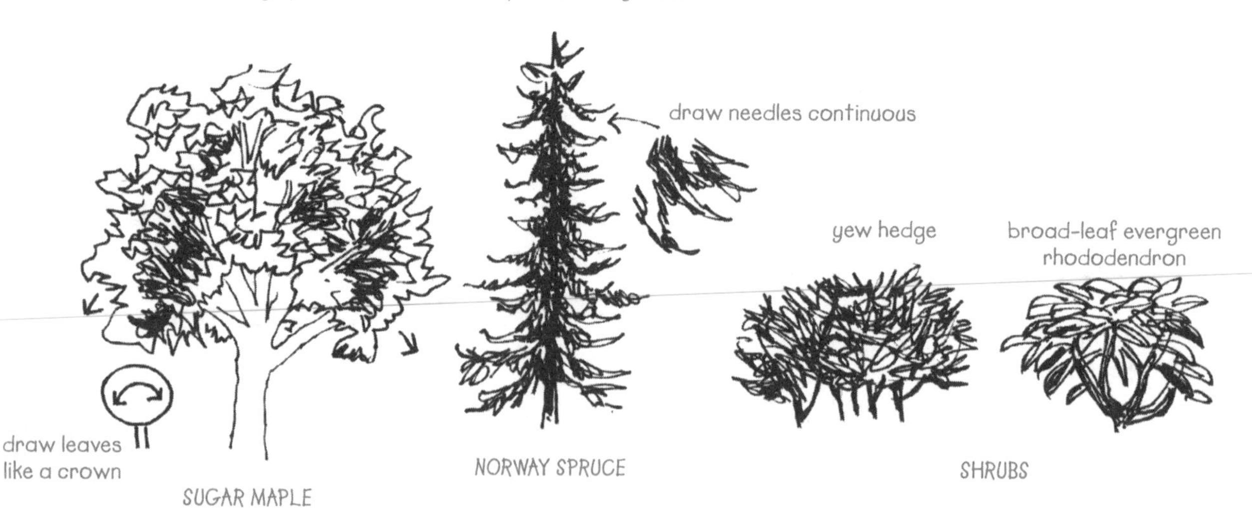

Draw a tree (or two) that grows near you. You can also take a photo or cut pictures from a magazine.

You might want to follow this tree through the seasons this year to see how it changes.

Date: Place: Time:

A Winter Tree Home

Animals need places to hide, rest, feed, and sleep during the cold winter months. A tree can provide shelter to lots of different animals.

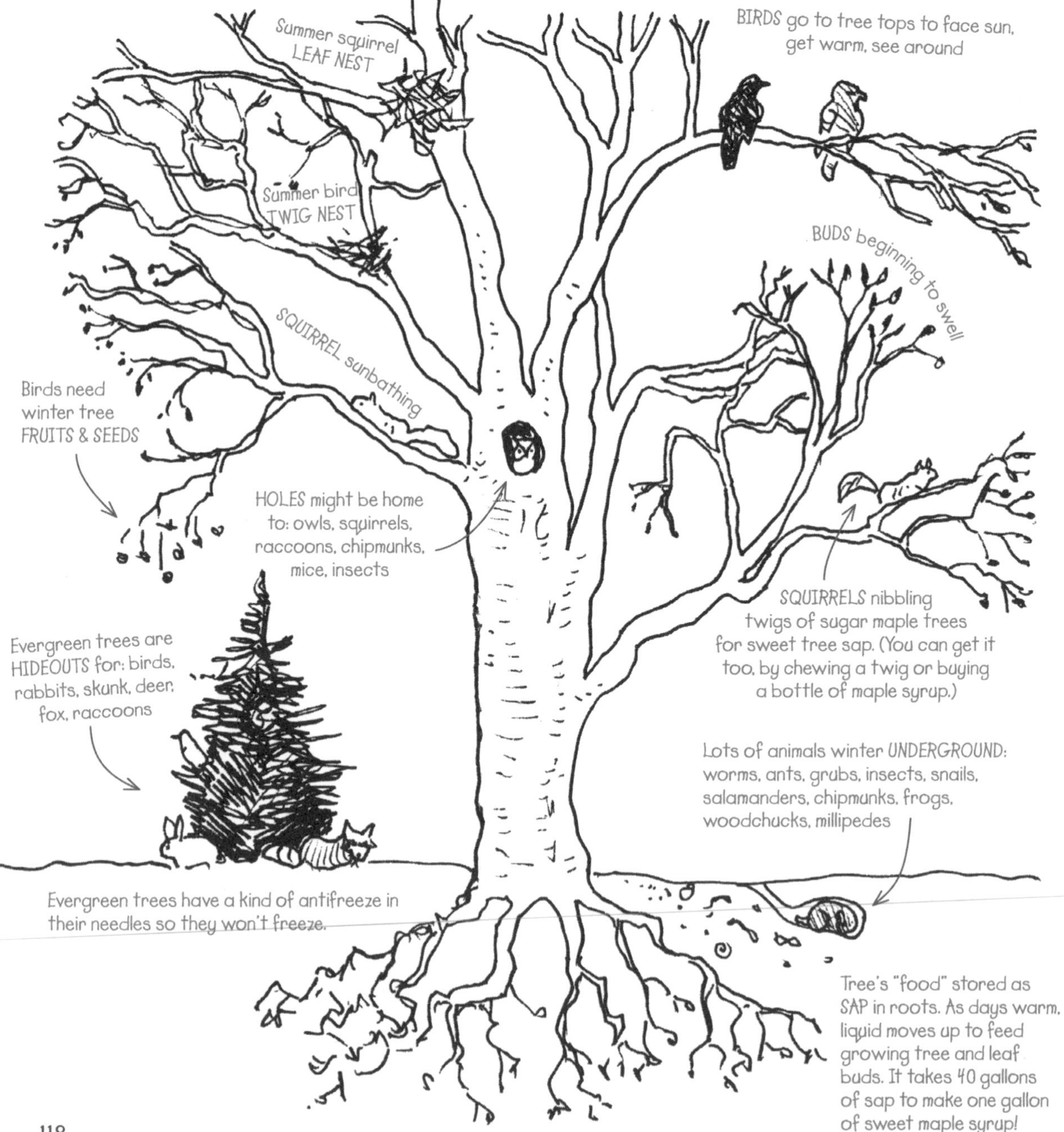

Draw your own tree home here with all the animals who might spend the winter in or around your tree.

If you are drawing an animal or insect from memory, don't hesitate to use a field guide for help. I often draw from books to get the shape and details correct.

Date: Place: Time:

Mysterious Shadows

You can't hold shadows or grab them, but you *can* see them and make them move. Many people have written poems about the mystery of shadows. Here is one I like.

MY SHADOW

I have a little shadow that goes in and out with me,
And what can be the use of him is more than I can see.
He is very, very like me from the heels up to the head;
And I see him jump before me, when I jump into my bed.
The funniest thing about him is the way he likes to grow —
Not at all like proper children, which is always very slow;
For he sometimes shoots up taller like an India-rubber ball,
And he sometimes gets so little that there's none of him at all.
He hasn't got a notion of how children ought to play,
And can only make a fool of me in every sort of way.
He stays so close beside me, he's a coward you can see;
I'd think shame to stick to nursie as that shadow sticks to me!
One morning, very early, before the sun was up,
I rose and found the shining dew on every buttercup;
But my lazy little shadow, like an arrant sleepy-head,
Had stayed at home behind me and was fast asleep in bed.

— ROBERT LOUIS STEVENSON, *A CHILD'S GARDEN OF VERSES*

Write your own shadow poem or story here.

More Things to Do

* **Play shadow tag** with a group of friends.
* **Read *Peter Pan*** by James Barrie or watch the movie. Remember how lost Peter feels without his shadow?
* **Look up British artist Andy Goldsworthy** and learn how he likes to use shadows in his outdoor sculptures.
* **Make a sculpture piece** of different shapes of cardboard and put it outside where there is bright sunlight. Notice how the shadows become a part of your art.

MARCH

Signs of Spring

MARCH IS A WONDERFUL MONTH OF HOPE. Winter's back has been broken and signs of spring are stirring, though it may still feel cold and dark. The old Roman calendar had only ten months. January and February weren't part of it; they were just called "the dead season." March was named by the Romans after Mars, the god of war and also of vegetation, which is fitting as this was the month that soldiers went to battle and farmers began planting.

The saying "March comes in like a lion and out like a lamb" refers to the constellations Leo the Lion and Aries the Ram — both are prominent in the March sky. Also, the weather is often ferocious in early March and gentler at the end of the month.

This is the month to begin looking for signs of new plant life. Go outside and listen to the chatter of the birds, feel the first warm breezes, smell the damp earth, and know that here and now, all is right. Be present to the sound of those birds, that rushing wind, the warming land.

As soon as he saw the Big Boots, Pooh knew that an Adventure was going to happen.

— A.A. MILNE, *WINNIE THE POOH*

MY NATURE NOTES

Date:	Time:
Place:	Temperature:
What's the weather like?	
Phase of the moon:	Time of sunrise:
	Time of sunset:
Look out the window or go outdoors, then jot down your observations, draw a picture, or describe a scene.	

To print out more pages like this, go to *www.storey.com/thenatureconnection.php.*

Go on a Nature Quest!

Start each month by taking a good look around. Go for a walk and see what you can find (use all your senses!) that gives a clue to the season. Try it on several different days and see how your answers change.

Can you find...	Describe what you notice.
☐ crocuses in a front yard	
☐ sparrows singing in a tree	
☐ mud — anywhere	
☐ salamanders under a log	

What else can you find?	
☐	
☐	
☐	
☐	
☐	
☐	
☐	
☐	
☐	

Picture of the Month

Choose one or two (or more!) things from your list to draw or photograph here.

Date: Place: Time:

Welcoming the Equinox

Just two months ago, the North Pole was in total darkness around the clock, while in the South Pole the sun shone 24 hours a day. Now, Earth has moved farther in its orbit around the sun, and we experience the spring (vernal) equinox. This means that for a few days around the 20th of March, the whole world experiences what the Equator has all year long: 12 hours of day and 12 hours of night. Baghdad, Paris, Sydney, Tokyo, Anchorage, Nairobi, New York, you name it, all enjoy the same amount of daylight.

The word *equinox* is from the Latin: *equi* (equal) and *nox* (night). *Vernal* comes from the Latin word for spring, *vernalis*.

NORTH POLE

SOUTH POLE

Right after the spring equinox, the equal balance between light and dark shifts as the days in the northern hemisphere grow longer than the nights and the days in the southern hemisphere grow shorter than the nights. This change continues until the summer (or winter) solstice in June (see page 172), which marks the longest (or shortest) day of the year.

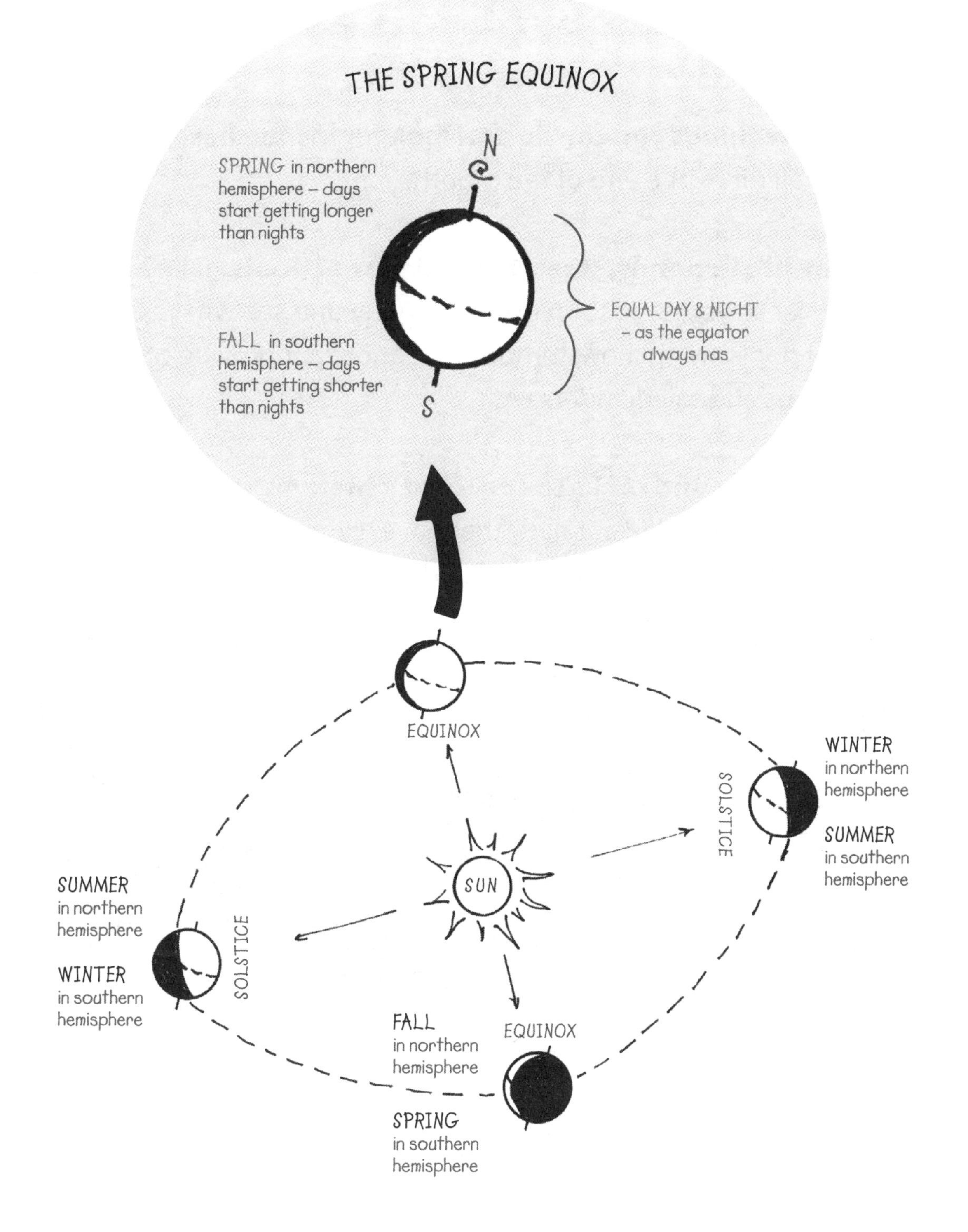
THE SPRING EQUINOX
N
SPRING in northern hemisphere – days start getting longer than nights
FALL in southern hemisphere – days start getting shorter than nights
S
EQUAL DAY & NIGHT – as the equator always has
EQUINOX
WINTER in northern hemisphere
SUMMER in southern hemisphere
SOLSTICE
SUN
SUMMER in northern hemisphere
WINTER in southern hemisphere
SOLSTICE
FALL in northern hemisphere
EQUINOX
SPRING in southern hemisphere

Pull on your rubber boots and go find some puddles to stomp in!

Here are some things you can do and look for in March. See if you can check them all off by the end of the month.

- [ ] **Look for life in ponds, streams, and vernal pools.** Take a net and a collecting jar so you can scoop up some water and see what's wiggling in it. (Vernal pools are shallow, temporary ponds that provide breeding places for frogs and salamanders.)

- [ ] **Turn over logs and rocks to see what's hiding there.** Numerous ectotherms (cold-blooded animals) that have wintered in the leaf litter can be found around rotting logs and under rocks.

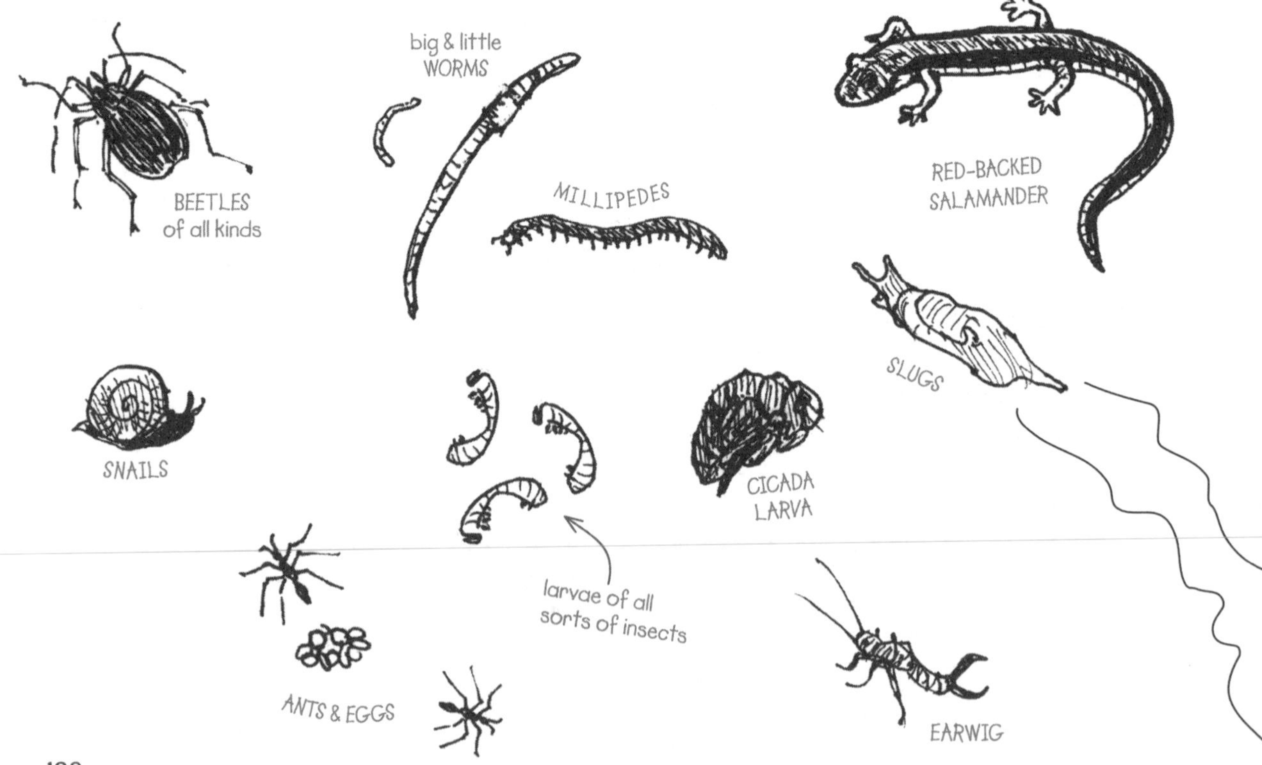

Ride your bike or skateboard to an open field or lot and see what new shoots are coming up.

Collect some nature things that speak of March to you. Bring them indoors to put in a bowl or on a platter. Draw the objects in pen or pencil or watercolors. Label them.

Go fly a kite! Did you know that kite-flying competitions are very popular in some other countries? See if you can find out more!

Cut some branches for forcing indoors. Many shrubs and trees are just waiting for warm weather to burst into bloom. You can clip several 8- to 12-inch branches of plants such as forsythia, cherry, apple, or star magnolia and put them in a vase of water. See how much earlier they open up than the ones outside.

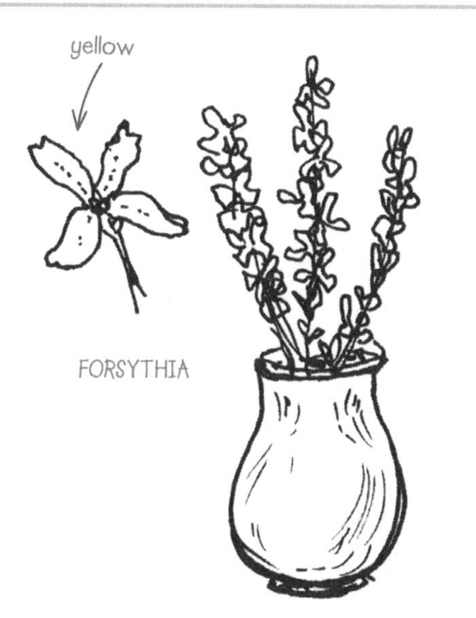

Unwind with a good book. Try *Roxaboxen* by Alice McLerran — it's about a bunch of kids living out in the Arizona desert, who build a village with forts out of rocks, plants, and other natural objects. Look in the illustrations for the little animals watching them!

Drawing What You See: Birds

Drawing birds is a good way to learn more about them. Practice drawing from photographs with clear profiles. You can find good ones in field guides and online.

Make some bird drawings here.

Date: Place: Time:

Nature at the End of a Leash

Take your dog for a walk and let his or her nose lead the way. (If you don't have a dog, maybe you can borrow a neighbor's, or invite a friend who has a dog to come along. I've even seen people in cities walking cats on leashes!) Notice where the dog sniffs and watch his nose follow the breeze. See if you can figure out what he smells. Think about what it would be like to have such a strong sense of smell.

If you don't have a dog, go for a walk on your own and see how many signs of spring you can notice. You can find them anywhere, even in a big city!

Here are some things to look and listen for (check them off as you find them):

- [ ] **Little green shoots** of plants and early flowers (snowdrops, crocuses, daffodils, tulips)
- [ ] **Birds** beginning to sing

- [ ] **Running, dripping, trickling water** as ice and snow melt

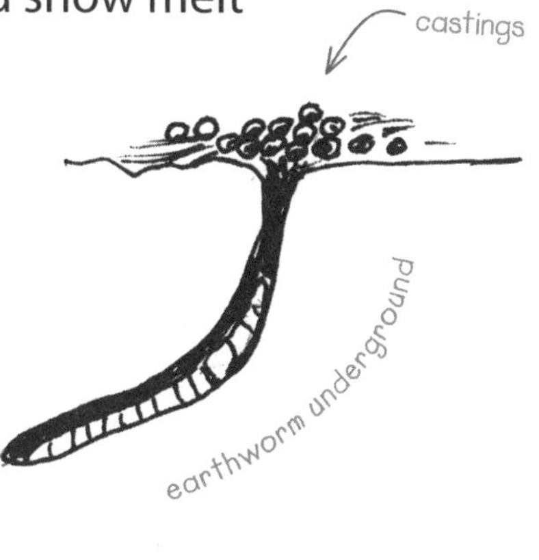

- [ ] **Earthworms** (Look for little piles of round dirt pellets called "castings." Earthworms eat their way through the ground, digesting and excreting the dirt, which enriches the soil.)
- [ ] **Scent of damp earth**
- [ ] **Mud!**
- [ ] **Warmer breezes and stronger sunlight** as the sun climbs higher
- [ ] **Insects** buzzing around (flies, beetles, bees)
- [ ] **Buds swelling** on trees and shrubs
- [ ] **Frogs calling** from ponds and vernal pools

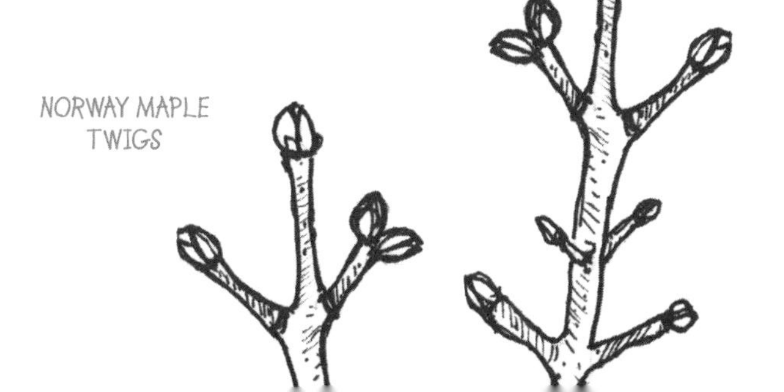

Signs of Spring: Green Things Growing

Where I live, the plant world changes a lot between the beginning of March and the end. Is this true where you live? With the longer days and warmer temperatures, I notice the grass turning green, the buds swelling on trees and shrubs, and early flowers appearing. March is my favorite month. It's so dramatic in its daily changes! The earth seems to be waking up, yawning, stretching, and giving us a big grin.

DAFFODILS begin to come up first in sunny, sheltered spots

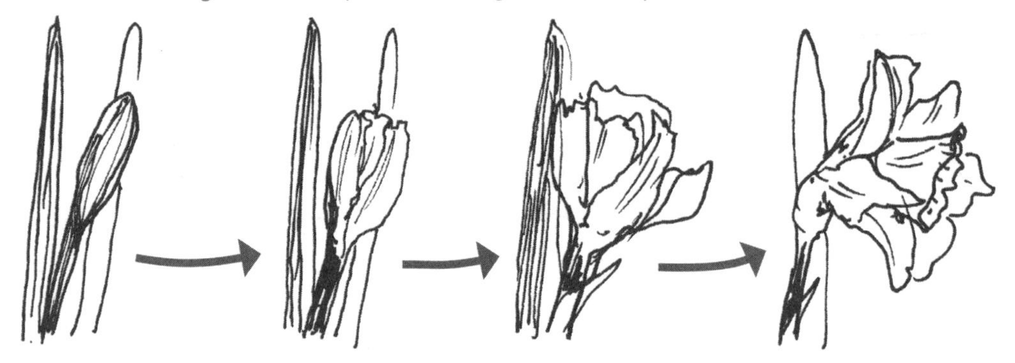

Some trees flowers come out early too:

MAGNOLIAS

early bees & ants love its pollen

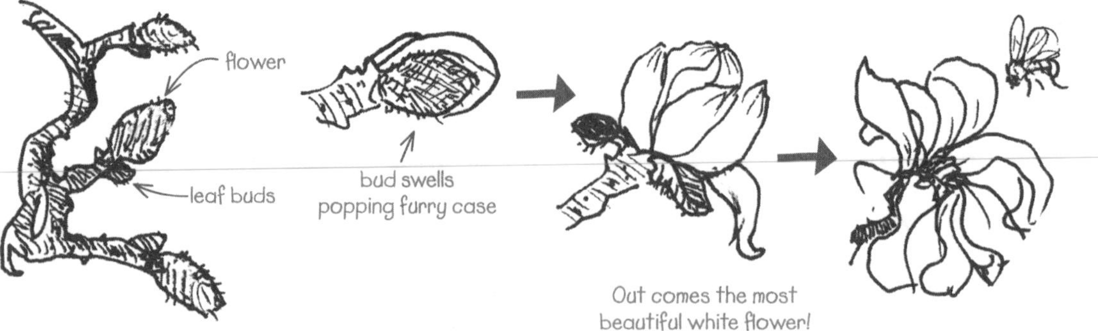

BUDDING TWIGS

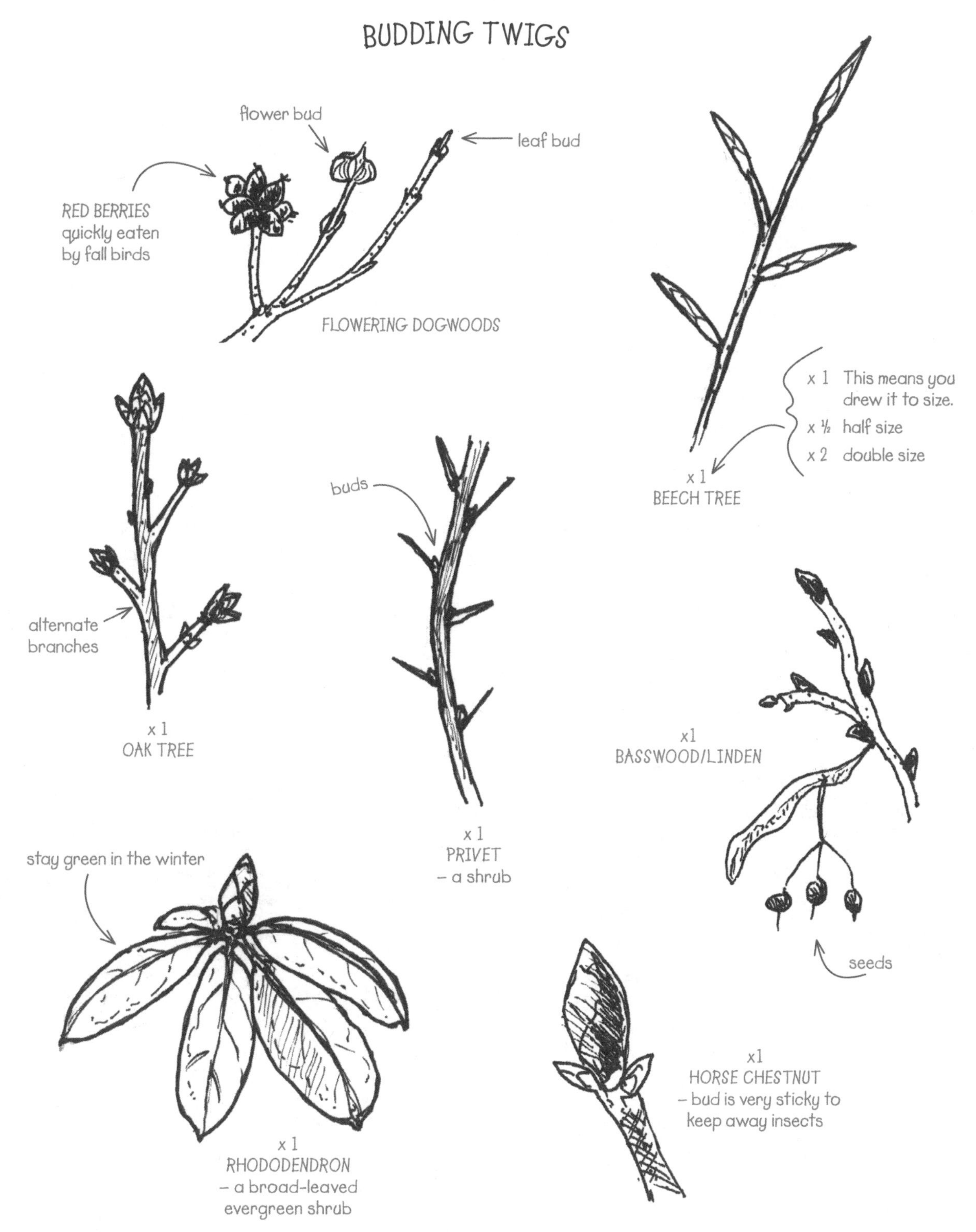

APRIL

The World Reawakens

APRIL IS ALL ABOUT REBIRTH AND GROWTH. The Romans named it after their word *aperire* meaning "to open or blossom." (And the word *Easter* comes from the names of several ancient goddesses of the dawn and spring — Eos, Astarte, Eostra.) In the northern calendar, it is the first full month of spring, a time when the days are considerably longer and the nights shorter. The sun is warming Earth as it has for billions of years.

Turtles, snakes, fish, frogs, and salamanders begin to emerge from their winter torpor. The first of the insects are out — various bees, early butterflies, little gnats, and flies. Earthworms are coming up from their winter underground holes. Local birds and returning migrants are hungrily eating those insects and will soon be looking for mates.

April begins the frenzy of awakening, breeding, gestation, birth, rearing, and growing up. For the farmer and gardener, the weather this month determines if the soil is warm and dry enough to begin plowing and if livestock can be turned out to pasture.

It's the land that feeds our children;
It's the land.
You cannot own the land;
The land owns you.

— DOUGIE MACLEAN, SCOTTISH FOLKSINGER

MY NATURE NOTES

Date:	Time:
Place:	Temperature:
What's the weather like?	
Phase of the moon:	Time of sunrise:
	Time of sunset:
Look out the window or go outdoors, then jot down your observations, draw a picture, or describe a scene.	

To print out more pages like this, go to *www.storey.com/thenatureconnection.php.*

Go on a Nature Quest!

Start each month by taking a good look around. Go for a walk and see what you can find (use all your senses!) that gives a clue to the season. Try it on several different days and see how your answers change.

Can you find...	Describe what you notice.
☐ tracks in mud	
☐ crows cawing	
☐ rain dripping	

What else can you find?

☐	
☐	
☐	
☐	
☐	
☐	
☐	
☐	
☐	
☐	

Picture of the Month

Choose one or two (or more!) things from your list to draw or photograph here.

Date: Place: Time:

What's a Reptile? What's an Amphibian?

Reptiles and amphibians may seem to be the same kind of animal at first. Both are ectothermic (see page 96), have skeletons, and reproduce by laying eggs. But reptiles lay their eggs on land, while amphibians start out life in the water, breathing through gills, and move to land as they develop into adults. (*Amphi* is the Greek word for "both.")

REPTILES

TURTLES, LIZARDS, SNAKES, CROCODILES, & ALLIGATORS are reptiles. Reptiles have tougher skin, covered with scales or plates.

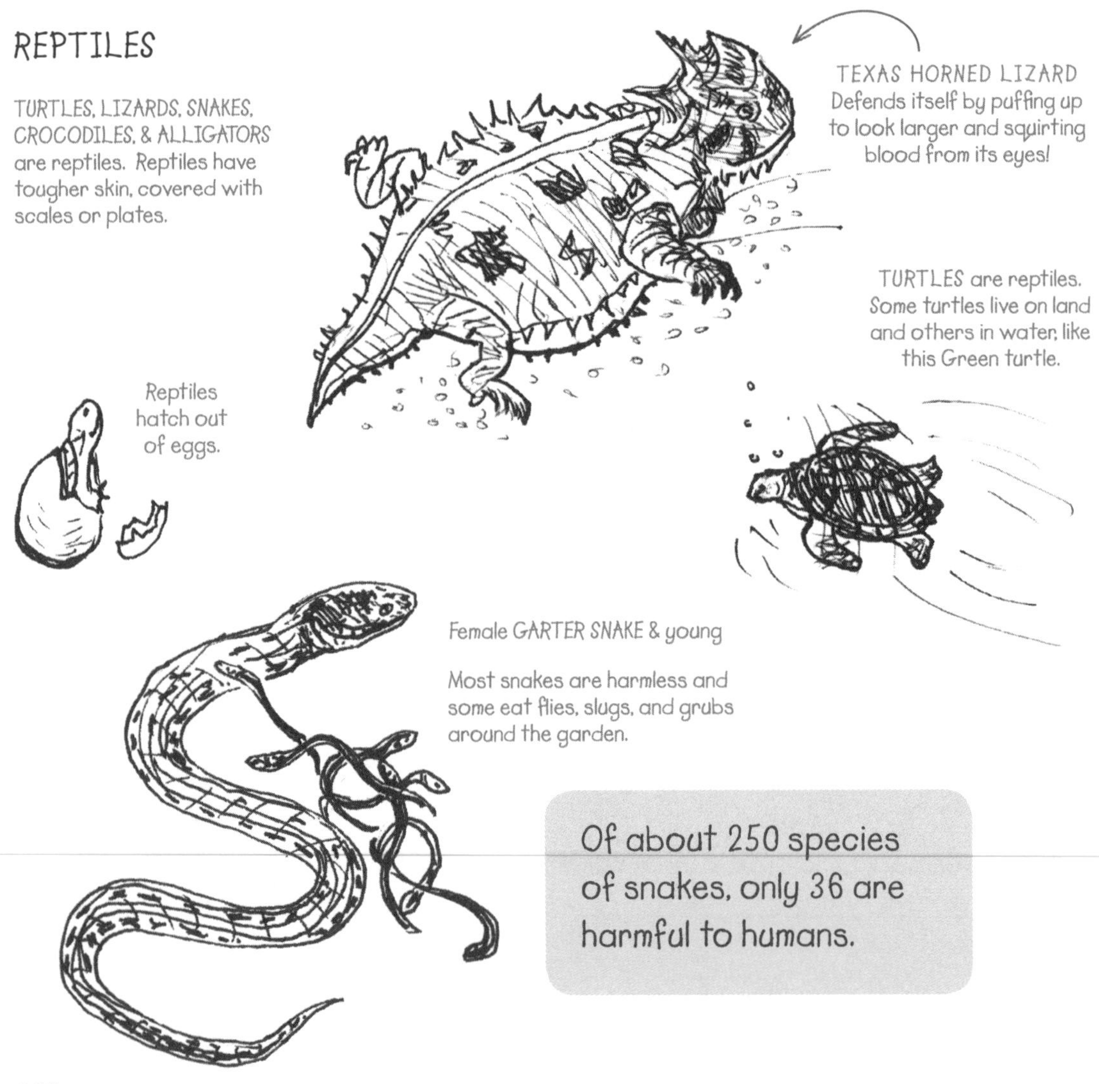

Of about 250 species of snakes, only 36 are harmful to humans.

AMPHIBIANS

FROGS, TOADS, NEWTS, & SALAMANDERS are amphibians. Amphibians develop from eggs, but in different stages.

AMERICAN TOAD (male) trilling for a mate. Toads are useful to have around as they eat slugs. Some people consider them good luck!

TOAD TADPOLES develop to adults within a few weeks and are fun to raise in a big container of water. Be sure they have a rock to hop up onto.

EGGS

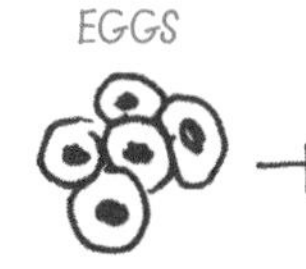

TADPOLE

growing legs & lungs

coming out of water

hops to land & grows bigger

RED-BACKED SALAMANDER
This common salamander is unusual in that it lays its eggs on land.

SPRING PEEPER
Hard to see, but easy to hear, these tiny frogs make their spring song by filling an air sac under their throats.

Eons ago, *amphibians* were the first creatures to come out of the water to live on land. They still live in moist environments and have smooth, porous skin. *Porous* means full of holes, which means that they easily absorb toxins and pollutants in ponds and streams.

The presence of amphibians indicates the health of an eco-system, and declining numbers of these animals are causing concern to environmentalists.

Celebrating Earth Day

In the month when we honor our planet, we owe it to our only home to seriously consider what we can do to make it a better place for all of us to live, even for the smallest of centipedes at our feet. Of course, as a naturalist, you try to make every day into Earth Day! And there are many ways you can do this.

Look online at these great sites to find nature projects you can be part of all year-round:

Cornell Lab of Ornithology
A variety of Bird Watch opportunities for kids.
www.birds.cornell.edu

National Wildlife Federation
Has the Backyard Habitat project and other activities.
www.nwf.org

You can search the Internet for summer camps and vacation ideas that have to do with the environment. Local, state, and national parks often have wonderful programs on nature. Check out your local nature center, animal shelter, or scouting organization too.

National Audubon Society
State Audubon chapters have their own projects for kids.
www.audubon.org

The Jane Goodall Institute
An international organization for children and the environment.
www.janegoodall.org

Journey North
A good resource site for all sorts of observation, record keeping and research projects.
www.journeynorth.org

National Geographic Kids
A fun site full of information on animals, nature, science, and other great stuff.
www.kids.nationalgeographic.com

What's the Deal with Fossil Fuel?

You have probably heard a lot about fossil fuels, carbon emissions, global climate change, and so on. What exactly does it all mean? Well, fossil fuels are called that because they come from fossils which are the squished remains of billions of ancient organisms (plants, animals, insects) that lived on Earth over 300 million years ago.

Fossil fuels are actually ancient plants – giant ferns, mosses, peat bogs, and vast forests – that once covered the land and decayed really slowly.

Eons later, what remains are various compounds of carbon, which humans have been burning in huge amounts for energy for the past 300 years or so. The pressure of tons of rock and soil compressed the carbon remains into a solid form (coal) or into liquid (oil or petroleum) or vapor (natural gas). Great pockets of oil, gas, and coal are found around the world wherever ancient plants and animals died and decomposed in large numbers and were buried.

Fossil fuels must be brought up from deep within the earth before we can burn them. Humans use vast amounts of fossil fuels to create electricity, grow food, build buildings, power our electronics, and run our daily lives. This creates two problems: Burning these fuels creates carbon dioxide (CO_2) and pollutes our air and ground. And the supply is limited, so we need to find other sources of energy. (See pages 176–177 for more on fossil fuels.)

Coal = hardened form of ancient plants, found within and beside mountains

Gas = a gaseous fuel, often found with petroleum; also methane, butane, propane

Oil = liquid petroleum (from the Latin *petra* "rock" and *oleum* "oil")

Rain or shine, this is a great month to see lots of things happening outside!

Here are some things you can do and look for in April. See if you can check them all off by the end of the month.

☐ **Track daily rainfall.** Compare the overall total to other months in your area. Are you still seeing snow or frost? Is there dew on the ground in the mornings?

☐ **Take a walk on the wet side!** Make a point of going outdoors in a rain shower. Notice raindrops on leaves and grass and spider webs. Look for little rivulets of water running downhill. What direction is the rain coming from? Is it a warm or a cold rain?

Notice images on raindrops are upside down.

☐ **Think about how animals find shelter from the rain.**

SQUIRREL

Have you ever seen a squirrel using its tail as an umbrella?

PIGEON

Many birds waterproof their feathers by keeping them oiled. They use their beaks to spread special oil from a gland near their tails.

HORSE

Many animals don't seem to mind getting wet. You often see cows and horses standing out in the rain, even if there is shelter nearby.

On a warm, sunny day, take an insect count. Can you find honeybees and bumblebees (what is the difference?). What about wasps? Look for ants, flies, gnats, butterflies, and moths. How many different kinds of beetles can you spot?

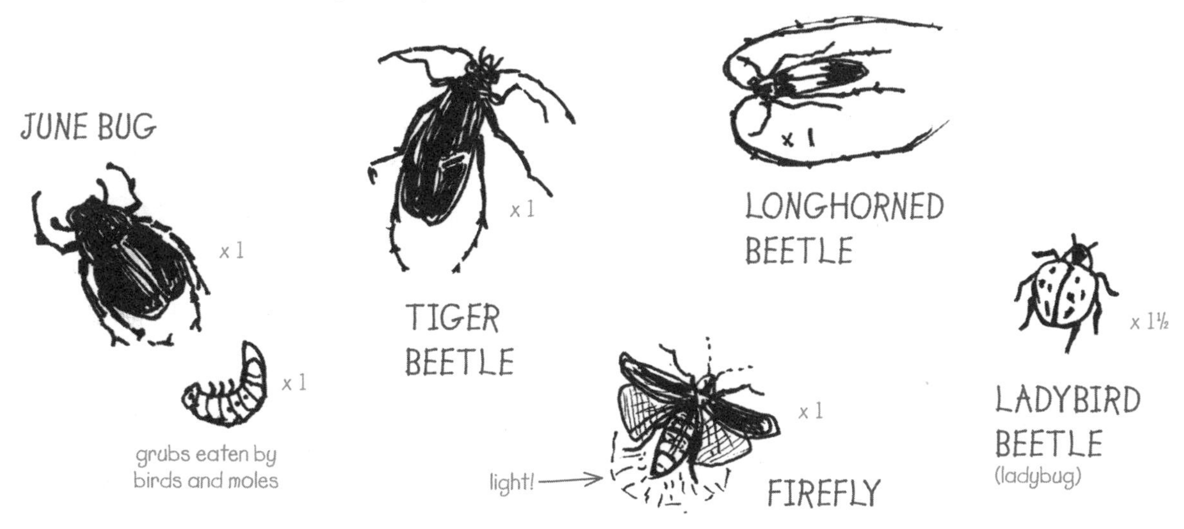

Give a helping hand to reptiles and amphibians. On rainy April nights in New England and elsewhere, people of all ages help yellow-spotted, blue-spotted, and red-backed salamanders and red efts cross roads to crawl into adjacent shallow ponds for mating and egg laying. Turtle, snake, and frog watchers also spend hours helping these slow creatures safely cross dangerous asphalt lanes so they too can successfully breed and lay eggs.

Curl up with a good book. Some nature writers I like are James Herriot, Gary Paulsen, Lois Lowry, and Robert Pyle. I also like these poets: Emily Dickinson, Walt Whitman, and Mary Oliver.

RED EFT

Spring Blossoms

Let's take a close look at some familiar flowers. How many different ones can you find blooming around your home, neighborhood, and school?

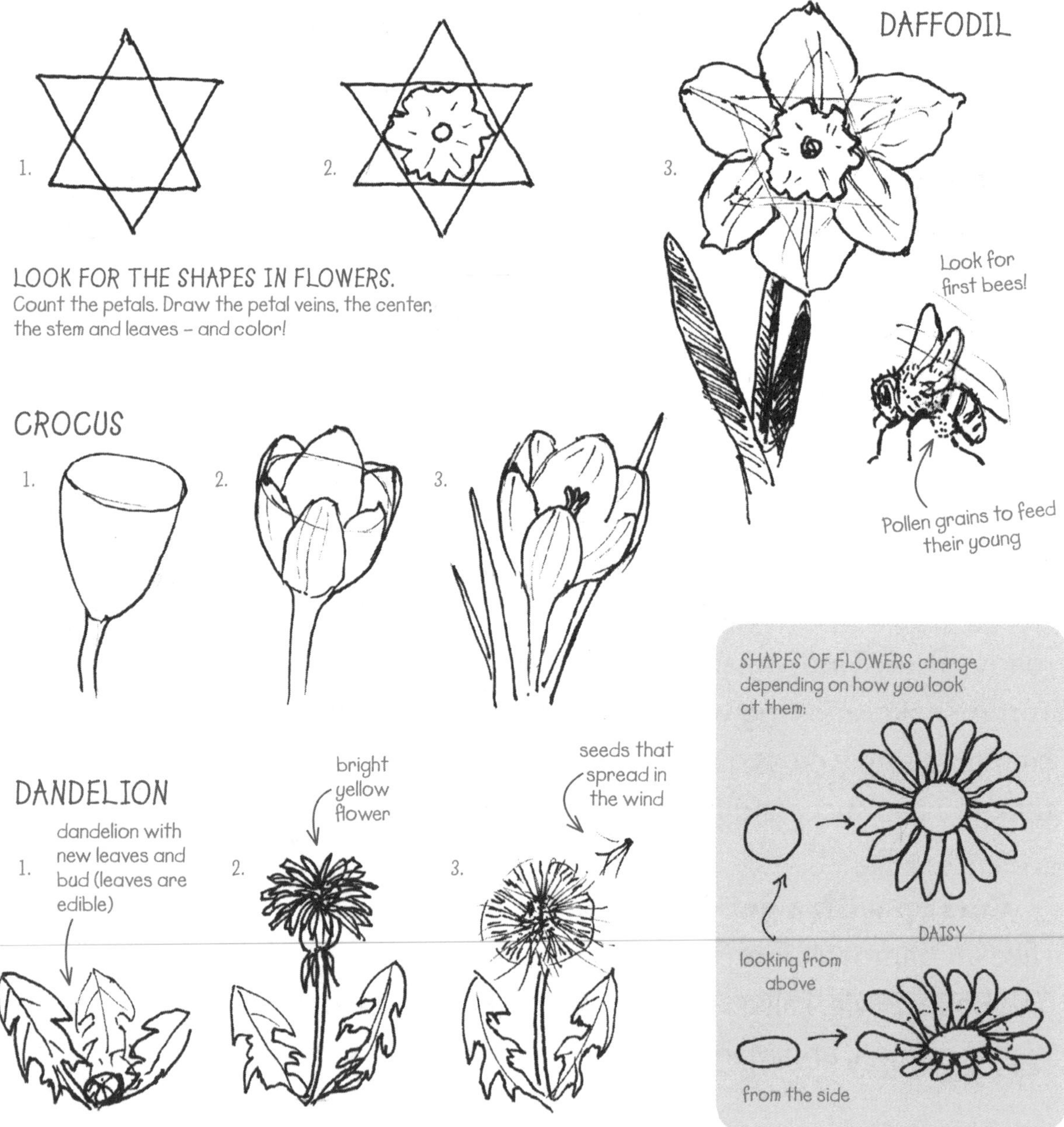

LOOK AT LEAVES TOO!

Leaves come in many different shapes and sizes and even colors, though most are green in the spring and summer. See pages 242–244 for more about leaves.

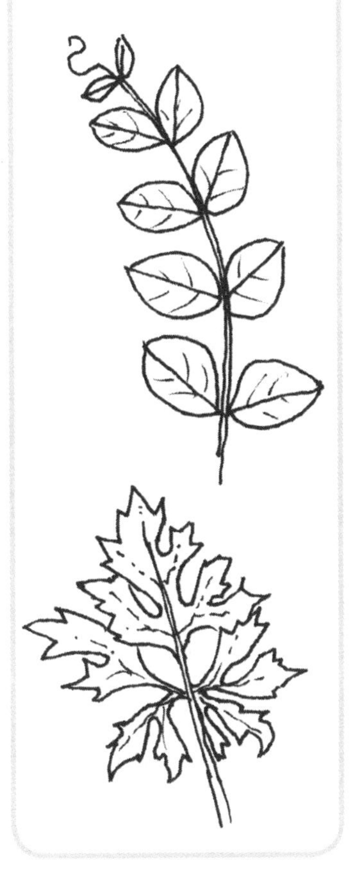

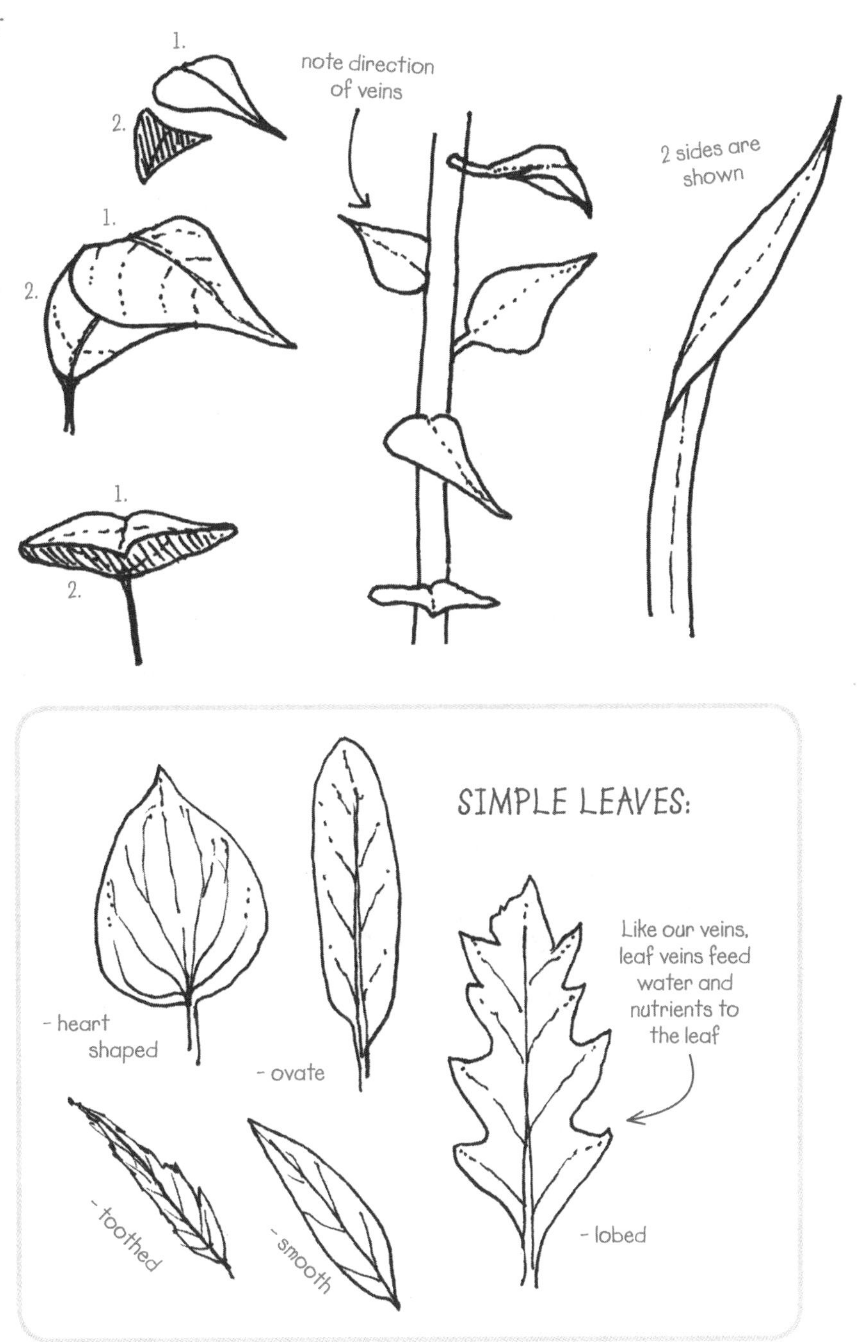

Wondering about the Weather

This is a good month to learn about the weather. "April showers bring May flowers" may or may not be the case, depending on where you live. In the Midwest, there can be dramatic flooding and tornadoes now and throughout the year. Areas in the far West might experience high winds, fires, mud slides, and late snows. In the high mountain states of the West and Northwest, blizzards and avalanches occur. In many parts of the country, April can bring ice and sudden snowstorms. In New England, we have mud!

As the snow melts in some places, MUD SEASON arrives before spring. The ground thaws and turns into gooey, sticky mud on many unpaved roads, which causes problems for cars and people.

Learn your local weather systems.

You can find many sources: the newspaper, the Internet, your local TV station, and of course, the library. Clip interesting articles about the weather (make sure to include the date) and paste them in a notebook. (See pages 54–56 for more on the weather.)

More Things to Do

* **Find out what weather fronts are** and how they affect the weather where you live. Draw a map to explain what you learn.
* **Do you know anyone who has experienced an extreme weather** event such as a tornado, hurricane, big blizzard, or mud slide? Interview them to learn what it was like and how they handled it.
* **Do some research on global climate change** and how it is affecting weather patterns, temperature changes, and water sources.

Put your weather research here.

Mapping Where You Live

It can still be pretty cold and wet in April in many areas. Here's a good way to spend a gloomy afternoon while still pretending to be outdoors.

Make a map of your town.
You can get an aerial map from your town hall or look for one at the local library or online. Using that as a guide, draw your map in this space. Color in with different markers the areas that are industrial, business, residential, and green space. Put in the major roads and mark in your house.

Draw your town map here.

Make a map of your state.

As we learn more about nature right around us, it becomes important to learn about the geography of where we live. Do you live in a town or city or out in the suburbs or country? Are there woods near you? How about a lake or stream or river? Knowing about the geography of where you live helps you understand why your area has certain land forms and weather patterns.

Draw your state map here.

MAY

A Happening Month

May is thought to be named after Maia Maiestas, the ancient Roman goddess of fertility. For the ancient Celts of Northern Europe, May 1 marked the coming of summer, the beginning of crop planting, and the delivery of healthy young livestock. Many of the old customs that celebrated the rebirth of life survive today, in the form of maypole dances, Morris dancing (an English men's folk dance), May baskets, and processions with garlands of flowers.

While humans celebrate, things are really gearing up in the world of nature. Flowers are popping into bloom, new leaves are coming out overnight, migratory birds are returning from the South, insects are appearing, animals and plants all around you are courting, mating, laying, hatching, and birthing babies so their genes will be passed on and their species will be guaranteed survival for another year. May is a fantastic month to be a naturalist!

The air is like a butterfly
With frail blue wings.
The happy earth looks at the sky
And sings.

—JOYCE KILMER, *SPRING*

MY NATURE NOTES

Date:	Time:
Place:	Temperature:
What's the weather like?	
Phase of the moon:	Time of sunrise:
	Time of sunset:
Look out the window or go outdoors, then jot down your observations, draw a picture, or describe a scene.	

To print out more pages like this, go to *www.storey.com/thenatureconnection.php.*

Go on a Nature Quest!

Start each month by taking a good look around. Go for a walk and see what you can find (use all your senses!) that gives a clue to the season. Try it on several different days and see how your answers change.

Can you find . . .	Describe what you notice.
☐ ants crawling on peonies	
☐ scent of apple blossoms	
☐ chimney swifts swooping	

What else can you find?

☐	
☐	
☐	
☐	
☐	
☐	
☐	
☐	
☐	
☐	

Picture of the Month

Choose one or two (or more!) things from your list to draw or photograph here.

Date: Place: Time:

May is a busy month in the world of nature.

Here are some things you can do and look for in May. See if you can check them all off by the end of the month.

☐ **Hold a May Day Celebration.** Read about the ancient Celts and about why May 1 was such an important time of year for them.

☐ **Take a walk outdoors and imagine you lived 2,500 years ago.** What would you be wearing and what would the land look like around you? As you walk, think about what it would have been like to live 800, 300, 100, 50, and 20 years ago. How has the land changed around you over the centuries and decades?

☐ **Lie under a tree for fun.** I love to lie under an apple tree in full blossom — all the better if there are plenty of dandelions around. See if you can find a tree in bloom (it doesn't have to be an apple tree!). Spend some time lying under it listening to the bees and watching the petals fall around you.

☐ **Imagine you live in some magical place** with magical animals. What would they look like? How would they behave?

☐ **Make a collage or a mobile of your local leaf shapes.** How many different ones can you find? Press the leaves dry and put them between clear contact paper or iron them in wax paper. Or paste dried leaves on a piece of cardboard in a wreath or other pattern. Draw the various leaves on stiff paper, then color them and cut them out to make a mobile using sticks and twigs. Count all the different leaf shapes you have.

☐ **Learn the leaves you should not pick,** such as stinging nettle, poison ivy, and poison oak. Are there others in your area?

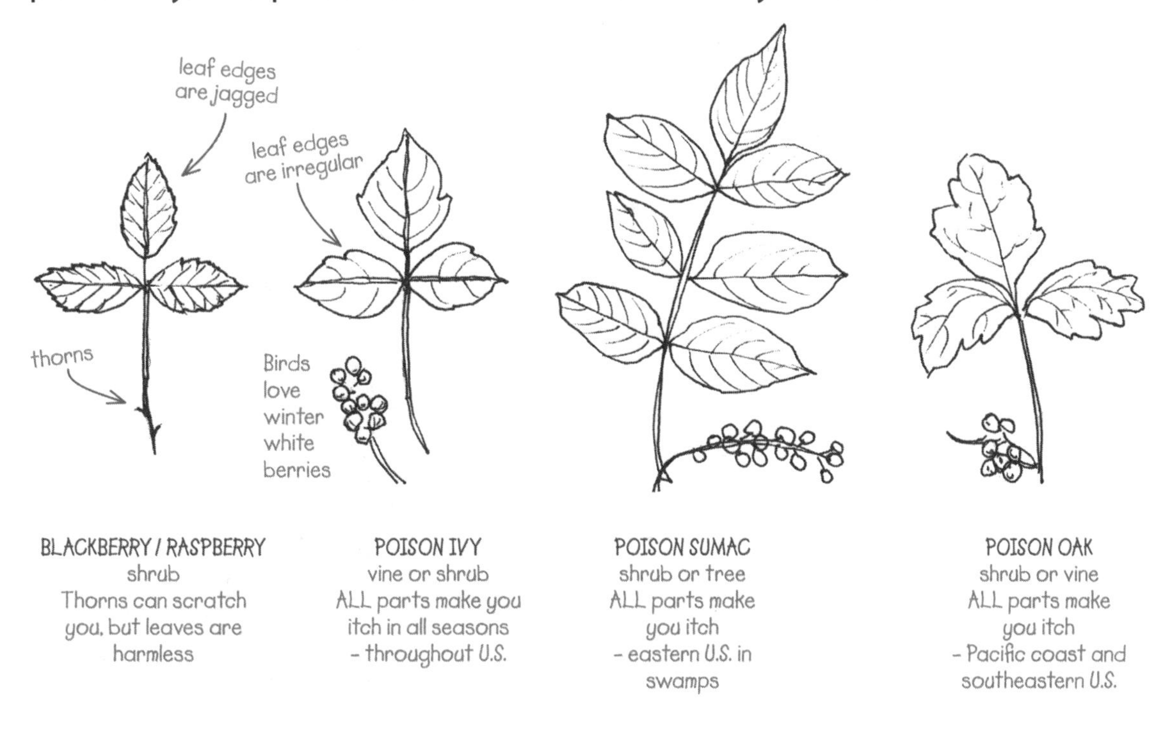

☐ **Relax with a good book.** Try *Redwall* and others in this series of fantasy adventures about woodland creatures by Brian Jacques; *Ida B. and Her Plans to Maximize Fun, Avoid Disaster and (Possibly) Save the World* by Katherine Hannigan; *Beatrix Potter: A Life in Nature* by Linda Lear.

An Incredible Journey

This is a big month for bird watchers as many songbirds, ducks and geese, shorebirds, herons, and hawks leave their winter homes and fly thousands of miles north. For generation upon generation, these birds have migrated to find the right food and nesting conditions to raise their families. Their offspring will cover those same flight routes, often without their parents.

Not all birds migrate; in fact, only 25 percent of the regularly recorded North American bird species migrate south of the United States border.

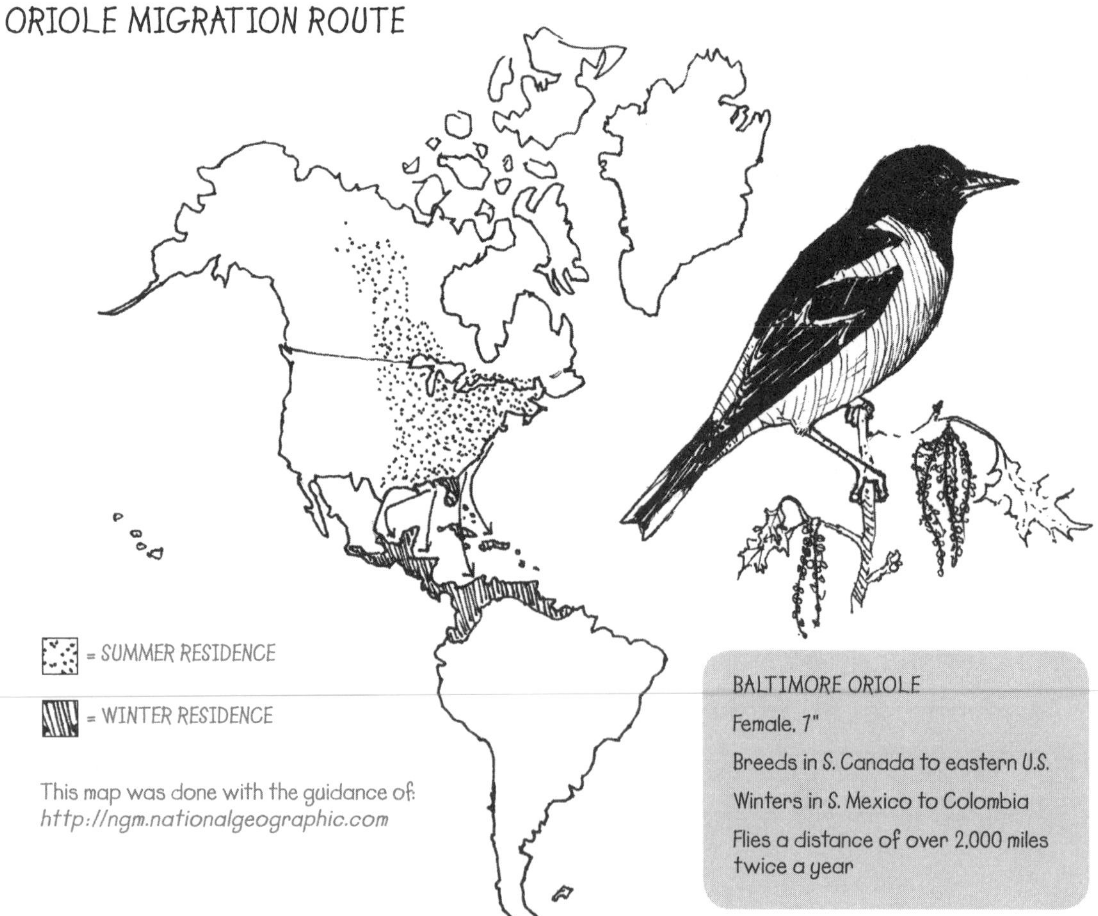

More and more species, such as the robin, mockingbird, cardinal, and Carolina wren, now stay all year long in their summer areas. Find out what birds live around you and if they stay or go for the winter months.

Why and how birds make this journey are questions even the best scientists are still figuring out, but you can have great fun researching this subject yourself. Search online, read books and journals, such as the Cornell Laboratory of Ornithology's *Living Bird*, and *The Birdwatcher's Companion* by Christopher Leahy.

SOME BIRD TYPES
(Over 700 species in N. America)

GREATER SCAUP
– breeds in the Arctic tundra and western Alaska; winters on the northeast Atlantic coast

GOLDEN PLOVER
– migrates from S. America to breed in Canada and Siberia

BARN SWALLOW
– found all over N. America; winters in S. America

BIRD FACTS

* Some scientists believe that migrations began at the end of the last ice age as the ice retreated and the northern lands became warmer.
* Birds can fly great distances without eating or sleeping, but somewhere along the way, they must stop to "refuel," as birders say.
* Birds use the stars, the sun, magnetic fields, and visual cues such as mountain ranges, rivers, and coastlines to find their way.
* The Arctic Tern migrates as much as 22,000 miles (35,400 km) round-trip. The Sooty Shearwater beats that, though – it travels 40,000 miles (64,370 km).

Learning Your Local Birds

Did you know that watching birds is one of the most popular outdoor activities? You can take a course, go on a field trip, or just find a place where birdwatchers go — most of them will be happy to help you learn. Or you can just go outside and make your own observations.

You already know that birds come in many different shapes and sizes, but they can be grouped into some general types. Here are a few of the more familiar ones.

* *Water fowl* (includes ducks, geese, swans, pelicans, egrets, herons) live near salt or fresh water. Many migrate great distances.

* *Raptors* (eagles, hawks, osprey, owls) are birds of prey, with strong hooked beaks and curved talons for hunting.

* *Songbirds* (finches, thrushes, warblers, wrens, sparrows) have adapted to habitats all over the world. Some migrate, others live year-round in one area. They are often our common backyard birds that we love to feed.

Make your bird notes or drawings, or paste your photos here.

Having a decent pair of binoculars and a good field guide will help a lot.

Date: Place: Time:

Spring Fever (and Hay Fever)

All during the spring, trees and flowers are bursting into bloom. Although we love the colorful display, those brightly colored petals are not designed for us, but to attract insects, birds, and even bats that will *pollinate* (fertilize) the plants. Pollination creates more seeds, which create more plants, which create more blossoms, so that more plants will grow. It's all about the survival of the species!

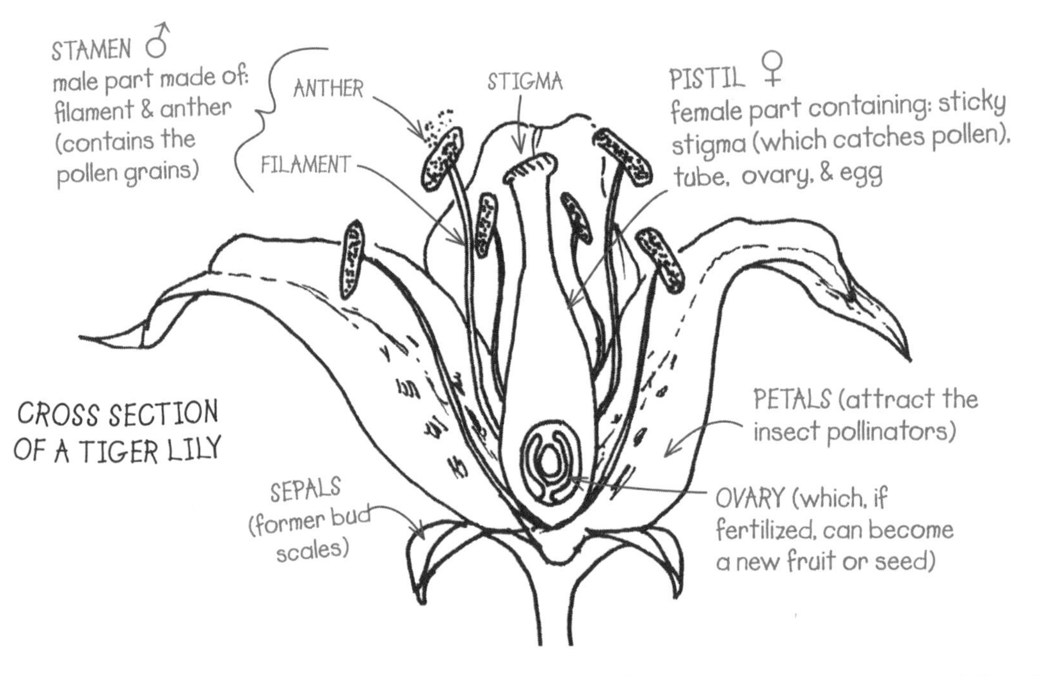

The pollinators fly to the blossoms seeking nectar to eat and feed their young. While they feed on the liquid nectar, they pick up tiny grains of pollen from the *stamen* (that's the male part of the flower). When they fly to another plant, the pollen falls onto the *pistil* (the female part, where the egg lies in the ovary). Once the pollen mixes with the egg, the fruit or seed will form.

TREES CAN HAVE:

FLOWERS THAT ARE POLLINATED BY THE WIND – usually before the leaves are out (includes evergreens, maple, birch, oak)

FLOWERS THAT ARE POLLINATED BY INSECTS – bees, ants, butterflies (includes apple, cherry, magnolia, lilac)

POLLEN FACTS

Pollen can be carried by the wind, instead of insects or birds. That kind of pollen, which comes from evergreens, oak trees, ragweed, and many grasses, among others, makes some people sneeze and itch with allergies.

When you see clouds of pollen swirling in the air, covering cars, and floating in puddles, you know it is just one of nature's many ways of surviving.

A funny way to remember what is happening is that the pollen making you sneeze is the male part of the flower. I call them the "bad dads."

Soon all those grains of pollen that didn't find a female plant to fertilize will lie scattered over the ground and become "dead dads." What's left? The "good moms," which are growing new flowers and fruits.

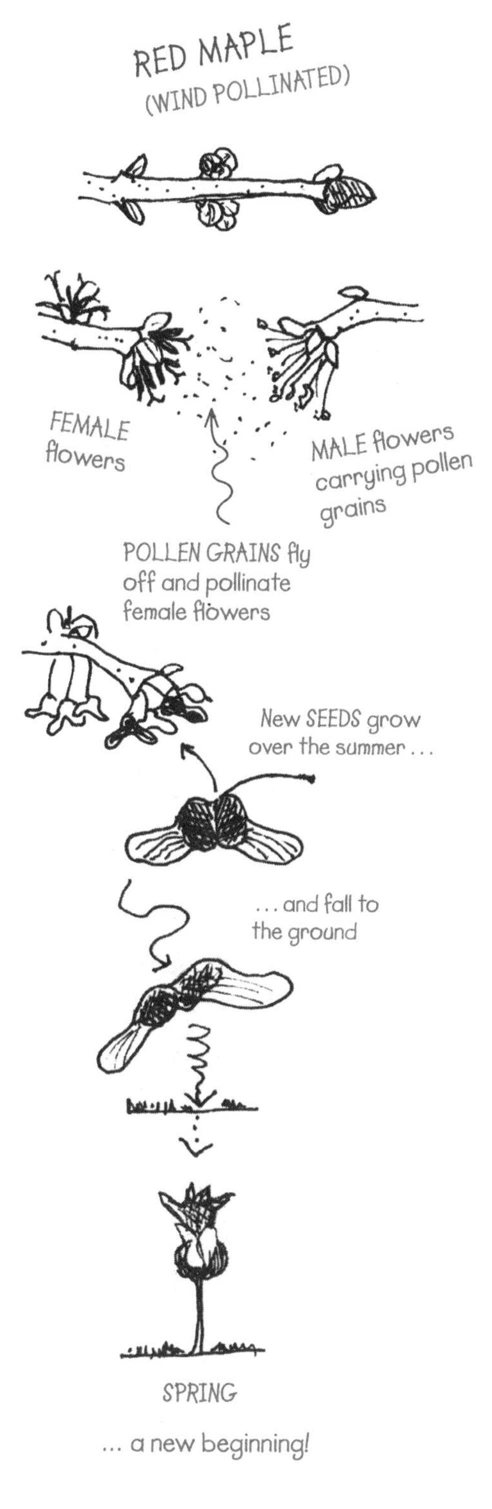

Quit Bugging Me!

Lots of insects appear in May and some of them can drive us crazy. Black flies, gnats, and mosquitoes might seem like awful pests, but they are an important part of the cycle of nature.

When one of these insects bites or stings you, it's not because it doesn't like you but because it needs you (your blood, actually) for food. But remember that all these insects taste very good to birds and bats and many other animals, like shrews, snakes, and frogs.

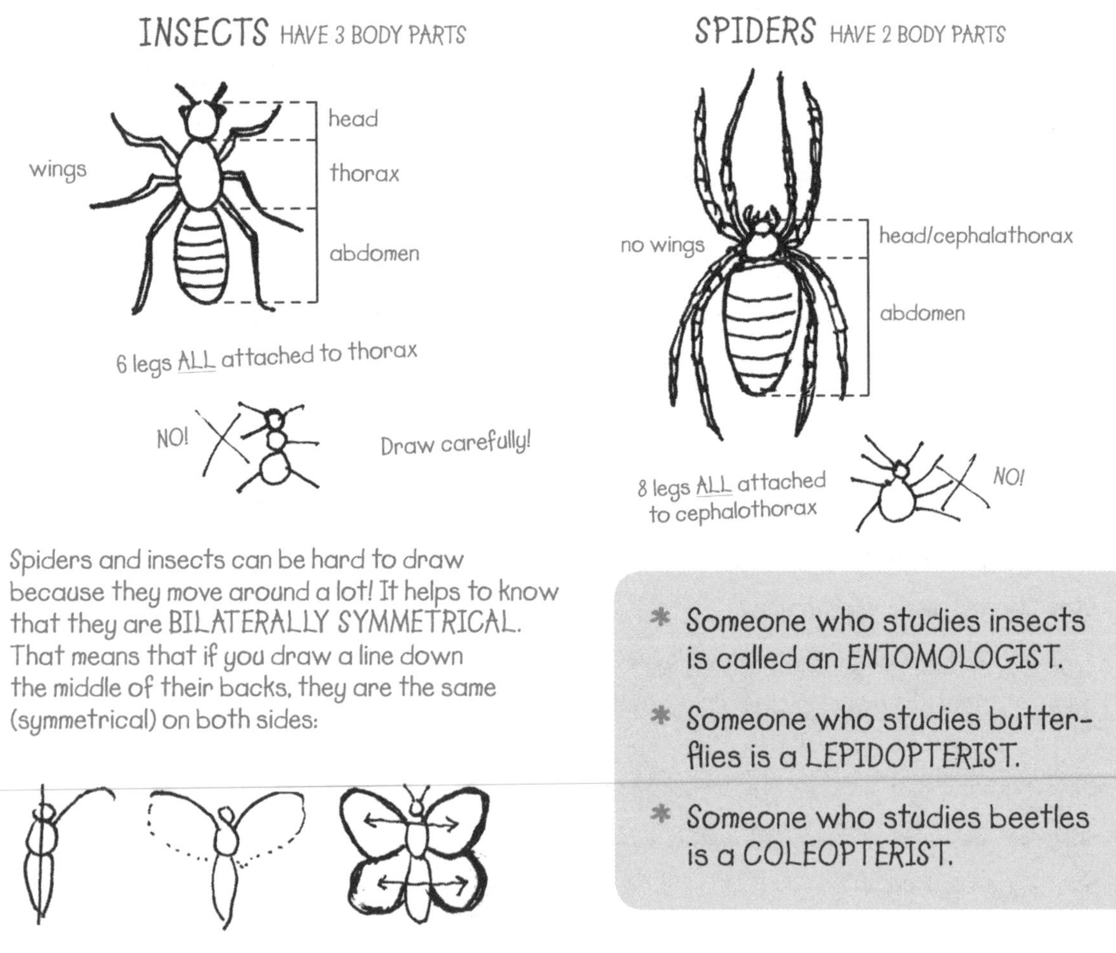

Spiders and insects can be hard to draw because they move around a lot! It helps to know that they are BILATERALLY SYMMETRICAL. That means that if you draw a line down the middle of their backs, they are the same (symmetrical) on both sides:

* Someone who studies insects is called an ENTOMOLOGIST.
* Someone who studies butterflies is a LEPIDOPTERIST.
* Someone who studies beetles is a COLEOPTERIST.

See pages 178–179 for more on bugs and insects and page 192 for more on butterflies and moths.

Make your drawings of insects or paste your photos here.

Date: Place: Time:

Make a Nature Treasure Map

Set out on a nature-sighting expedition in your neighborhood or school yard, or at a nearby park. You might want to take along binoculars and a hand lens so you can spot hidden things, too, like birds in the trees or small insects on the ground.

Make a map of your route, marking with an × all the spots where you found nature. Ask your family or friends to follow your map and see if they can find the same things. You could leave them little clues or surprises along the way!

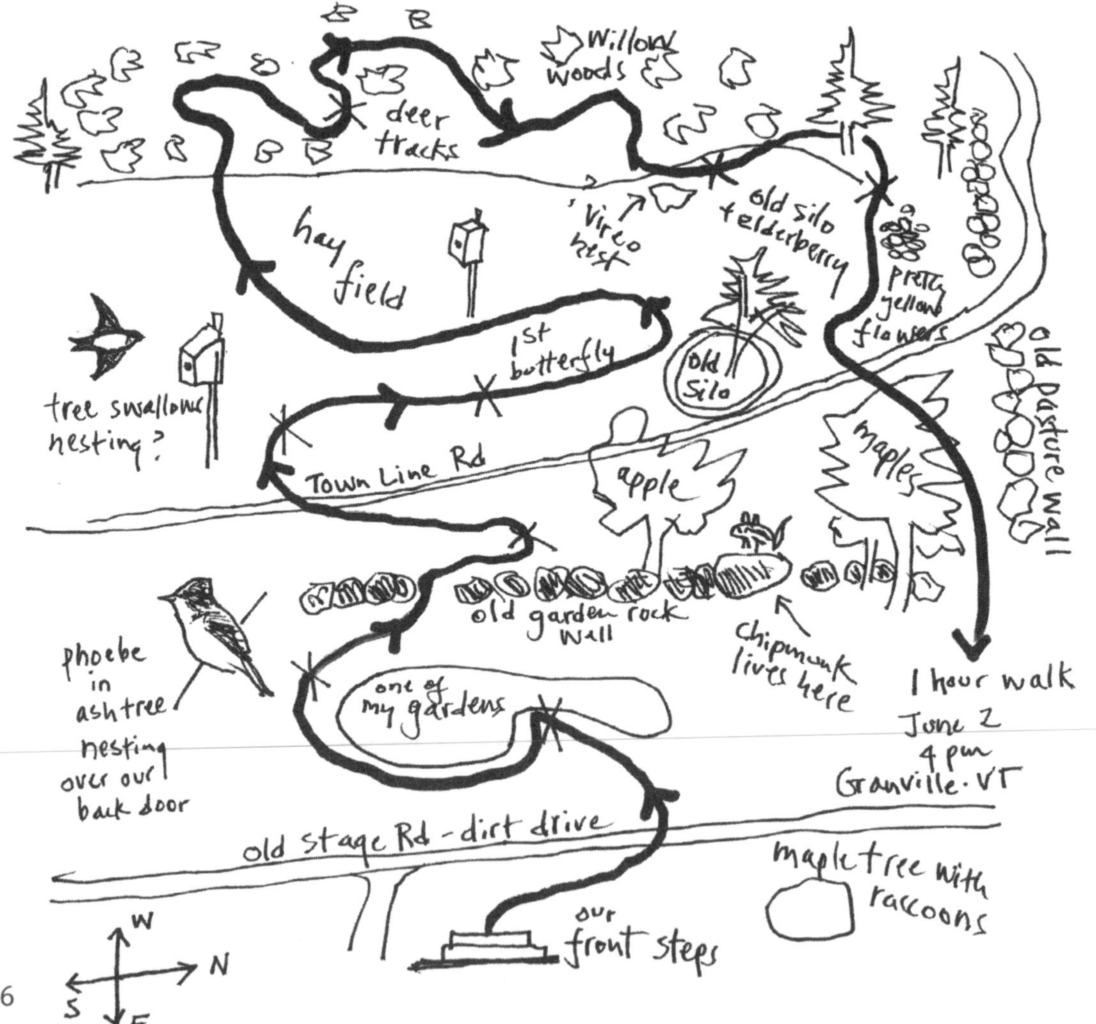

Draw your treasure map here.

Date: Place: Time:

JUNE

Lots of Babies Being Born

THE FIRST MONTH OF SUMMER is thought to be named after the Roman goddess, Juno, wife of Jupiter, the king of the gods, and queen of the heavens. Because Juno was the protector of women and guardian of marriages, June has been the favored month for marriages for many centuries.

This is the month of the summer solstice, which falls on June 20, 21, or 22, depending on the year. It is the day when the sun stays longest in the sky. The length of the day depends on where you live; in the far north, there is no night at all for many days.

June was called "midsummer month" by the northern European Anglo-Saxons, who celebrated the Longest Day Sun. In parts of America and northern Europe, people still light bonfires, set fireworks off, dance, and sing to honor the magnificent sun. There's a wonderful play about this time of year called *A Midsummer Night's Dream*.

Over hill, over dale,
Through brush, through brier,
Over park, over pale,
Through flood, through fire,
I do wander everywhere

— WILLIAM SHAKESPEARE, *A MIDSUMMER NIGHT'S DREAM* (ACT II, SCENE I)

MY NATURE NOTES

Date:	Time:
Place:	Temperature:
What's the weather like?	
Phase of the moon:	Time of sunrise:
	Time of sunset:
Look out the window or go outdoors, then jot down your observations, draw a picture, or describe a scene.	

To print out more pages like this, go to *www.storey.com/thenatureconnection.php.*

Go on a Nature Quest!

Start each month by taking a good look around. Go for a walk and see what you can find (use all your senses!) that gives a clue to the season. Try it on several different days and see how your answers change.

Can you find...	Describe what you notice.
☐ swallows hunting for bugs	__________
☐ cool cumulus cloud shapes	__________
☐ toads trilling at night	__________

What else can you find?

☐ __________	__________
☐ __________	__________
☐ __________	__________
☐ __________	__________
☐ __________	__________
☐ __________	__________
☐ __________	__________
☐ __________	__________
☐ __________	__________
☐ __________	__________

Picture of the Month

Choose one or two (or more!) things from your list to draw or photograph here.

Date: Place: Time:

The Summer Solstice

June is the month of the most daylight for the northern hemisphere. In the far north, the sun shines for 24 hours a day at this time of year. If you travel farther south, you will experience variations in day length until you reach the equator, where the days and nights are always of equal length. This has to do with the way the earth curves and how the sun's light hits it at different times.

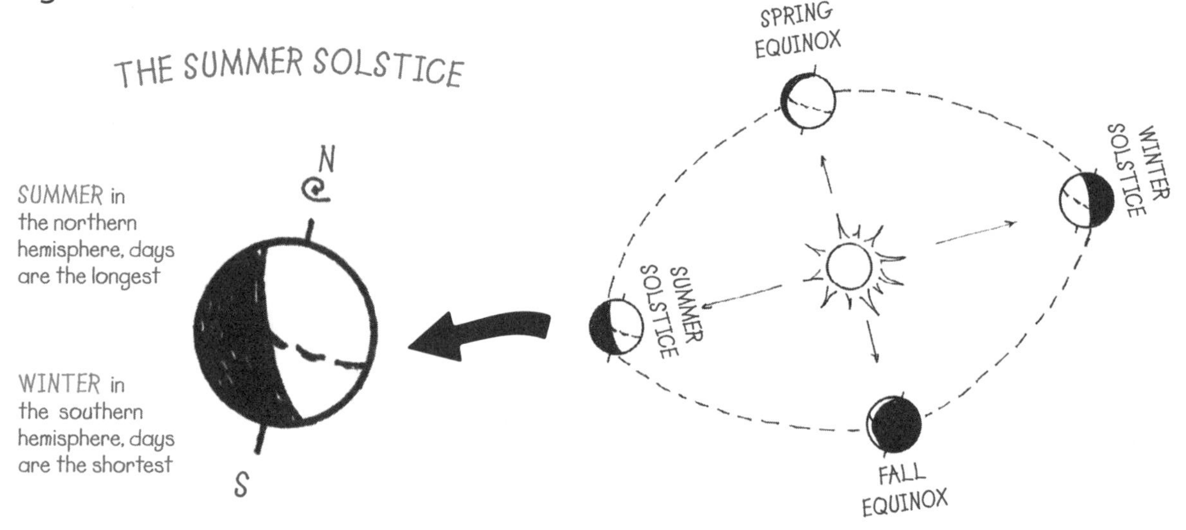

With Earth's rotation around the sun, the northern hemisphere is receiving the most light and the southern hemisphere the least. The longest days of the year fall on June 20, 21, or 22, and are called the summer solstice. Where I live, we have 15 hours and 17 minutes of daylight (at the winter solstice, we have only 9 hours and 4 minutes!).

No wonder the world of nature is so busy and active in the summer and quiet and sleeping in the winter. Don't you feel the difference? Check your own sunrises and sunsets for these two important seasonal times.

The word *solstice* comes from the Latin for "sun" (sol) and "stand still" (sistere). "Summer" comes from the Old English *sumor*, meaning "the warmest season."

Some cultures staged ritual plays that showed the death of the summer king at the hands of the winter king. At the time of the winter solstice, ritual plays showed the summer king rising to slay the winter king.

In some cultures long ago, people viewed the sun as the king, father, or ruler of all. The earth was the mother and the moon the sister. At this healthy time of year, between planting and harvest, people celebrated weddings, held great feasts, took voyages, and waged battles.

Even at the height of the summer, though, people knew that the great cycle would continue and winter would return. Much needed to be done during the healthy summer months to prepare for the harsh times to come.

PREPARING FOR WINTER IN SUMMER

Even at the summer solstice, you can see signs that winter is coming. What are some of the signs around you?

* Gardens planted with food to be eaten over the winter (corn, peas, beans, beets – what else?)
* Hay and grain fields growing and ripening
* Seeds setting on many trees and plants
* Long daylight hours for animals to hunt for food
* Fewer birds singing as they busily raise their young

School's out for summer! It's time to run around, play, and find new places!

Here are some things you can do and look for in June. See if you can check them all off by the end of the month.

☐ **June is a wonderful time to be out at night.** Grab a blanket, make some popcorn, bring some drinks, and go admire the night sky. Pitch a tent and spend the night in your backyard. See if you can find a spot by a meadow or in a clearing where fireflies gather by the thousands to find mates.

☐ **Look at your calendar.** Mark down some mornings and afternoons to just be outdoors. Don't schedule anything else! Invite friends or family to join you. Go exploring or fishing by a local stream. Visit a local nature center. Try a new hiking trail. Go for a bike ride. Build a fort and have a picnic there. Walk on the wild side for a while!

☐ **Create a naturalist's club with some friends.** Create a treasure hunt and see who can find the most birds, mammals, amphibians, reptiles, insects, fish, trees, plants, flowers, or rocks.

☐ **Absorb the colors of June.** How many different flowers can you find? How many shades of green do you see? What are sunsets like this time of year? Use watercolors or colored pencils or markers to create some June scenes.

☐ **Find a good book and learn about a new animal each week.** There are so many interesting animals, but here are a few to consider learning about:

* skunk
* bobcat
* beaver
* yellow-spotted salamander
* crane fly
* painted lady butterfly

* snapping turtle
* garter snake
* bluebird
* raven
* bluegill
* cottontail rabbit
* moose
* elk
* bison

Trees: Nature's Air Filter

Trees can indicate soil type, water amount, temperature, ecosystem, latitude, longitude, and health of the land and community. One of the most important things that trees do for the earth is keep the air clean. All plants and animals contain carbon. Most living organisms breathe in oxygen and give off carbon dioxide (CO_2). Plants do the opposite — they absorb CO_2 and emit oxygen back into the atmosphere. Fossil fuels also give off CO_2 when we burn them to produce energy.

For many millennia there was a balance between the amount of oxygen and CO_2 in the air. But since humans have started to use fossil fuels for energy and to cut down huge numbers of trees, that balance has changed. Now there is more CO_2 in the atmosphere, along with other pollutants, and those gases form a layer around Earth. This layer creates an effect like a greenhouse, trapping heat rather than releasing it.

THE CARBON CYCLE

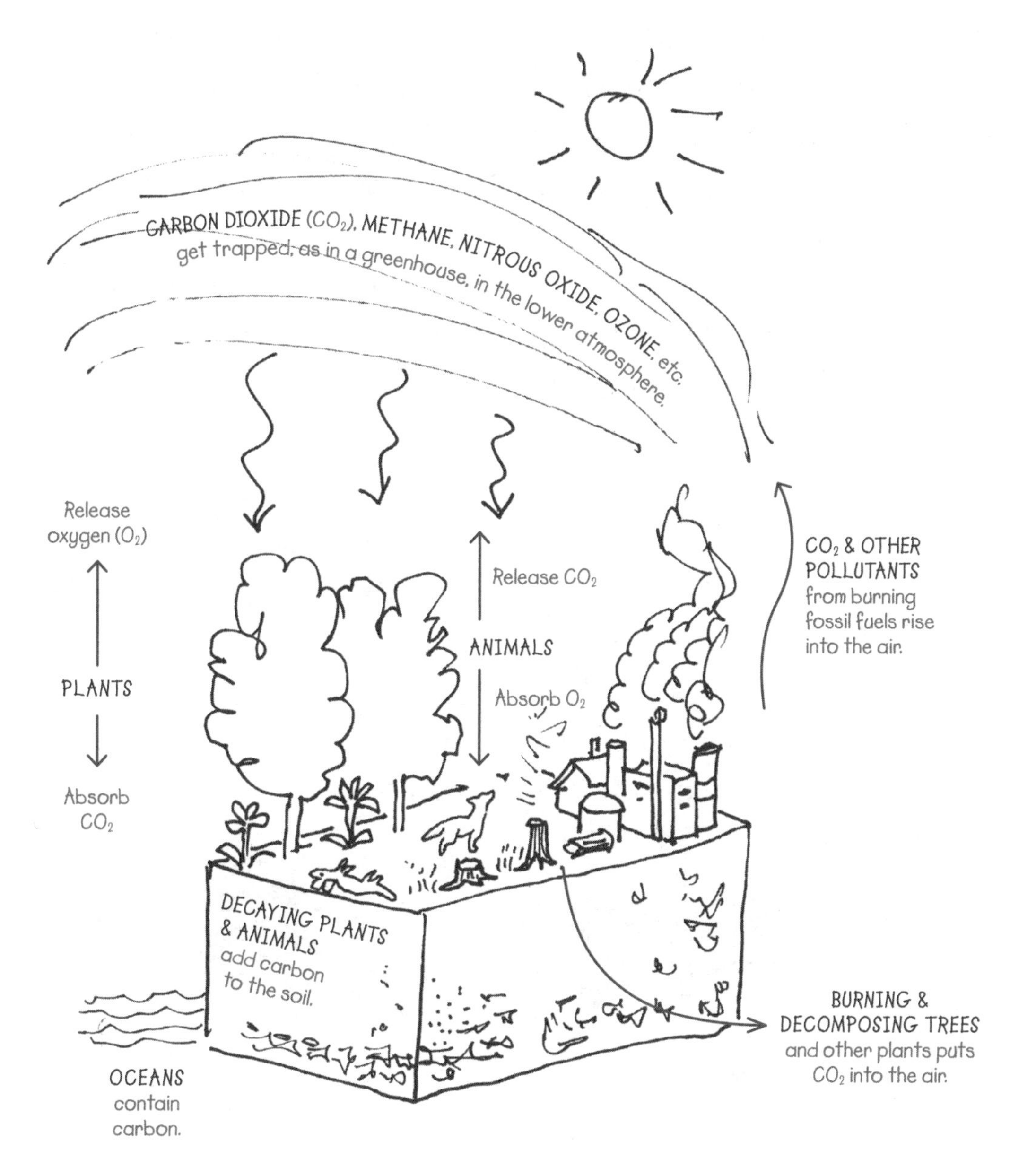

Bugs Are a Big Deal

If you have green plants and flowers, shady trees, or tall grasses in a backyard or meadow, you will have insects. Insects far outnumber all the rest of us living creatures, so give your six-legged neighbors some respect! The world couldn't survive without all the insects that pollinate plants, help the cycle of decomposition, and provide food for many other animals.

If they bite or sting, there is a reason: female mosquitoes and midges need a blood meal to *ovulate* (produce eggs), and bees and wasps only attack if they feel threatened.

MIDGE

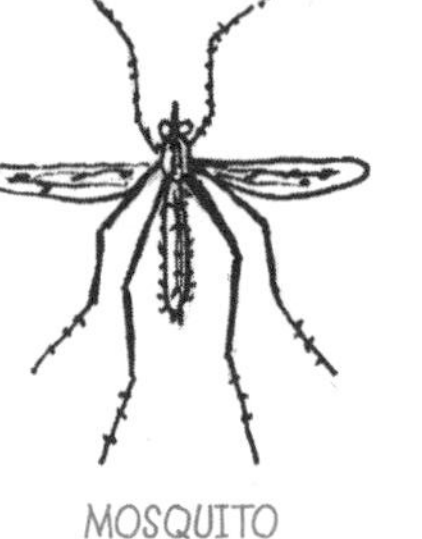

MOSQUITO

YELLOW JACKET

BUMBLEBEE

Most insects leave you alone and are fun to watch, like grasshoppers, butterflies, dragonflies, and praying mantises.

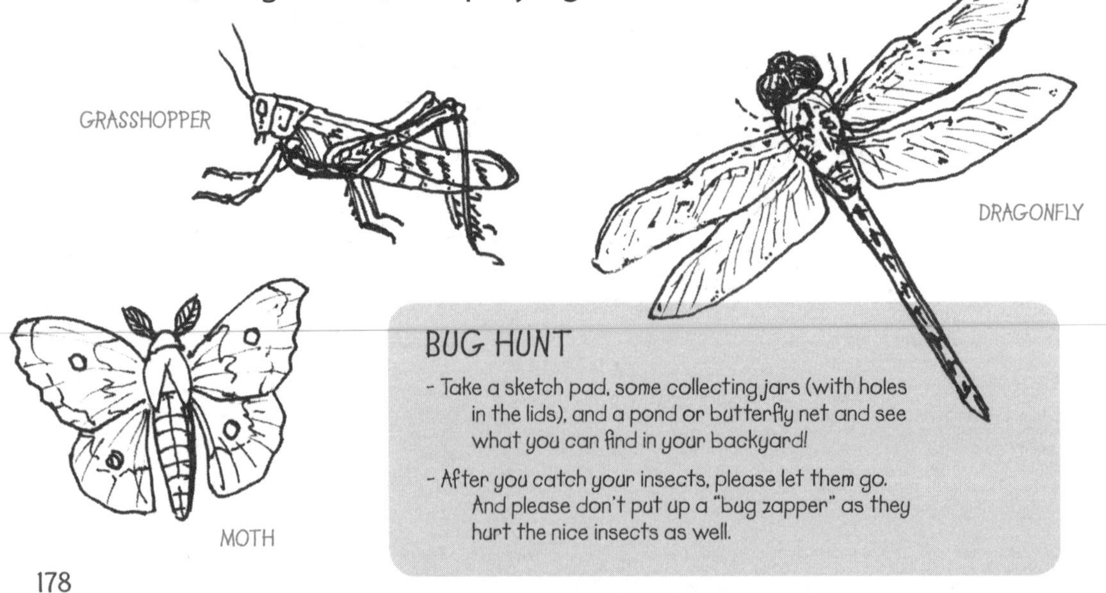

BUG HUNT

- Take a sketch pad, some collecting jars (with holes in the lids), and a pond or butterfly net and see what you can find in your backyard!
- After you catch your insects, please let them go. And please don't put up a "bug zapper" as they hurt the nice insects as well.

ALL BUGS ARE INSECTS, BUT NOT ALL INSECTS ARE BUGS

What's the difference between a bug and an insect, anyway? Insecta is the biological class that contains about 30 different orders or types, some of which are illustrated here. One of those orders is Hemiptera or "true bugs," which have two-part wings.

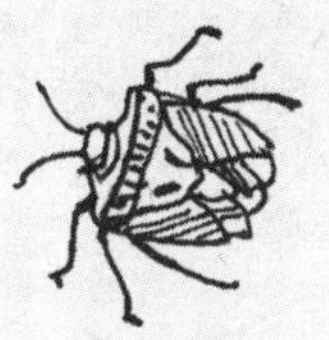

HEMIPTERA
Milkweed bugs, cicadas, stink bugs

HOMOPTERA
Leaf-hoppers, aphids

HYMENOPTERA
Bees, wasps, ants

LEPIDOPTERA
Butterflies, moths

ORTHOPTERA
Crickets, grasshoppers, locusts, cockroaches, praying mantises

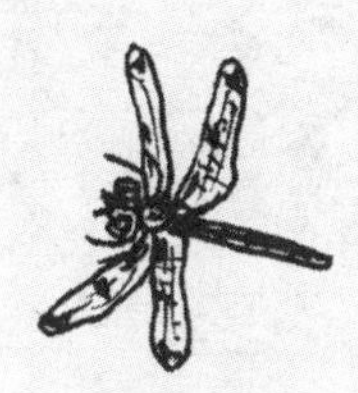

ODONATA
Dragonflies, damselflies

DIPTERA
Flies, mosquitoes, craneflies

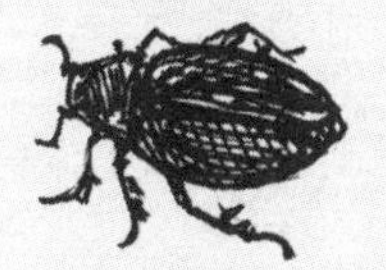

COLEOPTERA
All beetles

There are more species of beetles than any other species of animal – around 350,000 – with more being discovered every year. That means that one in every five animals in the world is a beetle!

While they come in an astonishing variety of shapes and colors, all insects have an external skeleton, a body divided into three parts (head, thorax, abdomen), and three pairs of legs. Most insects also have antennae and many have two pairs of wings.

June Drawings You Can Do

Baby animals are fun to draw. They look like their parents but they have proportionally bigger heads, with large, widely spaced eyes. Some have different markings when they are first born.

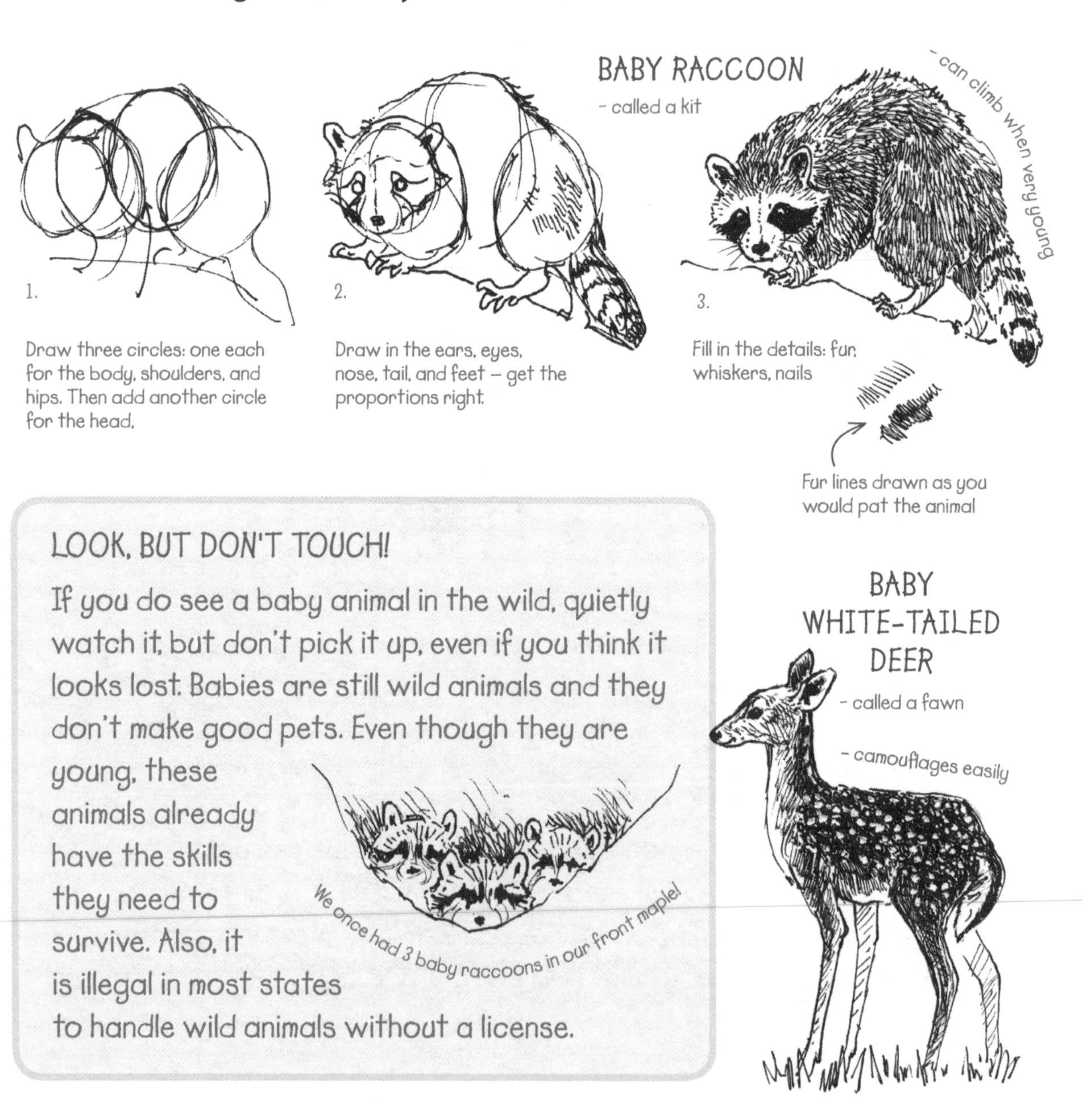

LOOK, BUT DON'T TOUCH!

If you do see a baby animal in the wild, quietly watch it, but don't pick it up, even if you think it looks lost. Babies are still wild animals and they don't make good pets. Even though they are young, these animals already have the skills they need to survive. Also, it is illegal in most states to handle wild animals without a license.

Take your notebook or camera to the zoo or a nature center to look for baby animals. You can also use pictures from a book – that's what I did for these drawings. Make your drawings here.

Date: Place: Time:

Feathering Their Nests

June is a busy time for birds, but you are probably hearing less singing because the parents are busy feeding and raising their young and keeping them safely hidden away. Scout quietly around your backyard or a field or patch of woods and listen carefully. You may hear the squeaking of baby birds as they beg for food, and you might see them as they start to leave their nests. Some birds have more than one brood each summer, raising young into late July.

Look carefully and you might also spy some nests tucked away in a tree or bush, or even right on your porch. Birds build all kinds of nests with all kinds of different materials. They know just what to use.

BIRDS' NESTS YOU MIGHT FIND:

RED-EYED VIREO nest hangs from a tree branch.

- nest made of plant fibers and birch bark strips
- lined with pine needles and spider silk

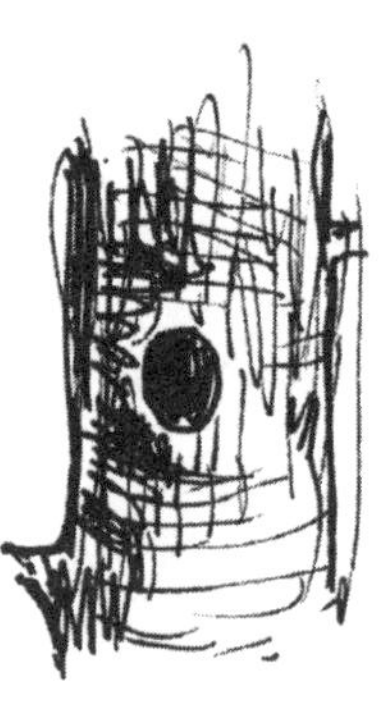

CHICKADEE or WOODPECKER
- nest in trees

Try building a nest yourself using toothpicks or pick-up sticks on top of a jam jar. How many do you have to use? Or collect some materials from outside and see if you can weave them together to make a nest. For a real challenge, just use your mouth!

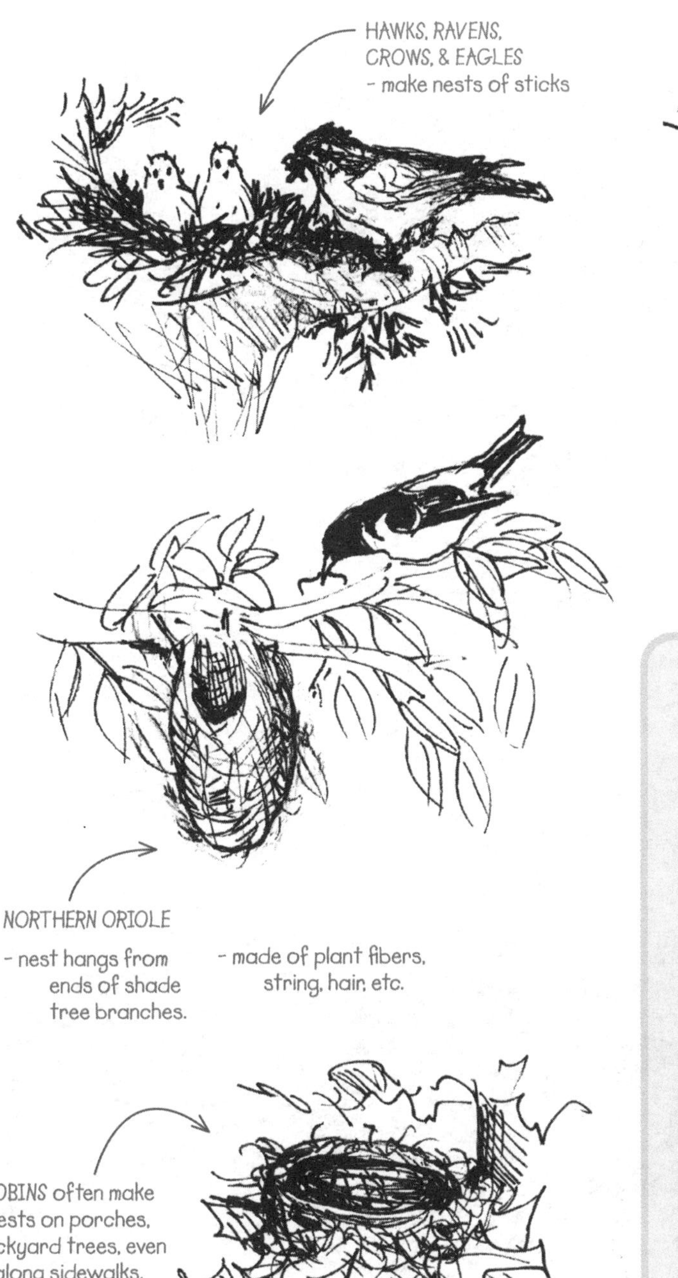

- nests made of rootlets, pine needles, string, grasses, and mud inside

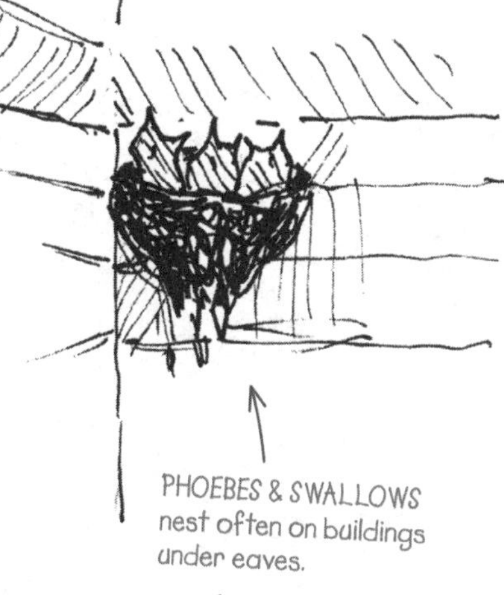

HELPING OUT

You can give your local birds some help in their nest-building work by putting out some materials for them. See if they will collect short lengths of yarn or string, lint from the dryer, hair from your hairbrush or from brushing your dog or cat, packing material made of shredded paper or straw – just don't put out anything made of plastic.

JULY

Everything Is Growing

July is named after the Roman statesman, Julius Caesar, who reformed the Roman calendar in 46 BCE, naming a number of the months after Roman statesmen or gods. And we still use those names today. The Northern Europeans called this month "hay-month," while some Native American tribes called the moon for this month "the hay moon."

That's because, in spite of the heat, farmers in many places are out madly cutting, drying, and baling their meadow grasses to sell as hay and to feed their livestock in the winter. Other crops are ripening now as well — what are some of your favorites? Corn? Blueberries? Peaches? Beans? Tomatoes?

July is an outdoor month. There are so many things for a blossoming naturalist to do outdoors. You can stick to the early mornings and evenings if the sun is too hot where you live. Think back to what 5:00 a.m. and 7:00 p.m. are like in the winter.

Summertime, and the living is easy,
Fish are jumping, and the cotton is high.

— GEORGE GERSHWIN, *PORGY AND BESS*

MY NATURE NOTES

Date:	Time:
Place:	Temperature:
What's the weather like?	
Phase of the moon:	Time of sunrise:
	Time of sunset:
Look out the window or go outdoors, then jot down your observations, draw a picture, or describe a scene.	

To print out more pages like this, go to *www.storey.com/thenatureconnection.php.*

Go on a Nature Quest!

Start each month by taking a good look around. Go for a walk and see what you can find (use all your senses!) that gives a clue to the season. Try it on several different days and see how your answers change.

Can you find...	Describe what you notice.
☐ cicadas buzzing	
☐ turkey vultures circling	
☐ smell of warm grass	

What else can you find?

☐	
☐	
☐	
☐	
☐	
☐	
☐	
☐	
☐	
☐	

Picture of the Month

Choose one or two (or more!) things from your list to draw or photograph here.

Date: Place: Time:

Spend as much time outside as you can!

Here are some things you can do and look for in July. See if you can check them all off by the end of the month.

☐ **Do something for Planet Earth:** go without air conditioning, turn off extra lights, use less water, walk or bike instead of driving. Clean up your backyard or neighborhood. Plant some flowers.

☐ **Do your favorite summer activity at different times of day.** While you're playing tennis or basketball, kayaking, biking, walking or running, notice the weather, light, clouds, sounds, animal activity, and so on. Think about how these things change over the course of the day.

☐ **Butterfly gardens have become very popular.** If you want to attract these lovely visitors, plant some bee balm, coneflowers, milkweed, butterfly bush, dill, and/or marigolds, for a start.

As this poem suggests, you might also see other things in your garden:

> *Where are the fairies?*
> *Where can we find them?...*
> *Why, in your garden surely they are dwelling!...*
> *Where there are flowers, there fairies are!*
>
> — CICELY MARY BARKER, *FLOWER FAIRIES OF THE GARDEN*

☐ **Track the temperature.** Follow the temperature charts for where you live. Are you having a heat wave? Is there drought? Or too much rain? Contrast your records with temperatures in other parts of the country.

☐ **This is the season for peaches, berries, melons, and lots more.** Go to a farmer's market and gather fresh, local fruit to make a big salad. If you have a backyard grill, try grilling peaches or nectarines with a little brown sugar — delicious!

☐ **Learn about the wild foods** and medicinal plants and herbs that people used before there were pharmacies and prescription drugs. Did you know that aspirin can be made from willow bark and that the foxglove gives us digitalis, a heart medication?

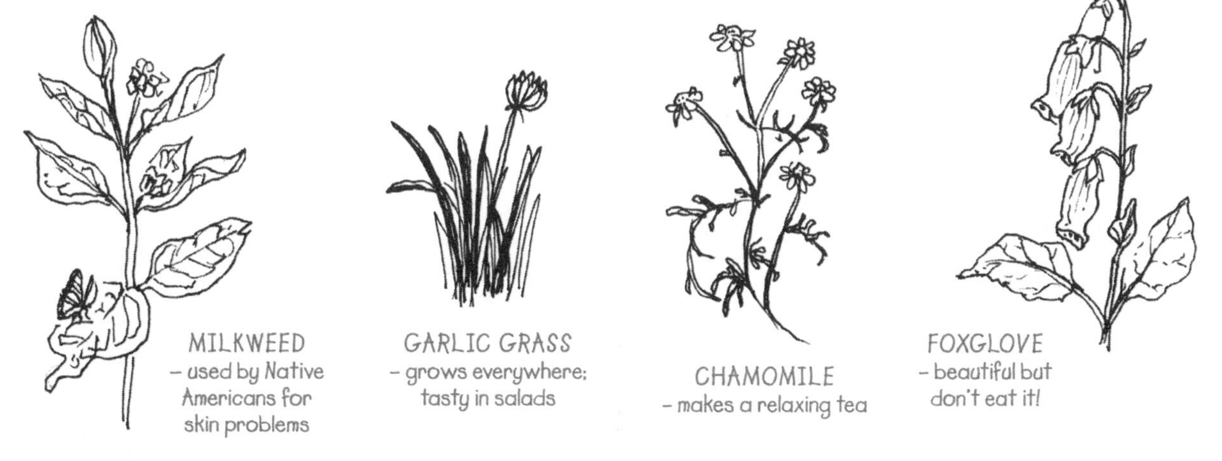

☐ **Sit under a tree and read a great book.** *Julie of the Wolves* by Jean Craighead George (and try her other books, too!) and *Rabbit Hill* by Robert Lawson; *The Life Cycles of Butterflies* by Judy Burris and Wayne Richards and *Butterflies and Moths* by Robert Mitchell and Herbert Zim.

Drawing Your Landscape

Landscapes are hard to draw, but fun. Keep them simple at first. Make notes of what you see. Draw inside a frame so you know where your picture ends! You can use a frame of any size and shape. I did this landscape to remember a place I didn't know; it took about 10 minutes.

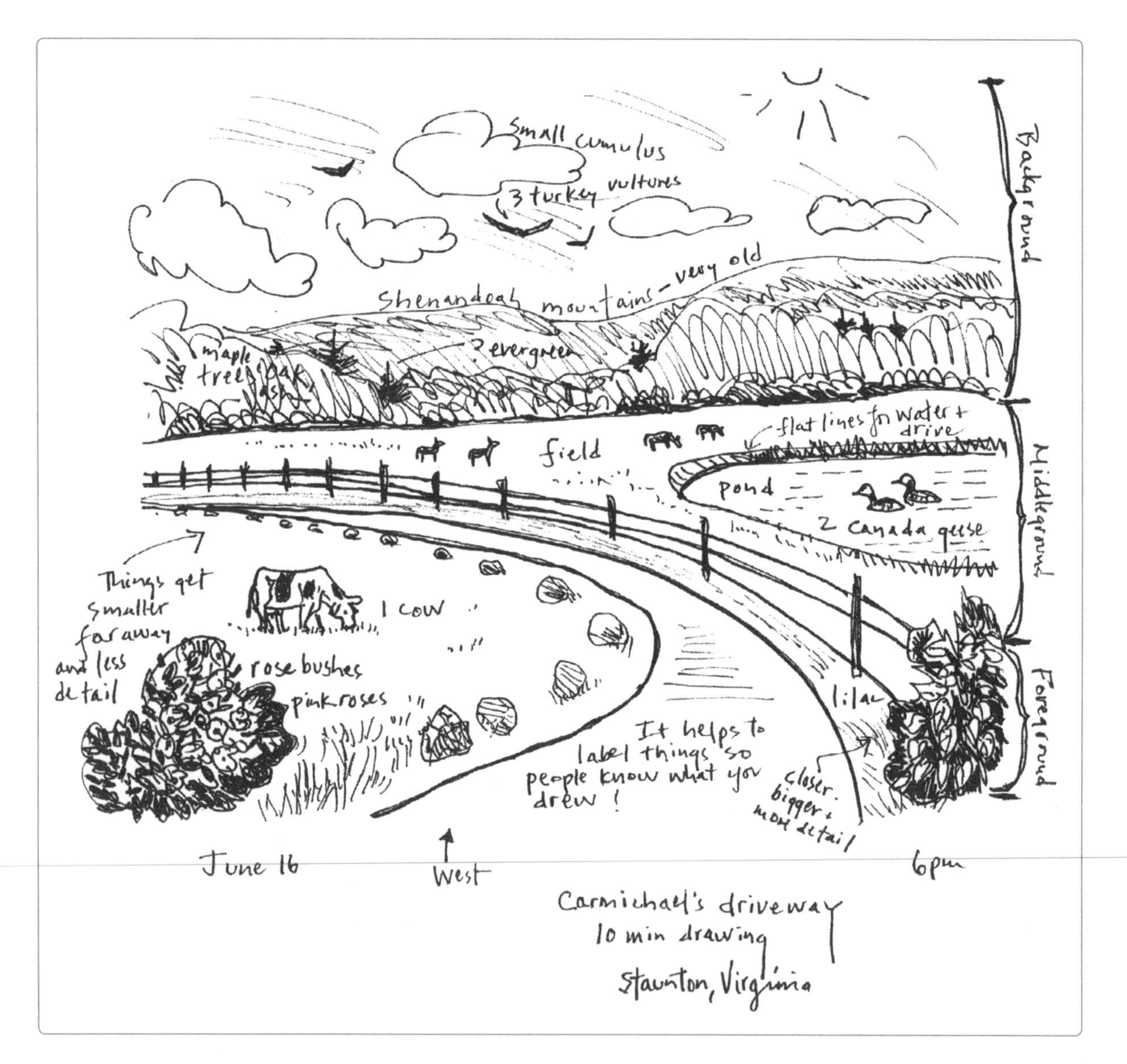

Put your landscape drawing here.

Date: Place: Time:

What's a Butterfly? What's a Moth?

One of the great pleasures of summer is learning about butterflies and moths. Did you know that moths have existed for many millions of years more than butterflies? There are a lot of other differences between them. For example, butterflies usually feed by day, and they rest with folded wings. Moths are more likely to feed and fly around at night and when they take a break, they usually spread their wings out. See what else you can discover by watching them.

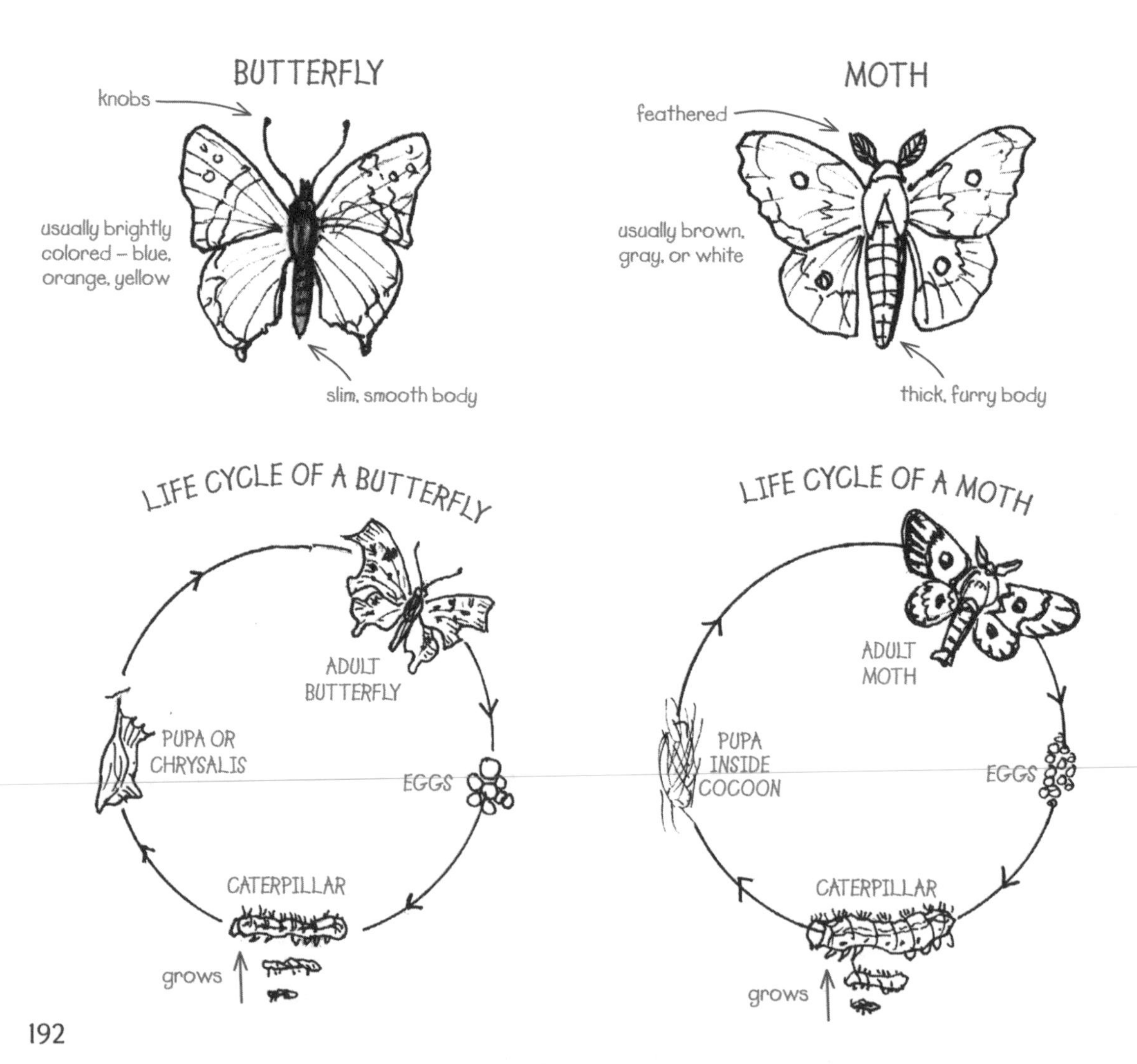

Date: Place: Time:

How Does Your Garden Grow?

All plants need periods of sun, water, perhaps some fertilizer and mulch, and, of course, weather that isn't too hot or too cold. Plants take nutrients from the soil, so it's important to have good, rich soil for your garden. The beauty of nature is that everything is recycled — leaves and dead plants fall to the ground and decay, creating a layer of humus that feeds the next generation of plants. Worms and other small creatures help the process by breaking down the decaying plant matter.

If you do have room for a garden, here are some questions to ask before you plant:

* **What do you want to plant?**
* **How much sun will your garden get?**
* **How will you keep it watered?**
* **Do you need to add compost** to make the soil more nutritious?
* **If you go on vacation,** who will look after your garden?

- Broccoli - Peas - Beets
- Kale - Beans

A pot of BASIL

If you don't have space for a garden, you can plant tomatoes or peppers in pots on a balcony or grow herbs in a sunny window. Find a spot to plant some impatiens or geraniums — maybe at your grandma's house.

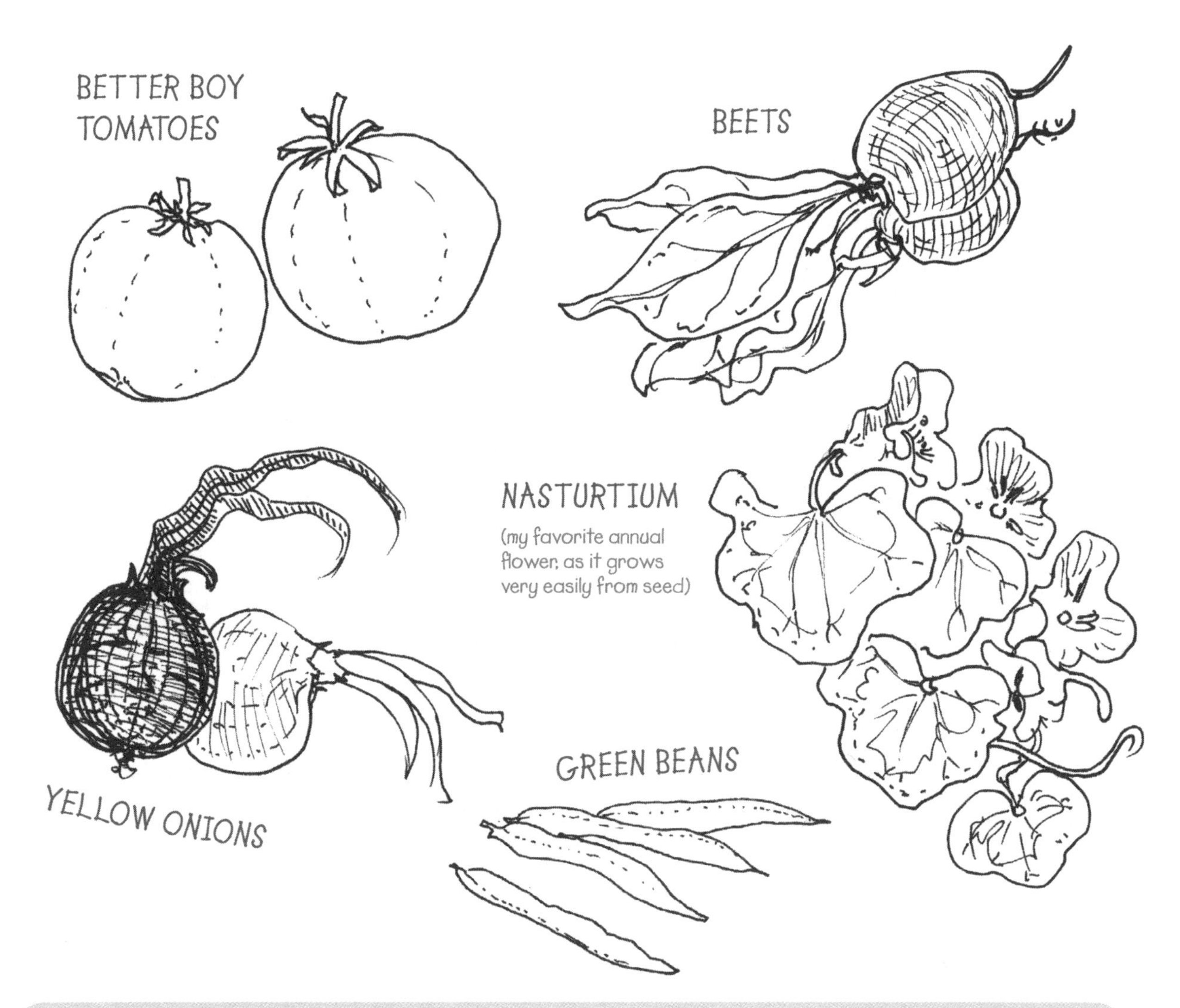

Depending on where you live, you could consider a YEAR-ROUND GARDEN.

My daughter, Anna, teaches at a school in New Orleans. She and her students built a garden in November and planted cabbage, broccoli, kale, and some herbs. Lots of schools have gardens these days – if yours doesn't, ask your teacher about starting one.

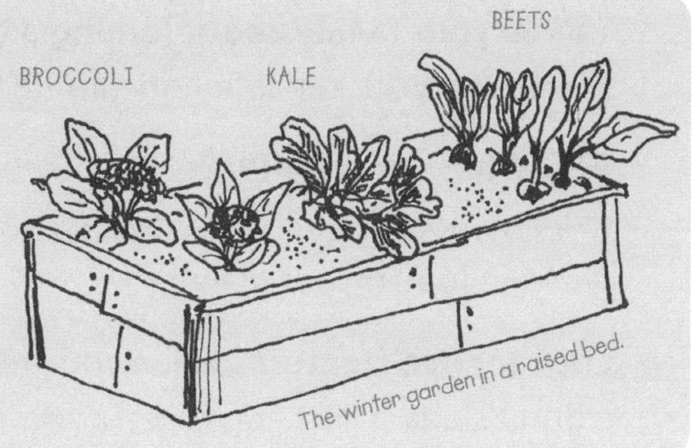

The winter garden in a raised bed.

More Fun in the Garden

You can grow herbs, vegetables, and flowers together or separately. Some flowers actually help keep pests away from your veggies. For example, chrysanthemums discourage Japanese beetles, nasturtiums keep squash bugs away, and marigolds ward off many different insects. Look in gardening books to find out about other plants that grow well together.

* **Annual plants** are ones that you must grow from seed or buy as seedlings and plant every year, as they can't survive through the winter. Most vegetables and many flowers are annuals.
* **Perennial plants** die back over the winter but return year after year. Some examples are daffodils, bleeding heart, coneflowers, and most daisies.

You can plant seeds directly in the ground or start them indoors before the ground is ready to plant. Look for seeds and seedlings at a plant nursery or garden center, even your grocery or hardware store.

More Things to Do

* **Talk to your family about joining a CSA** (Community Sustainable Agriculture) farm.
* **Visit What's on Your Plate? (***www.whatsonyourplateproject.org***)** to learn more about how kids can change the way we think about growing food on our planet.
* **Look for live creatures** when you are digging up your soil (earth-worms, slugs, insect egg cases, a sow bug, a beetle).

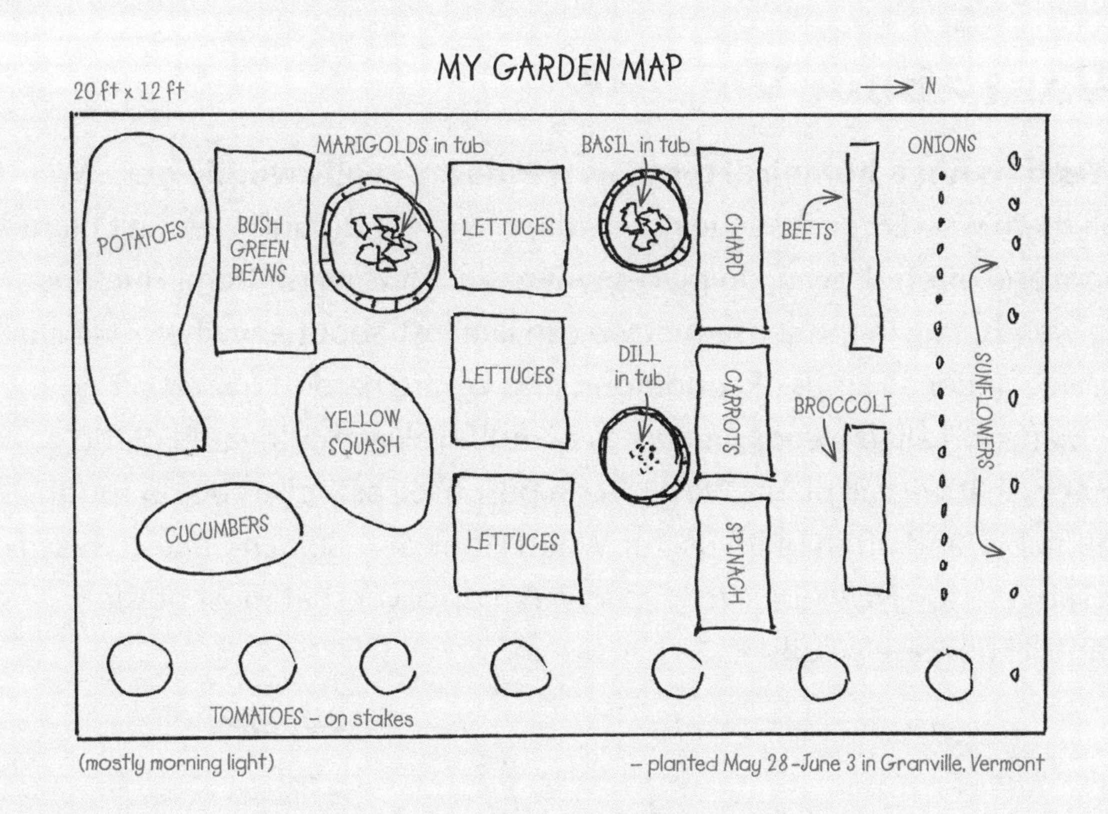

Make a map of your garden (or a neighbor's or an imaginary one).

What about Weeds?

"Weed" is not a botanical term, as weeds are really wildflowers. We call them weeds because they grow happily even though we don't plant them and often show up in places where we don't want them! Humans are weeds, too, in the sense that we can live just about anywhere, we can survive under all kinds of conditions, and we are hard to get rid of!

Many so-called weeds are just as beautiful as any cultivated plant (that's what we call plants we grow on purpose), as well as being tough, adaptable, and often quite useful. When I look at *A Golden Guide to Weeds* or *The Peterson Field Guide to Wildflowers*, I discover that most of the plants I know are weeds!

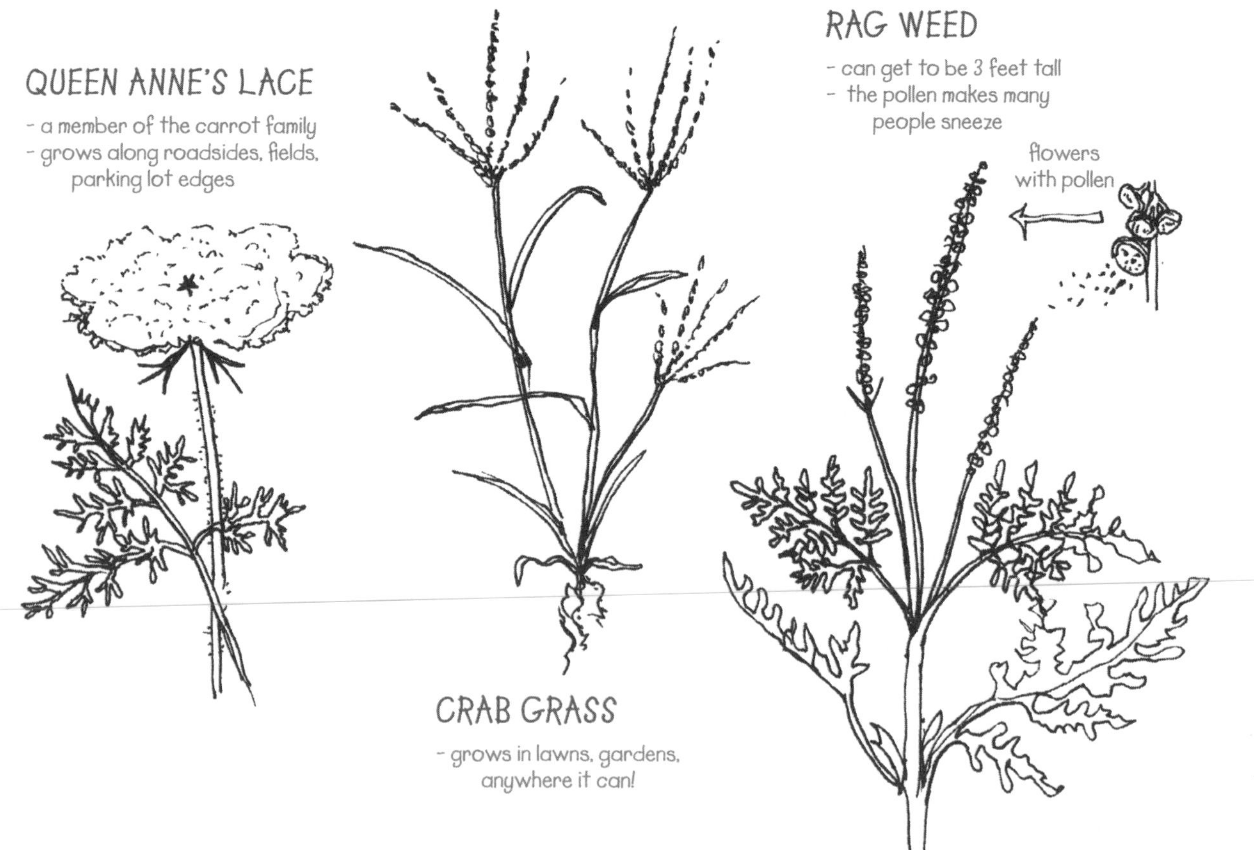

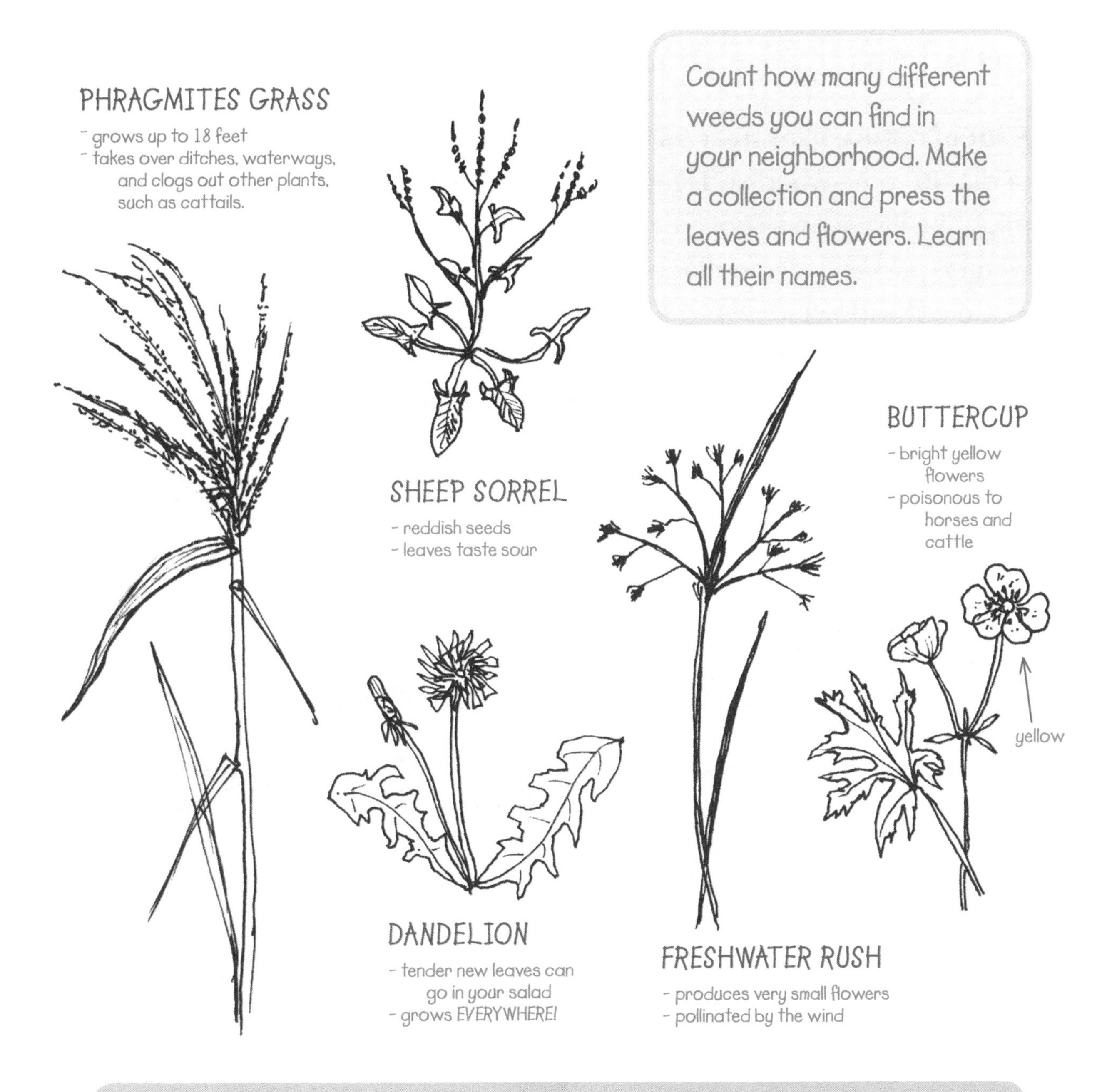

Count how many different weeds you can find in your neighborhood. Make a collection and press the leaves and flowers. Learn all their names.

Once you start noticing weeds, you'll see that they have many different ways of adapting to their environment. Look at the many kinds of leaves, seeds, and roots they have – no wonder they can grow almost anywhere!

Life Underneath

A lot of nature lives near us that we never see. Turn over a stone or log, or dig up some woodland leaves to find what is there. In the desert, who might be hiding in a cool crevice? In a marsh or stream, who floats in the watery grasses or camouflages itself on the pebbly bottom?

Go out with your eyes to the ground and find some of the dark places where animals might be hiding. Take a magnifying glass and perhaps a flashlight. Be careful not to hurt or harm anything you find and always roll logs and rocks back into place.

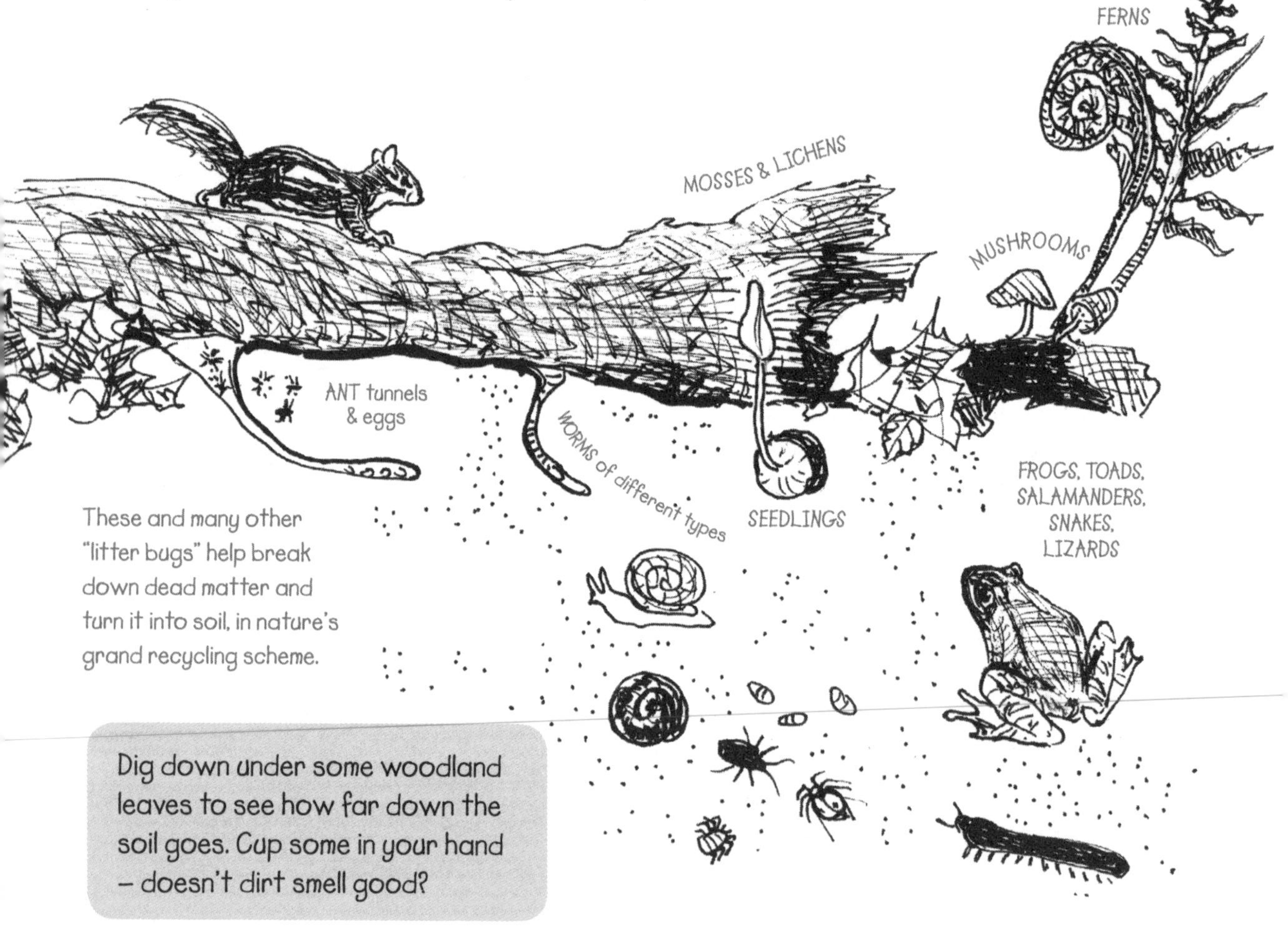

Dig down under some woodland leaves to see how far down the soil goes. Cup some in your hand – doesn't dirt smell good?

Draw/write your dark secret discoveries here.

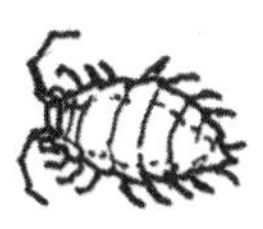

AUGUST

We All Need Water

THIS MONTH IS NAMED AFTER AUGUSTUS CAESAR, the Roman Emperor. It is often the time when people go on vacation. If you go on any trips or to camp, take your journal with you. Pretend that you are exploring a vast new region. Imagine that you are traveling with Charles Darwin or Lewis and Clark. You could be Magellan or James Audubon. These great explorers and naturalists brought back detailed reports and collections of unknown flora (plants) and fauna (animals) from their travels. This material often formed the basis of natural history museums, which were (and still are) of great interest to the general public.

With the hot days of summer in full blast, in the northern hemisphere anyway, August is also a good time to learn about water, from gentle summer rains to raging hurricanes, and from ponds to saltwater marshes. Don't forget all the plants and animals of the sea, beaches, islands, river deltas, and other bodies of water.

How beautiful is the rain!
After the dust and heat,
In the broad and fiery street,
In the narrow lane,
How beautiful is the rain!

— HENRY WADSWORTH LONGFELLOW

MY NATURE NOTES

Date:	Time:
Place:	Temperature:
What's the weather like?	
Phase of the moon:	Time of sunrise:
	Time of sunset:
Look out the window or go outdoors, then jot down your observations, draw a picture, or describe a scene.	

To print out more pages like this, go to *www.storey.com/thenatureconnection.php.*

Go on a Nature Quest!

Start each month by taking a good look around. Go for a walk and see what you can find (use all your senses!) that gives a clue to the season. Try it on several different days and see how your answers change.

Can you find…	Describe what you notice.
☐ crickets calling	
☐ monarch butterfly	
☐ shooting stars	

What else can you find?

☐	
☐	
☐	
☐	
☐	
☐	
☐	
☐	
☐	
☐	

Picture of the Month

Choose one or two (or more!) things from your list to draw or photograph here.

Date: Place: Time:

Water, Water, Everywhere

Most people live near some sort of water — a stream, creek, pond, fountain, reservoir, river, lake, ocean. Beneath the surface of the earth is an amazing system of ground water that feeds our wells and springs. Have you studied where your local water comes from?

You may have heard people say, "Water, water, everywhere, but not a drop to drink," but did you know that the line comes from a poem called *The Rime of the Ancient Mariner* by Samuel Taylor Coleridge?

It's about a ship that is becalmed on the ocean, and the crew has nothing to drink, in spite of the vast quantity of water all around. Why is that?

If you live in a city, your water comes through pipes, but from where? If you live in the suburbs or country, you may have a well, like we do in our house in Vermont. One summer our well went dry after a long summer drought. We had to use a neighbor's deeper well for drinking and cooking water. It made us realize that we have to use water wisely.

Did you know that 71 percent of the earth's surface is water? Much of that is salt water, tied up in our seas and oceans. A large amount of fresh water is frozen solid in glaciers and in the two polar ice caps.

Spring runoff from glaciers has been an important source of water for many mountain villages, and as the glaciers recede, people in some areas of the world are beginning to have trouble finding enough water.

In deserts, very little rain falls. What does fall evaporates quickly. How do plants, animals, and people adapt to these dry and hot places?

Where does water come from?

If you go to the ocean this month, or go to a lake, river, pond, swimming pool or opened fire hydrant, think where your water has come from. Water falls from the sky in many different ways: as a gentle rain or a pounding downpour, as a quiet fog or a noisy hailstorm, frozen into snow, and in a wild frenzy with hurricanes and typhoons.

Caribbean islanders named terrifying storms after their god of evil, *Huracán* – that's where the word "hurricane" comes from!

WATERSHEDS

Many of us are interested in learning about our watersheds. This is the land that water flows through as it seeks the lowest point, which is usually a stream, river, lake, or ocean. Every living thing is part of a watershed community, whether in farmland, prairie, mountains, even suburbs and cities. Our drinking water usually comes from local underground watersheds, so protecting them and keeping them healthy is very important.

August weather can surprise you — it can be hot or cold, wet or dry, pleasant or wild.

Here are some things you can do and look for in August. See if you can check them all off by the end of the month.

☐ **Visit an aquarium to learn about fish and other water dwellers.** If you see people fishing, ask what they are trying to catch — perch, sunnies, pickerel, bass, crabs?

☐ **Swing while singing some water songs.** Swings and hammocks are great places to invent and sing songs. So is the car on a long drive. There are many great songs about the ocean, sailing, battles at sea, whaling times and whales, and sad songs of loss at sea and lengthy ocean journeys. Start with *The Fireside Book of Songs.*

☐ **Learn about a river or stream or brook that is near you.** Which way does it flow? Where does it come from? Where does it go? Who uses water from it? Draw a map of how this body of water runs through your area. Look at a map to find states that have rivers or lakes as boundaries.

THE MISSISSIPPI RIVER

begins in the wild grasslands of northern Minnesota and, 2,351 miles later, flows out of Louisiana into the Gulf of Mexico. Think how Hurricane Katrina affected all the people along that river – and the wildlife too.

Do some experiments with water. Set out several different containers — tall and deep, wide and shallow — full of water.

* See how much rain has collected after a storm.
* Check in the early morning to see if dew has accumulated.
* Keep a record of the water level, from week to week.
* How long does it take for the water to evaporate?
* Does anything start to grow in the containers?
* Do you see insects or animals using the containers for drinking and bathing? (Watch out, though — our dog kept drinking our experiments!)

scoop out fluttering insects as they can't get out

Practice skipping flat stones across water.

Go on a freshwater or saltwater expedition with your family. Take whatever you need to explore: collecting pails, binoculars, bird guide, scoops, swimming suit, goggles, fishing pole, and a boat, canoe, kayak, or raft.

"The Owl and the Pussycat went to sea in a beautiful pea green boat . . ."

Pretend you are them for a day!

Go exploring with a good book. A good summertime read is *Pedro's Journal* by Pam Conrad, about a boy who travels with Christopher Columbus. Some of my favorite water adventure books are by Holling Clancy Holling — try *Paddle to the Sea* and *Seabird.*

Wondering about Water Creatures

Many animals live in the water all their lives. Fish are the obvious ones, but there are many other life forms to be found in both fresh and salt water. Fresh water includes ponds, lakes, streams, and rivers. Do you live near any of those? Here are some of the creatures you might find there.

BROOK TROUT 8–9"
- found in creeks, rivers, lakes

CYCLOPS HYDRA DAPHNIA
- larger creatures eat these tiny ones

MINNOW ¾–4"
- refers to many species of small fish

PUMPKINSEED 2–6"
– can you tell why this fish is called this?

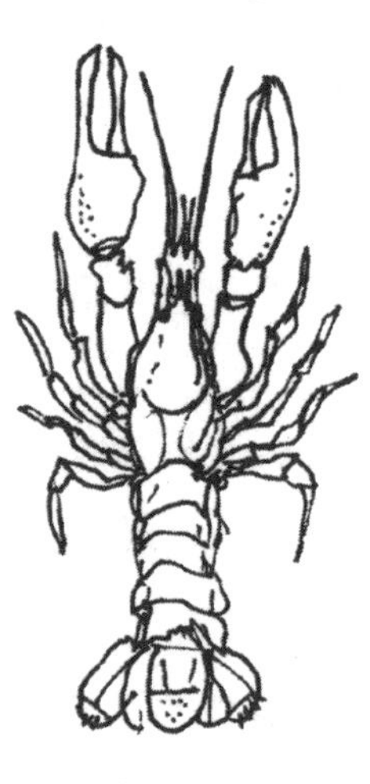

CRAYFISH 1–5"
- hides under rocks

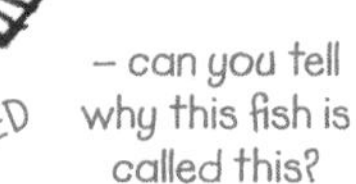

TADPOLE ¼–1"
- the beginning of frogs and toads

WATER BOATMAN ¾"
- found on surface of water

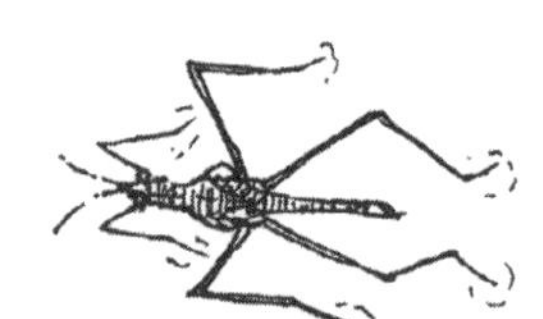

WATER STRIDER 1"
- skates on surface of quiet streams and ponds

Do you like to eat fish? As more and more people eat more and more fish, it's becoming harder and harder to find enough of them. It's important to eat fish responsibly and find out where it comes from and if there is a good supply of it. See if your local fish market can help with your questions.

Make your drawings of water creatures here.

Date: Place: Time:

Search for Water

Go outdoors and see where you can find water in nature. Are there droplets on grass blades? In a puddle? Under a leaf? Dripping from a faucet? How many places can you find water near your house?

Make a list of where you found water.

PLACE	DATE

How Do You Use Water?

In many parts of the world, water is scarce and people must treat it as a luxury. Imagine what it must be like to ration your drinking, cooking, and bathing water. Here are some things to think about if you're stuck inside on a rainy day this month.

First, make a list of all the ways that you use water.

____

____

____

____

Do you know where the water comes from when you turn on the kitchen faucet or where it goes when you flush the toilet? Do you have a well? Do you live near a creek or river, a pond or lake, the ocean? See if you can find the source of the water coming into your house and where the water going out of your house ends up.

Find out how much water you use to take a shower vs. taking a bath. Which uses more water: a dishwasher or hand washing? How much water does it take to run a load of laundry? Do different models of washing machines use different amounts of water?

Ocean Edges Are Important

Estuaries, wetlands, sandy beaches, and mudflats along the ocean's coastal edges are areas rich with nature. The mud flats and shallow beds created by the tides provide breeding and spawning grounds for many fish and other aquatic creatures. Thousands of birds, larger fish, and other animals forage and thrive on the food supply found here.

These areas are critical "supermarket" stops for migrating birds as they pass by in the spring and late summer. The large *blooms* (population explosions) of tiny sea creatures, called *krill*, along the coasts are an important food source for whales, dolphins, and sharks.

SANDERLINGS migrate up & down our coasts nesting in the High Arctic and wintering along the Gulf Coast.

Their 7½" bodies must refuel along the way, eating sand worms, tiny larvae, and crustaceans.

Earth has four oceans: the Pacific, the Atlantic, the Indian, and the Arctic. There are also four major seas: the Mediterranean Sea, the Black Sea, the Red Sea, and the Caspian Sea. (What's the difference between an ocean and a sea? Look it up!)

SALT WATER CREATURES

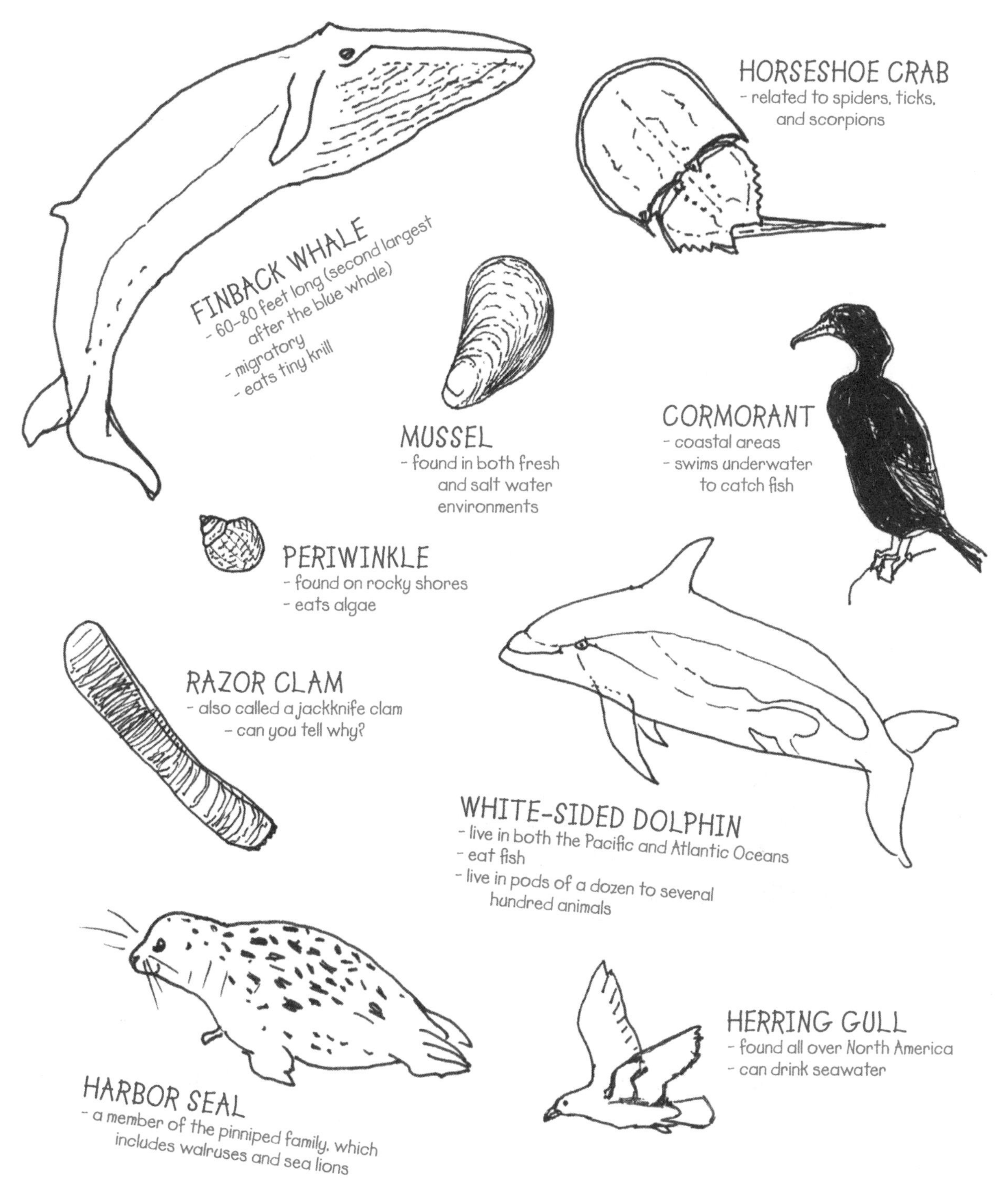

Keep a Vacation Journal

Pack up a vacation nature kit so you can have a good record to show your friends when you get home. See the equipment list on page 9. Be sure to take field guides with you for help in drawing.

Take time every day to jot down a few notes and observations about what you are seeing. Pretend you will have to make a report to your friends or family back home about the places you are visiting.

CREATE A CURIO CABINET

Collect objects from your outdoor adventures, whether you are by the beach, a rocky coast, the edge of a pond, in the woods, or by a meadow. Before you pick any live plants, find out from the local nature center or Audubon Society what local regulations are and if you should be watching out for any endangered species.

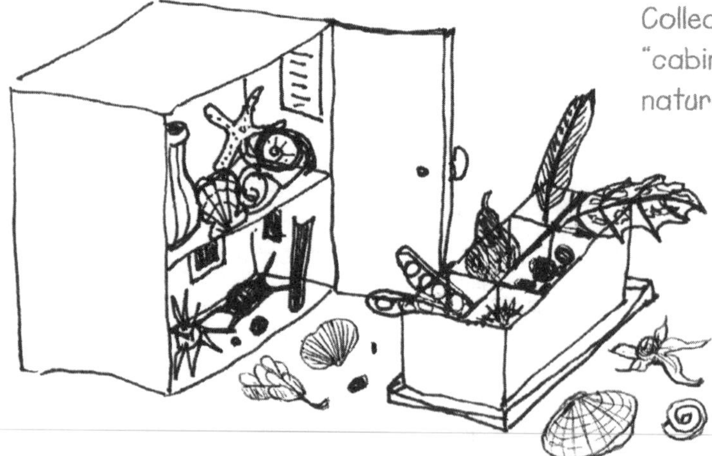

Collections like these were called "cabinets" by the nineteenth century naturalists, such as John James Audubon, Louis Agassiz, John Gould, William Bartram, and Henry D. Thoreau. These naturalists and their writings and collections were very much admired by the public.

Make a display of your objects by gluing them into a small cardboard box or egg carton. A shoebox works well. Use regular white glue. Make a label for each object.

NATURE NOTES ON VACATION

DATE	WEATHER	WHAT I NOTICED TODAY

You might enjoy reading *An Island Scrapbook* and *A Desert Scrapbook* by Virginia Wright-Frierson – she collects things just like you can.

Sleeping under the Stars

August is a great time to spend a night outdoors. Put up a tent or just take out a drop sheet, some blankets, and a pillow. When my kids were little, we did this a lot. It is fantastic to wake up with the dawn and realize that the sun rises every morning and on this particular day, you are seeing every minute of it!

* **Listen to the night rustlings of animals and harmless insects**. You might hear the late night chirps of a bird or the croak or peep of a single frog. Or you might be overwhelmed by an entire clanging of frogs or the zinging whine and buzz of crickets, grasshoppers, and cicadas.

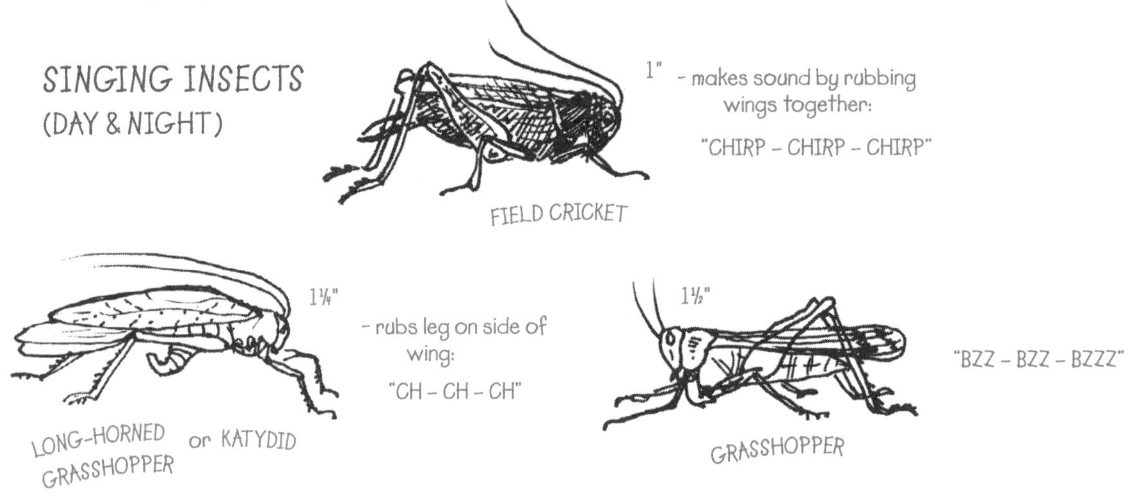

* Find out about the periodical cicada (not to be confused with a locust, which is actually a type of grasshopper). Cicadas have a very interesting and unusual life cycle — they live underground for many years and then emerge all at once to mate and lay eggs and start the cycle again.

1½–2"
CICADA
- climbs into trees on hot days and calls "ZZZZZZZ!"

* **Rig up a white sheet on a clothesline or drape it over a bush.** Shine a flashlight or lantern on it and wait patiently to see what nighttime insects are attracted to the light. (Or just watch the insects flying around your porch light.) You might even have a bat come looking for its evening meal!

* **The stars of the night sky are spectacular.** Find out when the meteor showers happen or what the brightest planets and constellations of your night sky are for this month. The Perseid showers are usually early to mid-August.

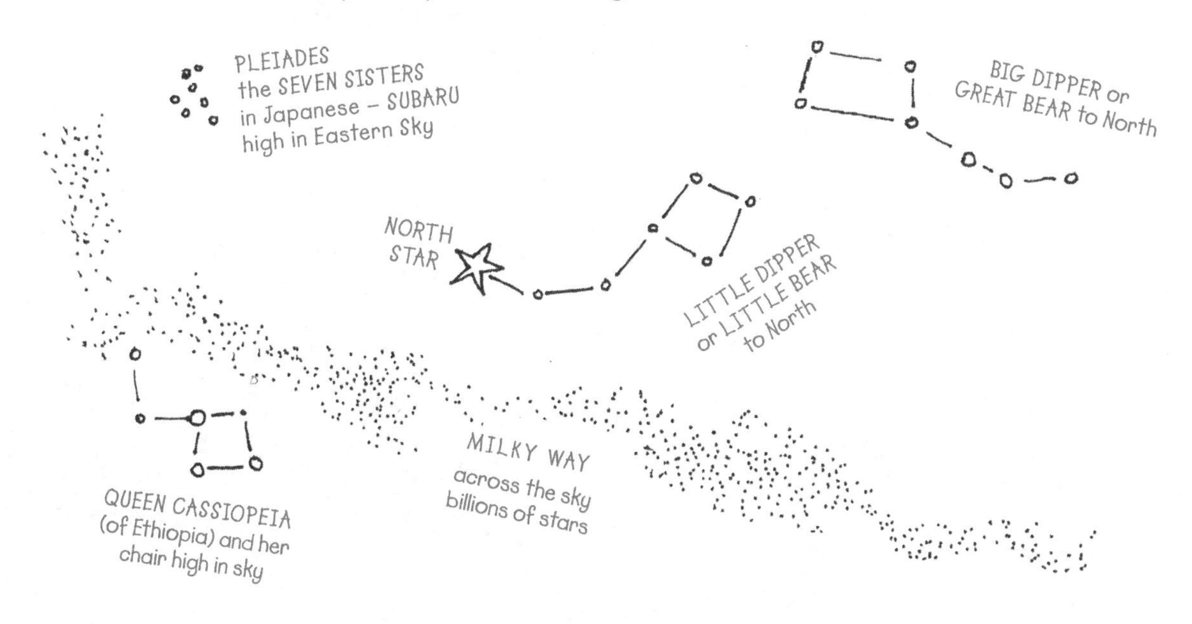

* **Read a story by firelight or flashlight** — ghost stories are always popular! Or read some folk tales about the nighttime. You can also find many wonderful stories about animals and what they do at night.

* **If you can have a campfire,** don't forget the s'mores!

SEPTEMBER

Change Is Coming

SEPTEMBER, A MONTH OF BEGINNINGS AND ENDINGS, was the seventh (*septem* means "seven" in Latin) month in the Roman calendar, which originally had ten months. (See more about that on page 122.)

The summer is ending. Kids and teachers go back to school. Dusk comes earlier and dawn comes later. Some flowers and leaves are shriveling but various plants are still blooming happily. The leaves on some trees are beginning to turn colors. In some places, summer's heat lingers, and September days can still be hot and muggy. In other places, frost may appear in the mornings.

In the world of nature, the decreasing daylight signals a time to start winding down. Some birds are migrating and many animals are busy eating, storing food, and looking for winter homes. The September full moon is sometimes called the Harvest Moon as this is often the last time crops can be harvested before the killing frosts of fall.

The crickets felt it was their duty
to warn everybody that summertime cannot last forever.
Even on the most beautiful days in the whole year,
the crickets spread the rumor of sadness and change.

— E.B. WHITE, *CHARLOTTE'S WEB*

MY NATURE NOTES

Date:	Time:
Place:	Temperature:
What's the weather like?	
Phase of the moon:	Time of sunrise:
	Time of sunset:
Look out the window or go outdoors, then jot down your observations, draw a picture, or describe a scene.	

To print out more pages like this, go to *www.storey.com/thenatureconnection.php.*

Go on a Nature Quest!

Start each month by taking a good look around. Go for a walk and see what you can find (use all your senses!) that gives a clue to the season. Try it on several different days and see how your answers change.

Can you find...	Describe what you notice.
☐ geese flying overhead	
☐ squirrel hiding an acorn	
☐ red berries on bushes	

What else can you find?

☐	
☐	
☐	
☐	
☐	
☐	
☐	
☐	
☐	
☐	

Picture of the Month

Choose one or two (or more!) things from your list to draw or photograph here.

Date: Place: Time:

Grass — So Much More than a Lawn

We usually think of green lawns when we hear the word "grass," but grasses grow everywhere — in marshes, high on mountains, in the tropics, in deserts, and in the empty lots and sidewalk cracks of cities all over the world. Prairie grass still covers vast acres of North America, though far fewer than a hundred years ago. Fortunately, many conservation organizations in Midwestern states are restoring areas of prairie land.

Have you ever watched a rabbit or a horse munching on grass or hay?

Grass is an important food source for many animals, including people. Surprised? Where do you think your breakfast cereal and sandwich bread come from? Wheat, oats, barley, rye, rice, and corn are all grasses, and we harvest the seeds, which we call grain. Horses, cows, and sheep eat grass or hay all year long (hay is grass that has been cut and dried so it will last through the winter).

Lots of wild animals feed on grass as well, including rabbits, mice, pronghorn antelope, bison, and prairie dogs. Meadows of grass and the tall grasses along ponds and marshes provide important shelter for many kinds of fish, crustaceans, birds, insects, and mammals.

I once had a friend, Lauren Brown, come visit me in Vermont. She wrote a book called *Grasses – An Identification Guide.* Within an hour, she had identified over 30 different grasses in the meadow near our house. I kept drawing them but couldn't keep up!

LEARN YOUR LOCAL GRASSES

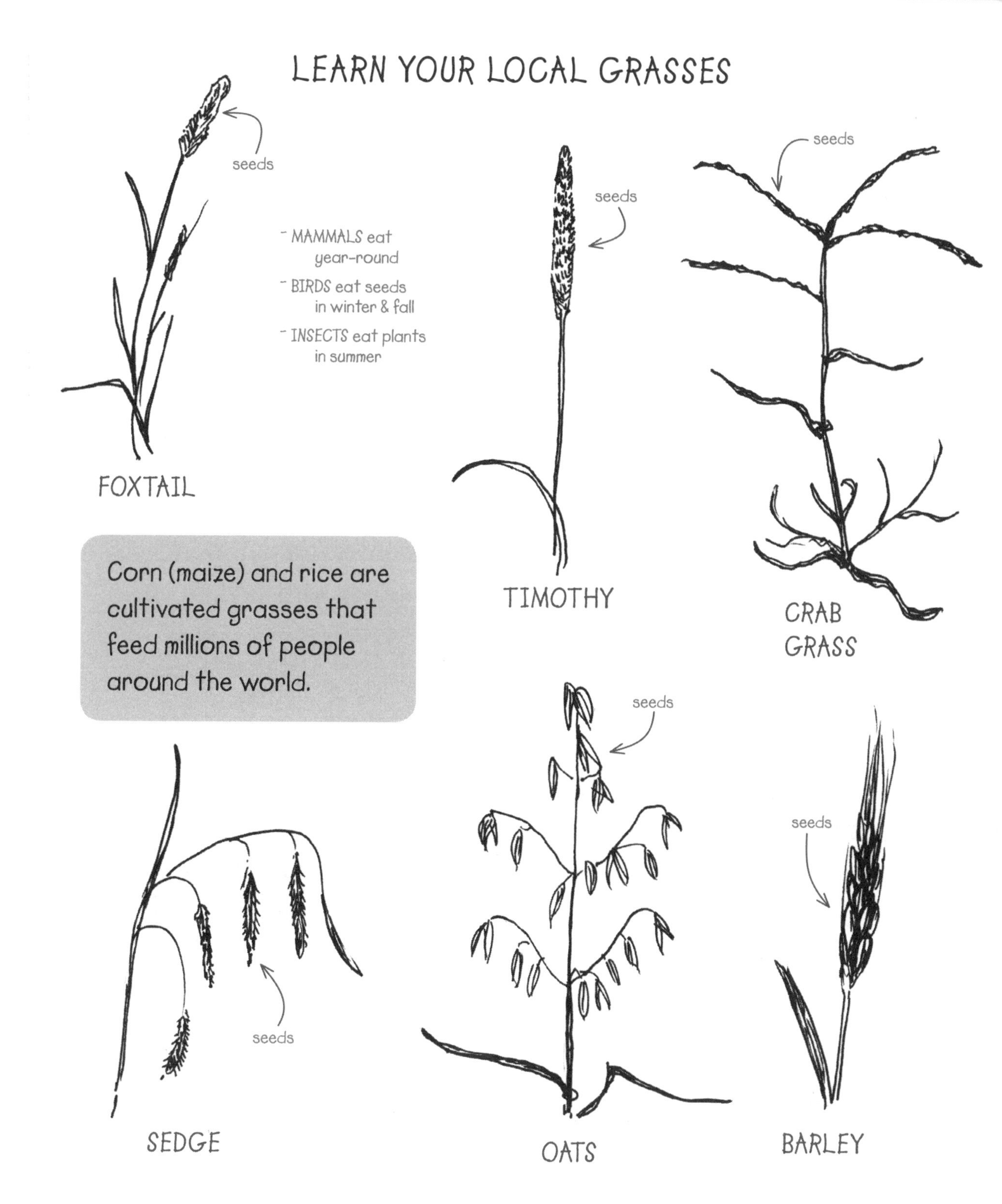

Corn (maize) and rice are cultivated grasses that feed millions of people around the world.

This is a beautiful time to enjoy nature — there's so much to do and see!

Here are some things you can do and look for in September. See if you can check them all off by the end of the month.

☐ **Choose one bird you have observed over the summer and do some research on its habits.** Write a report on your bird. If it migrates, include a map of its migration route. Draw pictures of the male and female birds, their eggs, and the nest. You could even make a three-dimensional model if you want.

☐ **Go outside with some friends and just play.** Jump rope, ride bikes, collect sticks and stones to build little houses with, or dam up a small stream. Just have fun being outside on these last warm days!

☐ **Collect a bunch of rocks of different sizes and shapes.** Rocks are very cool and so old. Learn about your local geology. Find a hard surface (a sidewalk or a large, flat stone) and try to break up the rocks with a hammer or a larger stone. What happens when you hit them? What do they look like inside? Be careful of your fingers!

Visit an observatory. If you have one nearby (check at a local college or university), they often have a public viewing night, especially if there is something very cool happening, like a comet or a lunar eclipse.

Afterward, you could write a story about the sky or do some research on a planet or constellation or make a painting of the dark night.

THE BIG DIPPER or THE GREAT BEAR (although named by people who knew that bears don't have long tails)

Watch the insects going about their business. There is so much to feed on at this time of year. Yellow jackets seem to appear from nowhere and often go after our sandwiches, juice, or fruit when we're eating outside. Don't be afraid and don't swat at them. Instead, watch closely and see if you can actually watch one of these insects sipping nectar or cleaning its mouth and legs.

Curl up with a good book. Try *Ring of Bright Water* by Gavin Maxwell (true tale about a pair of lively otters); *Never Cry Wolf* by Farley Mowat (a grand adventure with wolves in Alaska); and *Keepers of the Animals: Native American Stories and Wildlife Activities for Children* by Joseph Bruchac and Michael Caduto.

Going to Seed

As the season rushes toward winter, many plants are rapidly setting their seeds instead of blooming. Seeds guarantee a plant's survival into the following year and are an important food source for animals through the fall and winter. Seeds come in hundreds of different forms — from the tiny poppy seed to the giant coconut.

Did you know that nuts, such as walnuts and acorns, are seeds? All fruits contain seeds — apricots, apples, even bananas. Grasses have beautiful seed heads (see pages 224–225 for more on grasses).

More Things to Do

* **How many different seeds can you find?** Look for milkweed, daylily, crab apples, sunflower, and all kinds of grasses.
* **Collect a bunch of seeds into a "cabinet"** (see page 216) or use egg cartons to sort them. You can also glue them onto poster board. Don't forget to label them.
* **Find larger seeds** and see how far you can throw them.

WILD APPLES & CRABAPPLES help these animals make it through the winter:

- DEER
- TURKEYS
- BEAR
- PORCUPINE
- MICE
- ROBINS
- CEDAR WAXWINGS

MILKWEED SEEDS blow in the wind to a new place.

The beautiful WHITE CAMPION FLOWER shakes away its seeds from a dried pod.

HITCHHIKER SEEDS from flowers attach themselves to passing animals and get carried to a new place.

ACORNS get eaten or stored by squirrels, chipmunks, blue jays, some insects, bears.

Make some drawings of seeds you find.

Birds know which fruits have more sugars and which have more carbohydrates! Poison ivy berries, chokecherries, hackberries, and autumn olives are high in fat and are an important food source for birds flying south.

Date: Place: Time:

Getting Ready for Winter

When the light decreases to a certain amount each day, a sort of alarm clock goes off in the world of nature. Flowering plants put their energy into making seeds, while trees slow their production of food and, in many cases, prepare to lose their leaves.

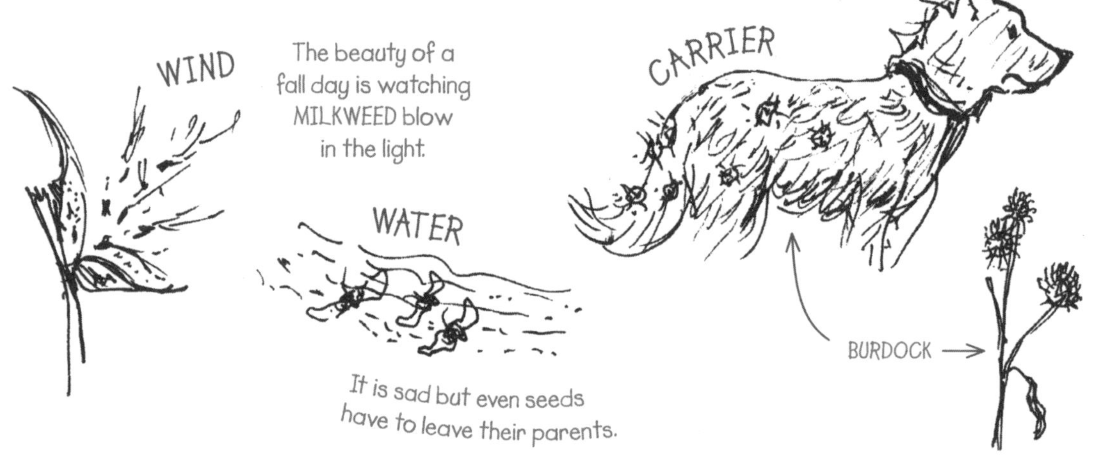

Mammals are eating, eating, eating, as they know food will be scarce in winter. Some, like the gray squirrel, store food away for later; you can watch them busily burying nuts. You might also see them carrying leaves up to tree holes for winter nests. Some animals will stay active and some will hibernate, but all act according to their inner clock.

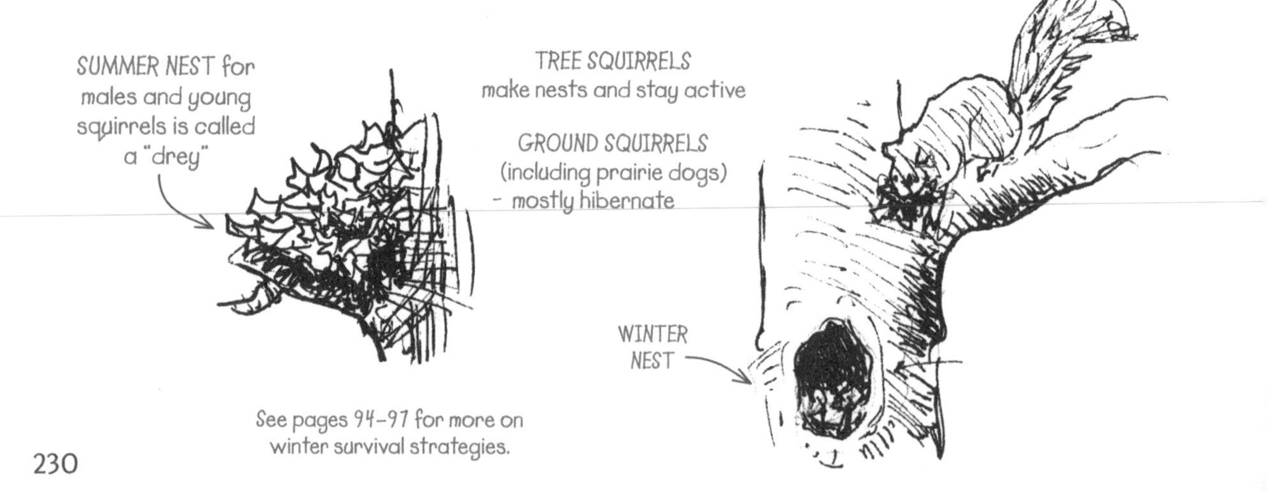

See pages 94–97 for more on winter survival strategies.

Birds are also busy in September. Not all birds migrate but many do. You can see them gathering in great flocks or flying far overhead.

SOUTH or southeast or southwest but south

SOME BIRDS THAT MIGRATE:

- swallows
- hummingbirds
- warblers
- vireos
- various ducks
- some sparrows
- blue birds
- phoebes

Toads, turtles, frogs, snakes, salamanders, and lizards are finding nice hiding places under logs or in ponds or deep in leaf litter so they can lie quiet all winter. Some actually freeze over the winter!

IS THERE WINTER IN THE DESERT?

Those of us who don't live in deserts may think of them as always being hot and dry, and they mostly are. During winter months, however, temperatures are lower and more rain may fall. A desert is an area with very little precipitation (rain and snow). Most are hot and sunny, but there are cold deserts in Greenland and the Antarctic. The plants and animals that live in these environments have adapted to the harsh conditions in many interesting ways – do some research and see what you discover!

An Animal Activity

As you notice the activity of the birds and other animals this month, think about how one particular animal is preparing for the winter. If you can, observe your animal over several days and make notes about its behavior. Take photos or draw a picture of what that animal is doing this month. Do research to back up your observations.

Put your drawings/photos and notes about animal activity here.

Date: Place: Time:

Take a Night Walk

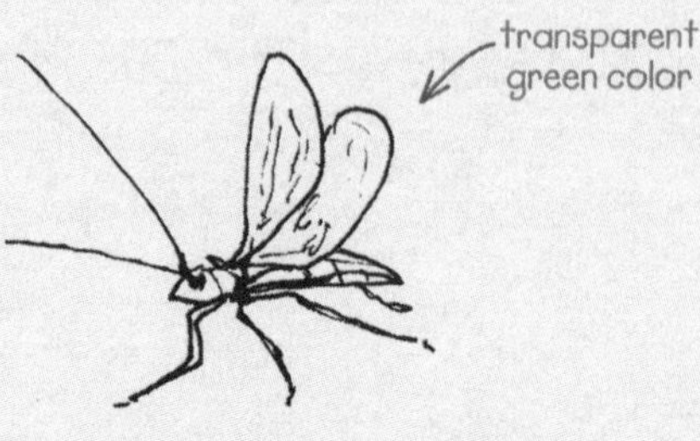

SNOWY TREE CRICKET
- sings by rubbing wings together "purr, purr, purr"

Being outside at night changes our way of relating to where we live. Go outside for a walk around your neighborhood after dark. Ask your family to join you. Hold hands if you are nervous. Take a flashlight if you want. (You can even do this blindfolded, but have someone lead you!)

You could go out for just 10 minutes or for a whole hour. Pay attention to everything you see, hear, or smell. When you come back inside, write your thoughts here.

How dark was it? Was it hard to see or did the moon provide some light?

___

___

What sounds did you hear?

___

___

What smells did you notice?

___

___

Write about how you felt walking in the night.

Draw a picture of nighttime shapes that you noticed.

Welcoming the Autumnal Equinox

Sunrises and sunsets for this month will change a lot. Where I live, we lose a total of 81 minutes of daylight between September 1 and 30. In the middle of the month comes the *autumnal* (fall) equinox, when day and night hours are about the same (12 hours each).

For a few days at this time of year, we share the same amount of daylight throughout the world, just as we do in March at the *vernal* (spring) equinox. (See page 126.) From now on, the days become shorter than the nights in the northern hemisphere, while in the southern hemisphere, the opposite happens.

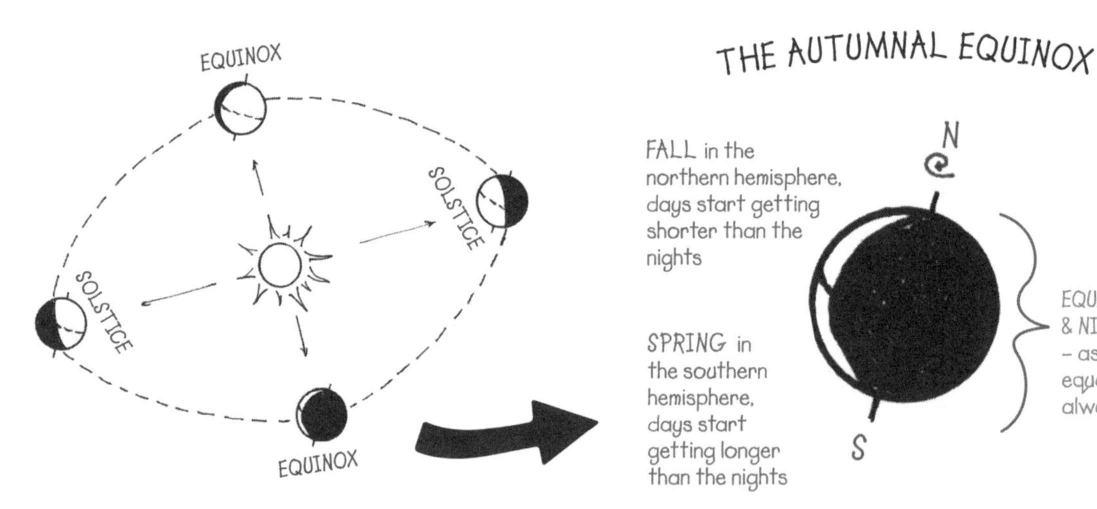

PATH OF SETTING SUN THROUGH ONE YEAR

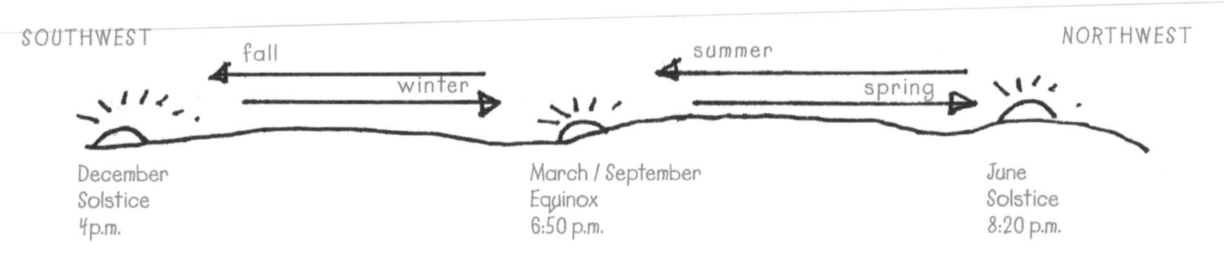

The height of the sun determines the amount of daylight we receive during any given season.

Summer
Spring/Fall
Winter

Measure the changing sun.
Put a stake outside in the ground. Record how the shadow changes as the month progresses. Try to check at the same time every day. You can use paint to mark the line, or plant a series of smaller stakes.

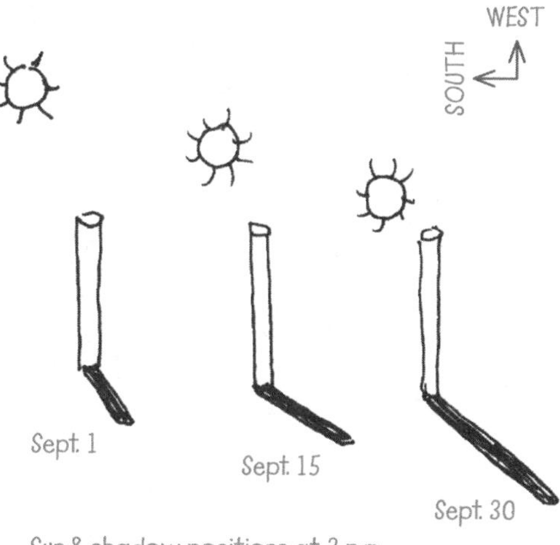

Sun & shadow positions at 3 p.m.

The position of the sun in the sky is a major determinant in the next stage of life for many plants and animals. Scientists still don't know a lot about how this trigger works, but they do know that the coming of the autumnal equinox stimulates the migration of birds, butterflies, and whales, and it signals a period of food gathering, mating, egg laying, and other changes in behavior. Plants respond to less light by releasing seeds, changing leaf color, and dying back.

As the daylight decreases, who around you is madly eating, storing food, or leaving for warmer places?

OCTOBER

The Last Hurrah

OCTOBER WAS THE EIGHTH MONTH in the ten-month Roman calendar (*octo* is Latin for "eight"). The ancient Anglo-Saxons, farther to the north, called it "Winterfylleth" because winter was said to begin on the full moon of this month.

In the Celtic lands of northern Europe, people celebrated October 31 as the end of their agricultural year and the beginning of a new year. Tribes gathered from all over for a three-day festival of *Samhain* — Gaelic for "year's end." Families came together to honor the dead, trade livestock, and light fires to banish the old year and bring in the new.

Eventually this important Celtic festival became what we know today as Halloween (meaning "holy evening" and coming before All Saint's Day) and *Dia de los Muertos* ("Day of the Dead," a remembrance of departed loved ones).

Look into nature
and then you will understand
everything better.

— **ALBERT EINSTEIN**

MY NATURE NOTES

Date:	Time:
Place:	Temperature:
What's the weather like?	
Phase of the moon:	Time of sunrise:
	Time of sunset:
Look out the window or go outdoors, then jot down your observations, draw a picture, or describe a scene.	

To print out more pages like this, go to *www.storey.com/thenatureconnection.php.*

Go on a Nature Quest!

Start each month by taking a good look around. Go for a walk and see what you can find (use all your senses!) that gives a clue to the season. Try it on several different days and see how your answers change.

Can you find…	Describe what you notice.
☐ bluejays calling	________________
☐ red & yellow leaves	________________
☐ morning frost	________________

What else can you find?

☐ ________________	________________
☐ ________________	________________
☐ ________________	________________
☐ ________________	________________
☐ ________________	________________
☐ ________________	________________
☐ ________________	________________
☐ ________________	________________
☐ ________________	________________
☐ ________________	________________

Picture of the Month

Choose one or two (or more!) things from your list to draw or photograph here.

Date: Place: Time:

Why Do Leaves Turn Color?

Trees that drop their leaves and turn colors are called *deciduous*. When daylight grows shorter and temperatures drop, a sort of "computer chip" in these trees kicks in. Twigs cut off the supply of water to their leaves. The chemical *chlorophyll* in the leaves can no longer make food. The dominant green color breaks down and the yellows (*xanthophylls*), reds (*anthocyanins*), and oranges (*carotenes*) appear. The browns you see are the *tannin* chemicals left as the leaves of oak, beech, and sycamore die.

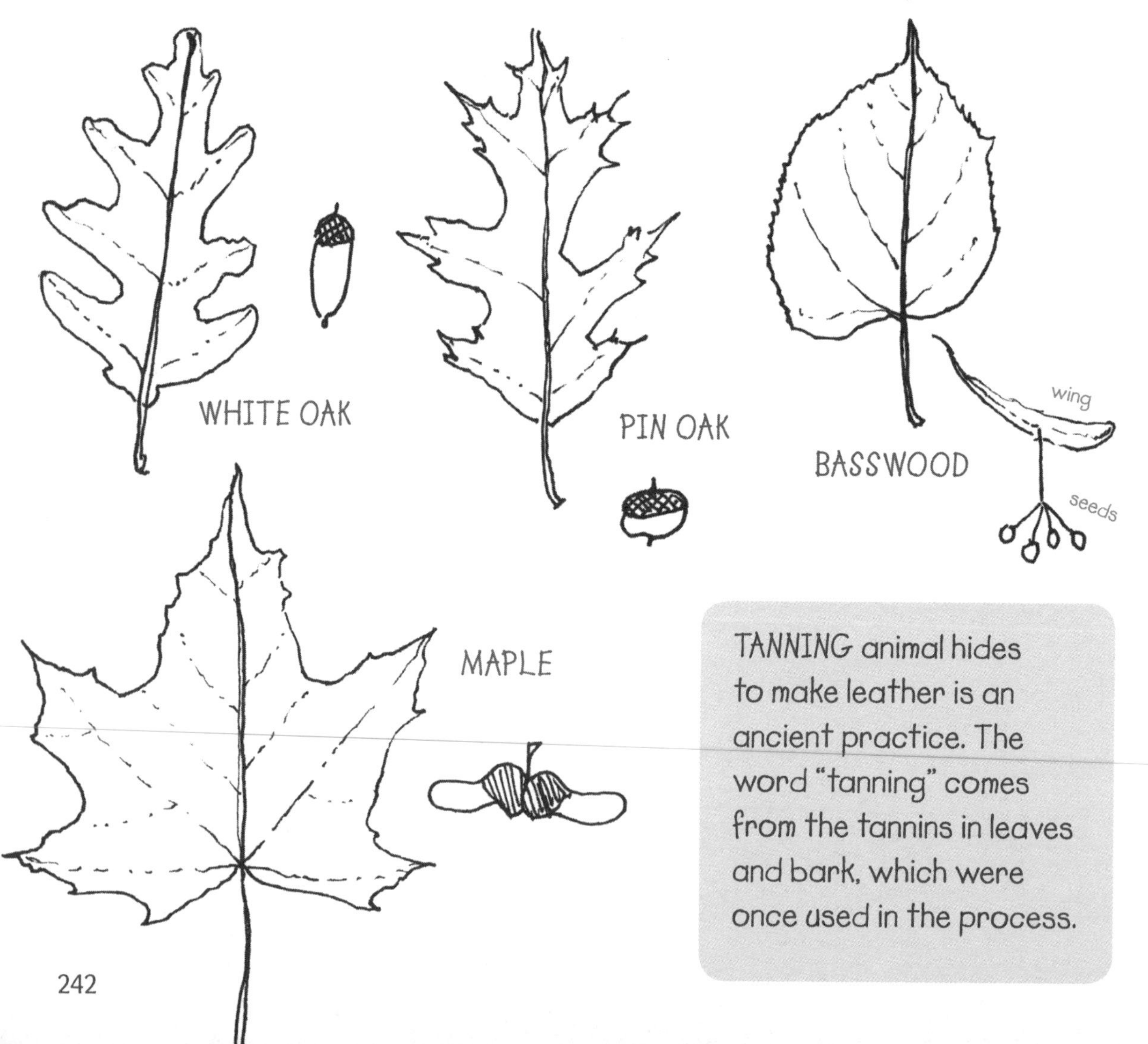

TANNING animal hides to make leather is an ancient practice. The word "tanning" comes from the tannins in leaves and bark, which were once used in the process.

Broad-leaved evergreens keep their leaves and stay green throughout the winter, replacing them slowly over the year. Examples of these include rhododendrons, mountain laurels, palms, and southern live oak. Notice their thick and waxy leaves. Many of them grow in places where the temperature rarely goes below freezing. Others thrive in desert climes.

Conifers, such as pines, spruces, cedars, and arborvitaes, grow cones instead of flowers and have needles that withstand any winter cold. The surface area of the needles is small, and their sap actually contains a form of antifreeze. Conifer branches are elastic enough to withstand strong winds and heavy snows.

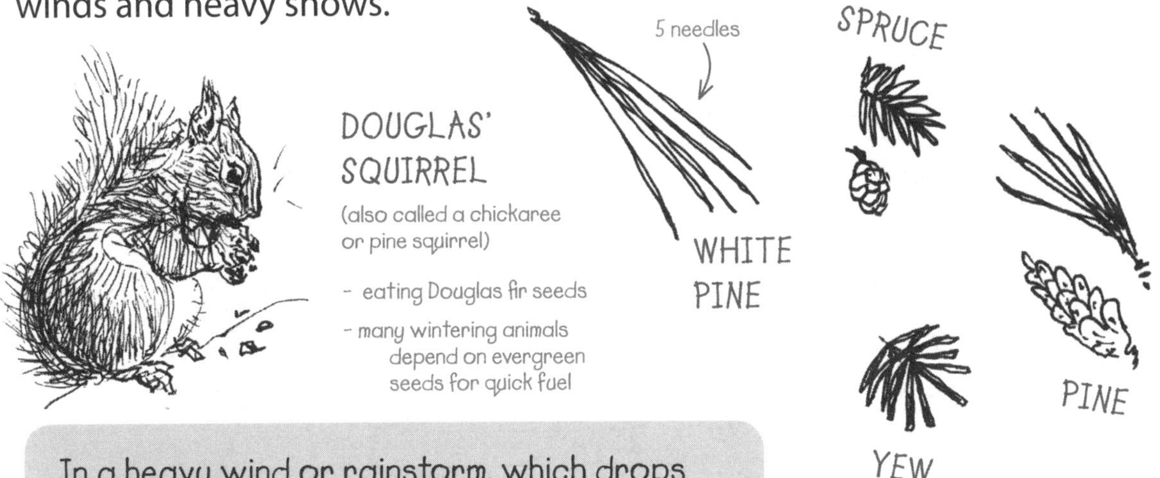

In a heavy wind or rainstorm, which drops fewer branches: deciduous or evergreen?

Drawing Leaves

Leaves are fun to draw because they come in so many different shapes and sizes. There are two basic types: *simple* and *compound*. Simple leaves have one blade (leaf) to a stem, while compound leaves have several blades (sometimes called leaflets) on a single stem. Within those groups, leaves have an amazing variety of patterns — see how many you can find!

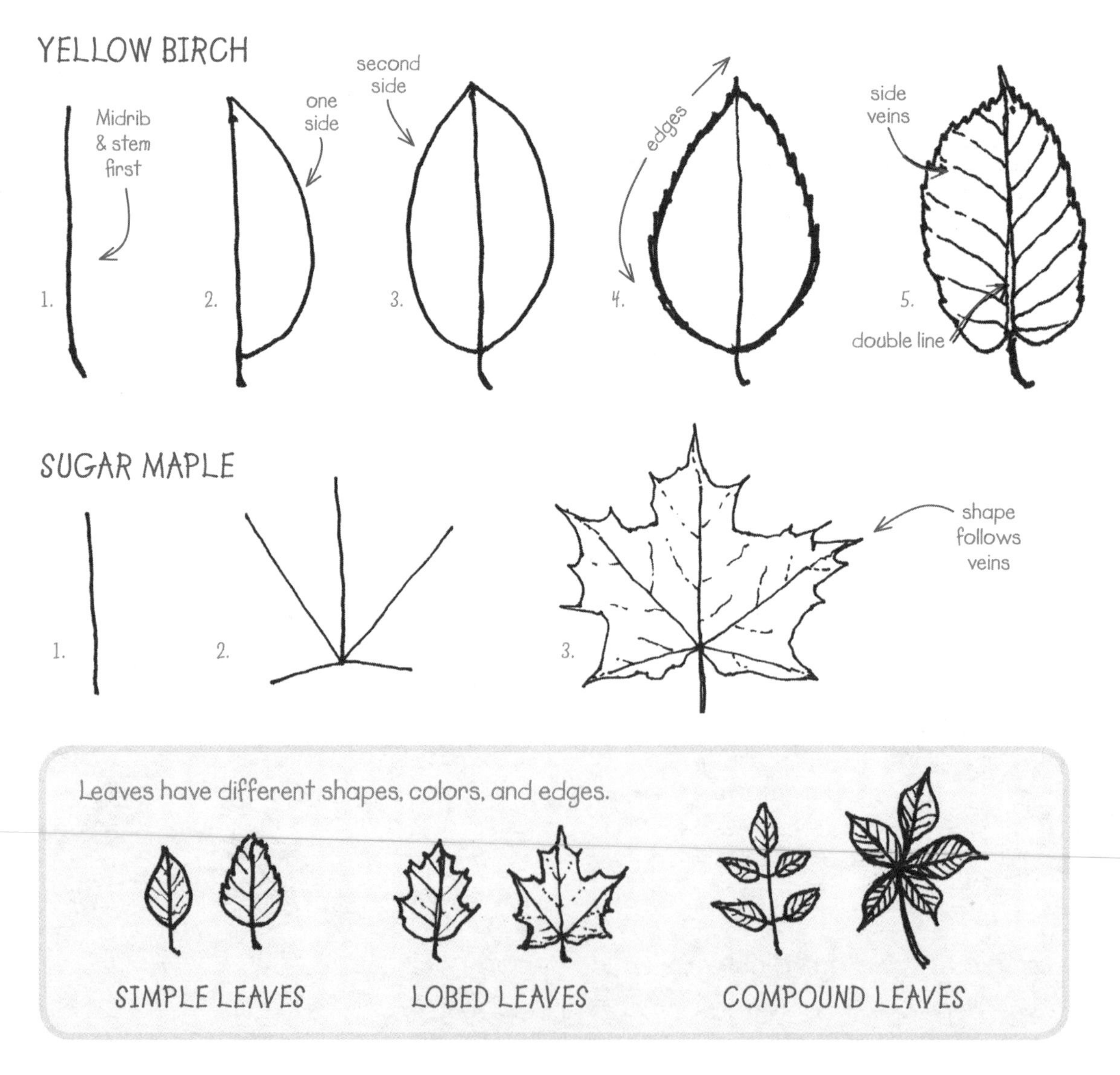

Put your leaf drawings here.

Date: Place: Time:

It's hard to stay inside in October!

Here are some things you can do and look for in October. See if you can check them all off by the end of the month.

☐ **Plan for spring and plant some bulbs.** This is the best time, before it gets too cold and the ground hardens. We plant crocuses, daffodils, snowdrops, squill, and tulips. Planting bulbs is easy. You can make a garden bed for them or just plant directly into your lawn. Bulbs are the winter food storage part of the plant and will happily winter over underground and burst into bloom come spring.

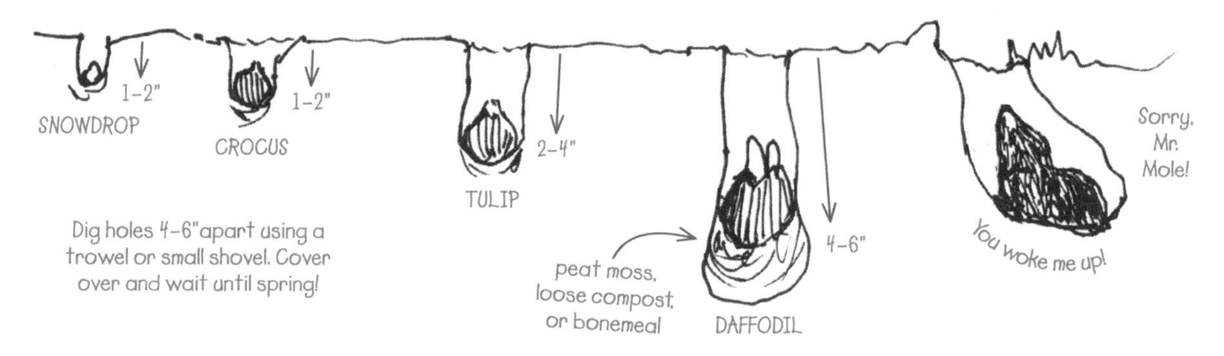

☐ **Collect a variety of leaves and seeds and make art work.**

* **Make leaf prints** using tempera paints or printer's ink.
* **Draw or trace the leaves** onto paper and color them.
* **Press them** for a few days between a couple of heavy books, then make a collage or paste them into your journal.
* **Iron a pattern of leaves** between two sheets of wax paper (using low heat!) or mount them between clear contact paper and hang in a window.

☐ **Rake up a big pile of leaves** with some friends and then jump in it. Run through the pile and rake it up again.

* Bury each other in leaves!
* Offer to help an elderly neighbor or relative by raking and collecting their leaves.
* Make a lean-to shelter from fallen branches (don't break them off), bunches of leaves, and other material.
* Leave a pile of brush in your yard to provide winter shelter for birds and other wildlife.

☐ **Play "Pooh sticks" on a bridge.** If you don't know how, read about it in *The House at Pooh Corner* by A.A. Milne. And then look up the World Poohsticks Championships online!

☐ **Snuggle up with a good book.** *My Side of the Mountain* and *Frightful's Mountain* by Jean Craighead George tell the story of a boy who lives on his own in the woods and befriends a hawk.

My Favorite Tree

As you wander around your neighborhood, notice the different kinds of trees that live there. Adopt one that you can visit regularly and watch it change over the seasons. Spend some time really looking at it. Examine the bark. Study the shape of the leaves or needles. Notice how the branches grow out of the trunk.

WHITE OAK

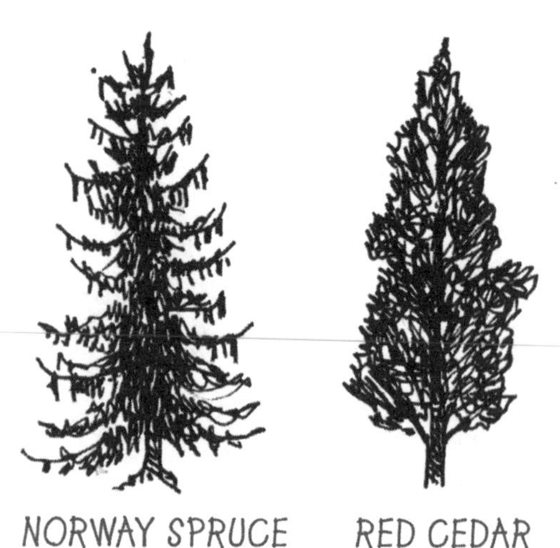

Find a tree guide to learn more about your tree and use as reference for your drawings. I use *Eastern Trees* by George A. Petrides and *The Sibley Guide to Trees* by David Sibley.

Draw some pictures of your tree.

Date: Place: Time:

What Is Moss? What Are Fungi?

The carpets of moss that you see in shady, damp spots are made up of thousands of tiny individual plants. *Mosses* need droplets of water to grow and reproduce, as they lack roots and can't transport water from the soil. By spreading over an area, they help retain moisture in the soil. Most mosses look and feel soft and fluffy but they have a waxy coating that keeps them from drying out.

Fungi is a kingdom of organisms that is classified separately from plants, animals, and bacteria. Fungi are crucial in the cycle of decomposition and recycling of organic material that occurs in nature. This grouping includes molds and yeasts, but the most familiar is the mushroom, which grows all over the world in many different forms.

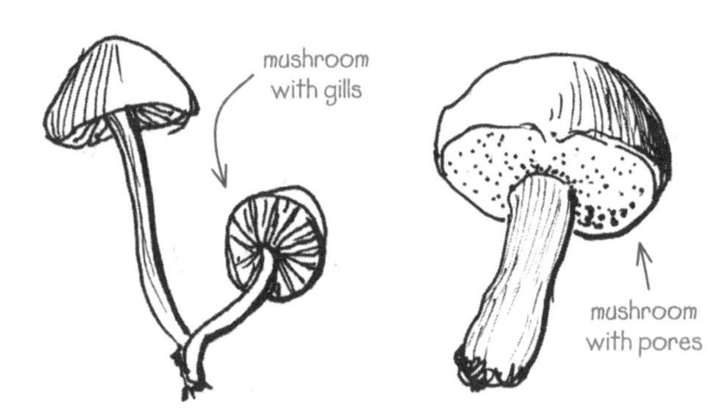

What you see above ground is called the FRUITING BODY of this plant. It gets its food from tiny rootlets that attach to the soil or decaying wood.

Some FUNGI (that's the plural of fungus) have names that describe them.

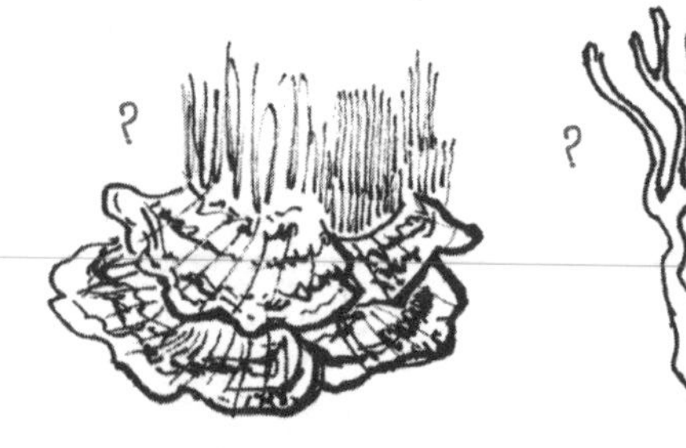

Can you guess which of these is the TURKEY TAIL FUNGUS and which is the CORAL FUNGUS?

Many mushrooms are edible (and delicious!) but a few are highly poisonous. Never eat a wild mushroom unless a knowledgeable adult says it's safe!

AND WHAT ABOUT LICHEN?

Lichens are primitive and ancient plants. They are a combination of fungus and alga that together create a *symbiotic* organism. Symbiotic means two things that live very closely together, each benefiting the other. In this case, the fungus provides the structure and the alga produces the food. Lichens break down the rocks and trees that they live on, eventually creating soil that nourishes more life.

I used the *Golden Guide to Non-Flowering Plants* to draw these examples.

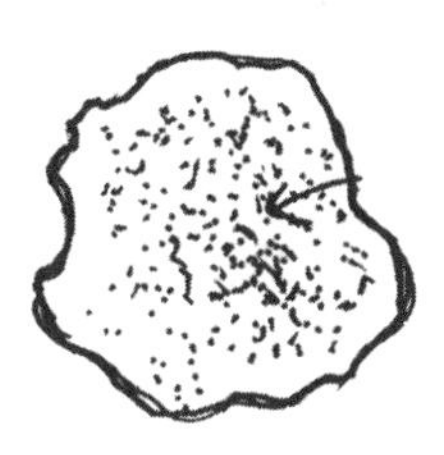

CRUSTOSE LICHEN
(FLAT)
1–3"

FRUTICOSE LICHEN
(SHRUBBY)
1–1½"

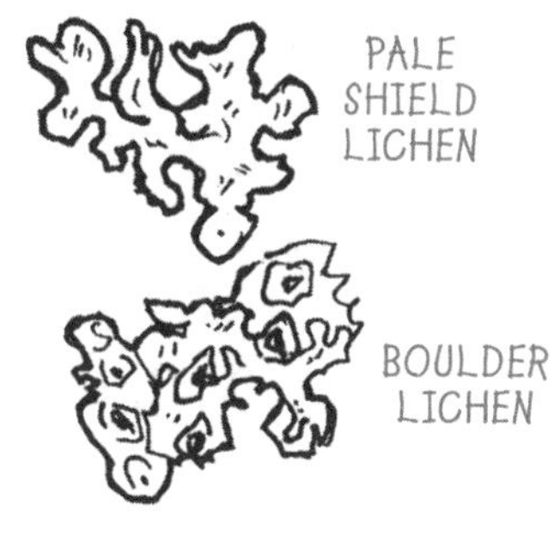

FOLIOSE LICHEN
(LEAFY)
1–5"

FERNS

Ferns are another type of plant entirely. They grow all over the world, but like mosses, most varieties prefer moist, shady spots and are often found growing in forest environments. They have roots to draw nutrients from the soil but are unusual in that they do not produce flowers and seeds. Instead they reproduce from spores, which form on separate stalks or under the leaves and fall to the ground or are released into the air.

spore (fruiting stalk)

leaf frond

Storing Food for Winter

All through the autumn, animals have been busily eating to store energy for the winter and in some cases, gathering food to stash away for later. Humans, too, are harvesting food and preparing it for storage. This is the season of harvest festivals and country fairs.

In this age of global grocery stores, it may seem that we don't need to worry about storing food for a long winter, but if you take a look around your kitchen, you'll find lots of foods that are prepared in ways that your great-great-grandparents would recognize. Some examples are popcorn, raisins and other dried fruit, jams and chutneys, and pickles.

What are some others that you can think of?

Harvest Festival Time

This is the time of gathering the harvest in preparation for the long winter. The first Thanksgiving feast of American legend was actually celebrated earlier in the autumn of 1621. November would have been too cold and too late for many crops, and the local Wampanoag tribes would have gone to their winter homes inland to what is now Rhode Island. Today we still give thanks for family, health, and good harvest by preparing foods similar to those grown 400 years ago.

NOVEMBER

A Quiet Time

As you may have guessed from September and October, November (from the Latin *novem* or "nine") was the ninth month of the Roman calendar. In the northern hemisphere, this is a time when the outdoor world settles into a long period of quiet and rest. Just as people have a daily cycle of activity and sleep, so does nature.

This is an important time of dormancy and gestation for many plants and animals in nature. With the woods and fields easier to get into and winter coming on, hunting is a popular activity in many parts of North America through November and December. Depending on where you live, hunters might be out looking for grouse, squirrel, elk, rabbit, deer, turkey, even bear and moose.

Some people hunt for the sport alone, but many also do it for food and income and as a tradition, carried down through families. Many hunters and hunting organizations, such as Ducks Unlimited, are actively involved in protecting land and wildlife.

The Lakota was a true naturalist — a love of Nature.
He loved the earth and all the things of the earth . . .
Kinship with all the creatures of the earth, sky, and water
was a real and active principle.

— CHIEF LUTHER STANDING BEAR

MY NATURE NOTES

Date:	Time:
Place:	Temperature:
What's the weather like?	
Phase of the moon:	Time of sunrise:
	Time of sunset:
Look out the window or go outdoors, then jot down your observations, draw a picture, or describe a scene.	

To print out more pages like this, go to *www.storey.com/thenatureconnection.php.*

Go on a Nature Quest!

Start each month by taking a good look around. Go for a walk and see what you can find (use all your senses!) that gives a clue to the season. Try it on several different days and see how your answers change.

Can you find...	Describe what you notice.
☐ late blooming flowers	
☐ ice on puddles	
☐ cold wind blowing	

What else can you find?

☐	
☐	
☐	
☐	
☐	
☐	
☐	
☐	
☐	
☐	

Picture of the Month

Choose one or two (or more!) things from your list to draw or photograph here.

Date: Place: Time:

Looking at Geology around You

If geology means the study of the earth, where would you go to learn about the land under your feet and all around you? Begin right where you are, by looking at the rocks or pebbles in your backyard. Where did they come from? (Did you know that asphalt is a kind of rock? It's made from sandstone mixed with petroleum.)

Scientists believe that Earth is some 4.6 billion years old. Hills and mountains may look as though they've been there forever, but geology changes as the eons pass. The New England mountains, now much smaller than the mighty Rockies of the west, used to be as high as Mount Everest.

Mile-high glaciers once covered vast areas of Earth and carved out different land formations. Volcanoes erupting in the oceans formed islands; in many parts of the world, volcanoes are still active and changing the landscape.

A STRANGE STONE

In a schoolyard in Boston, my students and I found interesting outcroppings of a black and bubbly-looking rock called "Roxbury puddingstone." It was formed by volcanoes millions of years ago, cooled by retreating glaciers, mixed with river stones, and buried far under the earth.

ROXBURY PUDDINGSTONE

MINERALS

Quartz, copper, talc, mica, garnet, and gold are some of the building blocks for rocks.

QUARTZ
- formed of six-sided crystals

Here are some types of rocks that you can learn more about. Get a good book on geology (I like the *Golden Guide to Geology* by Frank Rhodes.) Collect different rocks, stones, and pebbles from various places as you explore. Hammer them open and see what they look like inside. See if you can figure out what type they are.

SEDIMENTARY

Sand, pebbles, shells, and others on the earth's surface are cemented together over time. The sedimentary layer is often a good place to find fossils.

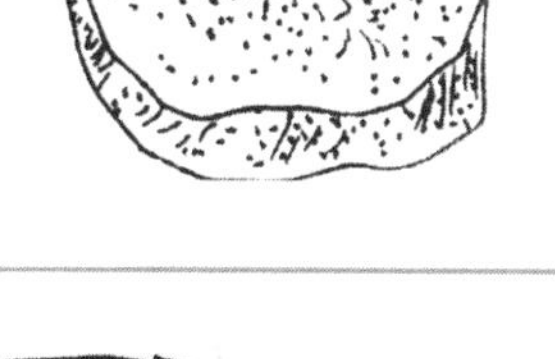

SANDSTONE is made of sand, of course!

METAMORPHIC

Sedimentary rocks are buried in layers and crushed by the earth's heat and pressure, forming metamorphic rocks such as quartzite, schist, and slate

SLATE is formed from layers of shale.

IGNEUS

Metamorphic rocks from deep underground melt; if they come to the surface in the form of molten lava from a volcano, they cool into a rock such as basalt. If it cools underground, it becomes something like granite.

GRANITE sometimes has different minerals embedded in it.

FOSSILS

The remains of ancient plants and animals, often marine, preserved in sedimentary or metamorphic rock (some are 400–500 million years old)

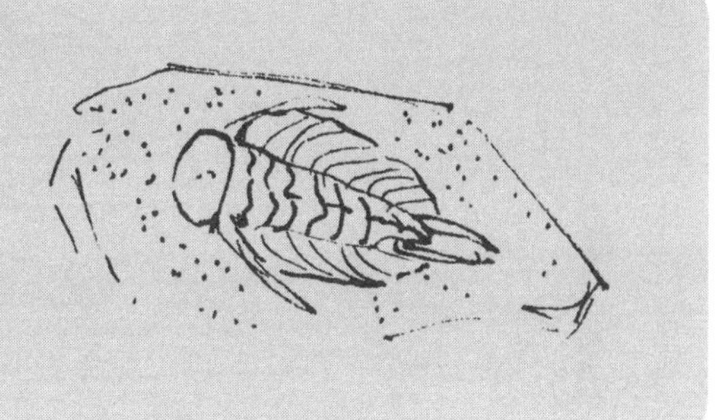

Even when it's dark and cold, you can always find a reason to step outdoors.

Here are some things you can do and look for in November. See if you can check them all off by the end of the month.

☐ **Make a point of listening to the quiet.** Bundle up and go outside at several different times of day and just stand still and notice what sounds you can hear in the frosty air.

☐ **What can you see around your house or favorite play area now that all the leaves are down?** If you live in a warmer climate, how does a familiar scene look different than it did six months ago?

☐ **Study different ice formations as the temperature drops.** Look for places where icicles form or where melting water freezes overnight. Pour a cup of water into several different-sized containers of water, put them outside, and measure how quickly they freeze. Does the time differ with the temperature or location?

Leave a bottle full of water out overnight when it is below freezing and see what happens. Try both glass and plastic (leave the cap off!).

☐ **Make a sculpture or mobile of collected objects** — twigs, berries, seeds, dried leaves, feathers. Your creation should last the rest of the winter as all those materials have dried out by now. (Don't use the small white berries from poison ivy vines!)

☐ **Write your own poem of thanksgiving.** Here's mine: *Thanks for the sun. Thanks for friends. Thanks for the trees beside me tall. Thanks for the cardinal so red and for the inky night. Thanks for my family's health as this year quiets down.*

☐ **Do a series of paintings of November.** What colors would you use? I know I will use a lot of burnt umbers, grays, ultramarine blues, ochre, and rusty browns. Sometimes I like to sprinkle a little silver glitter on my paintings to show the iciness of the season.

☐ **Create a play about nature where you live.** Set the play somewhere in your town. The characters could be a blue jay, mouse, coyote, deer, or whatever you want. Make up a story about them and act it out with some friends. It could be a winter play, or you could have one act for each season.

☐ **Curl up with a good book.** Read the Little House series by Laura Ingalls Wilder. They all offer a detailed picture of life long ago, but *The Long Hard Winter* tells the story of people struggling to survive an unusually harsh winter on the prairie.

Birds in Your Backyard (and Beyond)

Learning about birds is a great way to study nature. No matter where you live, they are easy to find, do interesting things, and are often very pretty. It can be hard to say the same about studying clams or jellyfish or bumblebees, though scientists are interested in all creatures.

Get to know a few birds in your neighborhood and you will learn a lot about where you live, whether it's urban, suburban, or rural. It's often hard for the birds that don't migrate to find enough food in the winter. They need lots of energy to keep warm and to keep looking for food so they can keep warm!

Put out a birdfeeder and see who comes. You can buy an inexpensive plastic feeder at a hardware store or you can make one out of a half-gallon milk or juice jug: Cut three or four 3-sided windows with the flap out so the birds can perch.

Build a brush pile for birds to find shelter in. You can put out your old Christmas tree — no tinsel, though! If you have a big enough yard, ask your parents to think about planting some evergreen bushes or trees to protect birds in the winter.

Try hanging PINECONES smeared with lots of peanut butter!

SUET FEEDER
- WOODPECKERS and NUTHATCHES like suet feeders

How Many Birds?

Birds are a valuable indicator of the health of an environment and of the shifting climate locally as well as globally. Numerous organizations and programs monitor birds at feeders as well as seasonal counts of birds in towns and states. One is Project FeederWatch (*www.feederwatch.org*), sponsored by the Cornell Lab of Ornithology.

Kids all over the world are doing interesting and important things to help the environment. If you're interested in birds, your nearest Audubon chapter or local environmental center will have information on other fun and useful bird-related things you can do.

Keep a list of the birds you see in November. Depending on where you live, some birds will have migrated away or have come to your area for the winter. Others stay year-round. Do you have juncos, robins, or hawks?

Make your list here.

How Do You Feel about Hunting?

For hundreds of years, hunting animals was the only way that people could obtain meat. Today, hunting is still an important source of food for many families around the world, although some hunters are more interested in finding trophy animals. You may not have thought of it like this, but hunters need to be naturalists in order to be successful.

Why? Because if you don't understand the habits and behaviors of your prey, you won't be able to find it even if you spend many hours searching. Responsible hunters spend much of their time watching, waiting, and studying the land.

It's natural for some animals to be hunters and others to be hunted, but the age-old balance between predator and prey has been upset. Humans have killed off many large predators, such as wolves and wild cats, causing the population of some prey species, like deer and rabbits, to explode in some areas.

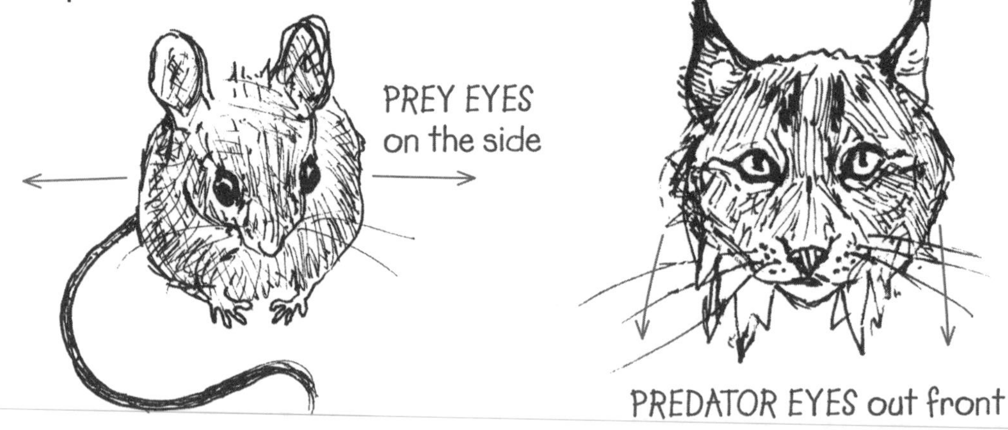

You can learn more about hunting from your state's Department of Fish and Wildlife, and from groups like Ducks Unlimited (*www.ducks.org*).

Write your ideas about hunting here.

Have an Outdoor Adventure

Invite your family or a few friends on a winter treasure hunt. See how many different colors, sounds, smells, and shapes you can each find. Put your lists together to create one long list and post it on your refrigerator or send it around as an e-mail.

Keep the game going and have people add to the list every day. After a week, see who found the most items or the most unusual!

Draw some of the things you find here.

Date: Place: Time:

NATURE TREASURE SIGHTINGS

COLORS	DATE/PLACE/TIME	WHO SAW IT?
SOUNDS	DATE/PLACE/TIME	WHO SAW IT?
SMELLS	DATE/PLACE/TIME	WHO SAW IT?
SHAPES	DATE/PLACE/TIME	WHO SAW IT?

DECEMBER

Year's End

IN OUR CALENDAR, December (from the Latin *decem* for "ten") is the last month of the year. We may think of December as a month of endings. Plants have died back. Animals are finding ways to survive until spring or have left altogether. The weather has become harsh, with cold winds and even snow. The days are short and the nights are long. But in nature's calendar, there are no named months or numbered days, and no final endings. There is rest, germination, gestation, rebirth, growth, reproduction, death, and so on in an endless cycle.

We are indoors more and connected to the natural world less. This time of year, we may not notice the tree silhouettes, the night stars, the waxing and waning moon, the frost on grass blades, the vivid sunsets, the huddled squirrels, or the red-tailed hawk hunting overhead, but they are out there whether we are watching or not!

Good King Wenceslas looked out
On the feast of Stephen,
When the snow lay round about
Deep and crisp and even.
Brightly shone the moon that night,
Though the frost was cruel…

— **TRADITIONAL CAROL**

MY NATURE NOTES

Date:	Time:
Place:	Temperature:
What's the weather like?	
Phase of the moon:	Time of sunrise:
	Time of sunset:
Look out the window or go outdoors, then jot down your observations, draw a picture, or describe a scene.	

To print out more pages like this, go to *www.storey.com/thenatureconnection.php.*

Go on a Nature Quest!

Start each month by taking a good look around. Go for a walk and see what you can find (use all your senses!) that gives a clue to the season. Try it on several different days and see how your answers change.

Can you find...	Describe what you notice.
☐ snow squeaking underfoot	
☐ chickadees feeding	
☐ sun glinting on ice	

What else can you find?

☐	
☐	
☐	
☐	
☐	
☐	
☐	
☐	
☐	
☐	

Picture of the Month

Choose one or two (or more!) things from your list to draw or photograph here.

Date: Place: Time:

It's Holiday Time

December is the month of numerous celebrations, and all of them feature lights: Saturnalia, Hanukkah, Santa Lucia Day, the winter solstice, Yule, Kwanza, and Christmas. For centuries, this time of year was a terrifying time for many cultures. People didn't know if the sun would come back. They hoped they had enough food to survive. They hoped their families would not get sick.

For many centuries people have sought to keep the cold and dark at bay and encourage the sun to return by putting candles in windows and lighting bonfires. And it worked! At this time of year, the sun makes its lowest arc across the southern sky, creating the shortest days of the year. But after the solstice, which falls around December 22, the days slowly begin to increase in length, moving again toward the renewing days of spring.

This time of year was called "Hweolor-tid," yuletide. The Yule log was brought in and lit, to symbolize the sun's return and warmth in the house.

APPLES symbolized food, health, and life.

MISTLETOE

HOLLY, IVY, WINTERGREENS. Red and green are symbols of life in winter.

Mistletoe was a symbol of life and love for the ancient Norse and Druids.

Often a Sun image was put on top.

EVERGREEN and OAK trees, both outdoors and in, decorated for many centuries in Europe to symbolize eternal life.

DID YOU KNOW?
The legend of Saint Nicolas came from Turkey and his reindeer came from Norway.

Have you noticed that ANGELS have bird wings?

Bright, cold winter days can be the perfect time to explore nature.

Here are some things you can do and look for in December. See if you can check them all off by the end of the month.

☐ **Take a long walk outdoors on a sunny day.** Bundle up for the weather and just listen, watch, and breathe in deeply as you look for signs of nature. Count them in your mind. I count them on my fingers and will return and write them down, from remembering 8 fingers or 6 fingers.

☐ **Watch for the winter owls, ducks, and geese that come down from frozen tundras.** Winter bird watching is cold but exciting. Find a bird club, nature center, or individual who has a telescope, a field guide, lots of enthusiasm, and knows where to go.

MY FAVORITE TIME OF YEAR TO GO BIRD WATCHING IS DECEMBER. The marshes have turned a glorious copper and ochre, the sky is steel gray, the tidal marsh ripples and glints with light from the sky. The hours of light are few, so your attention is tight and your mind is only on birds.

Think about all the different kinds of beaks that birds have. From your observations of birds, make some lists of ones that you've seen that have beaks like the ones I've drawn here.

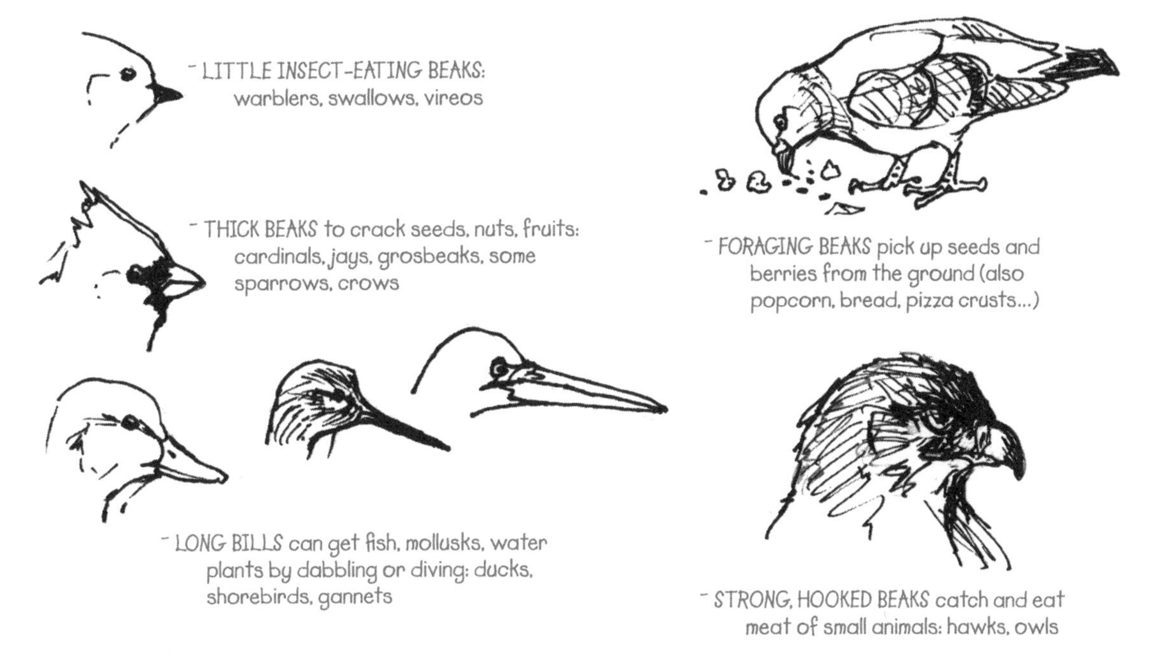

Make a calendar for yourself or as a gift. Every month has its colors. Every month has its nature features. Paint, draw, color, or collage a panel for each month. Go through your nature journal or any observations that you've made. Use some of the pictures you've created over the year or make new ones. At the end, write a poem blessing the elements of nature that have made up your year.

Settle in with a good book. Find some books about winter myths, celebrations, and beliefs. Try *Dear Rebecca, Winter Is Here* by Jean Craighead George or the classic nature information book by Don Stokes, *A Guide to Nature in Winter.*

The Winter Solstice

The movement of the earth around the sun determines the seasonal flow of the year and the cycle of light and dark. The winter solstice marks the time of year when the days are short and cold in the northern hemisphere but long and warm in the southern hemisphere. (See pages 60–65, 126–127, 172–173, and 236–237 for more.)

Find out from the Internet, your local newspaper, or your weather channel, what times the sun rises and sets where you live this month. In Cambridge, Massachusetts, the earliest sunset is not on the actual solstice but in early December, when it typically happens at 4:12 p.m. and remains the same for a number of days in a row. By December 21, the sun is already setting at 4:15 p.m. The sunrise, however, doesn't start getting later until the first week in January. Find out the time of your own sunrises and sunsets at this time of year.

ABOVE THE ARCTIC CIRCLE

Here the sun sets in November and doesn't reappear until early February. Communities living that far north don't celebrate the winter solstice. They celebrate the return of the sun, even though it may only appear for 15 minutes at first sometime in January.

FINDING THE SUN

This is an exercise I like to do with my classes to help them understand the solstices. Imagine you are Earth, in winter and in summer. Use your belt or waistband as the equator. In the winter, bend away from the sun and in the summer, bend toward it. Which part of you gets the most sun and in which season?

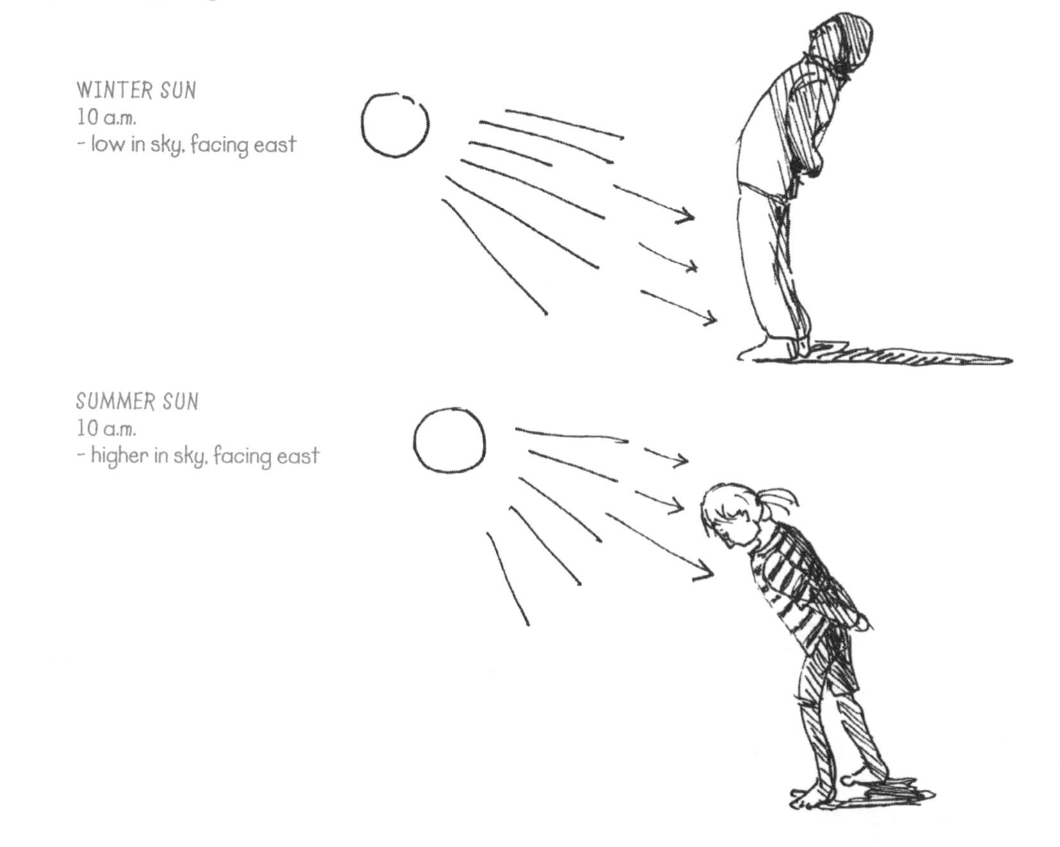

Notice how plants and animals turn to the sun. Watch birds on a winter day finding its warmth. What are the warmest and coolest sides of your house or school building? Where do plants come up first in the spring?

December Landscapes

Where are all the animals? What are they doing to stay warm? How are the trees living through the cold? What kinds of shelter do birds and animals find? What are they eating? (You can find out more in January and February sections.)

Here's a quiz for you:

* How many different plants and animals can you find on these two pages?
* What other animals might be hiding unseen?

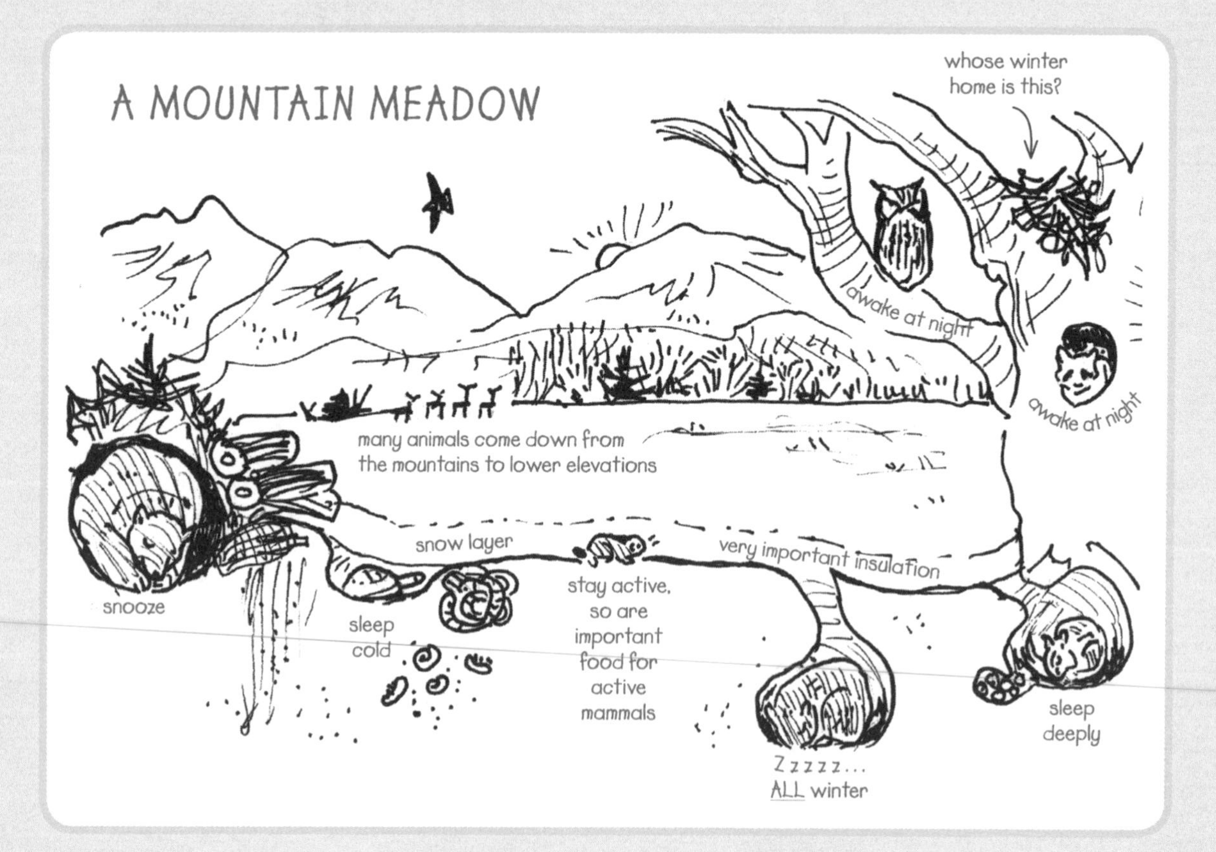

IN THE WOODS
Evergreen trees are shelter for birds, rabbits, deer, moose, and other animals.
UNDER THE WATER
All sorts of insects, larvae, and crustaceans sleep away in the mud.

Appendix

The path into the woods near our house in Vermont was a little bit scary and dark. When Eric and Anna were small, my husband and I frequently took them exploring down there. As they got older and braver, they would disappear into the woods for hours on their own. Now we wait for them to come visit and ask us to go for a walk!

A Special Note to Parents and Teachers

When I was raising my two children twenty-some years ago, we simply didn't have all the cool stuff that kids have today to keep them happily plugged in indoors. We moved back and forth between a small city apartment and an old country farmhouse. Frogs visited our bathtub, hurt birds and dragonflies lived in cardboard boxes, and the kids and their friends played endless games through both city streets and open fields.

We never once thought, in those days of the late 1980s, "Oh, our children are playing outdoors." They just were. And aside from the usual squabbles and cut knees, the children seemed quite happy and absorbed. Today, Eric and Anna are busy with jobs and grown-up lives. But they still enjoy being outdoors and happily return to those outside places where they once played with their friends.

One day my kids put 15 green frogs in our bathtub!

So often, when I mention my childhood and that of my children, other adults chime in, "Oh, I used to hop on my bike after school and go off exploring. Why don't kids do that today?" Well, they can and they still do, but most kids are doing a great many other activities as well. Yet wherever I go, I find that kids still love being outdoors. They just need to be shown how. A curious adult can make a wonderful companion! Exploring nature with your child is easy, fun, inexpensive, and takes no special skills — just a little time and interest.

You can easily take a walk in the woods with your family, or write a poem about the moon with your granddaughter, or lie on your backs in a fresh pile of snow and make a snow angel, or climb a tree or build a fort. It's time to renew the practice of spending time outdoors as a family. I hope this book will become your companion in this exploration.

As a parent and a teacher, I know how hard it can be to find the time to be outdoors with a child or a class. We only have so many hours in the day and so many priorities filling them and often we have no reason to go outdoors. But time and time again, in talking with both parents and teachers, watching children, and noticing my own feelings, I realize that we are all happier and more relaxed after just 15 minutes outdoors. I'm sure you've noticed how eager and engaged children become while watching a hawk soar overhead, following deer tracks in the snow, or just running freely through an open field.

Our world is full of information that previous generations had to know when they lived closer to nature. These days, most people don't know the phases of the moon, or the times of the tides, or the names of birds. But all these things are still here to learn about, and knowing about them will help you and your children feel more a part of the world around you.

You might begin your nature study by reading Rachel Carson's inspirational book, *The Sense of Wonder*. She based much of her writing on the time she spent outside her home in Maine. Carson had a very important philosophy, which I share and teach by: "Wonder... leads to Curiosity... leads to Information... leads to Responsibility... leads to Action."

British primatologist and humanitarian Jane Goodall founded her successful Roots and Shoots Program, for kids of all ages, on this same premise. She says, "If people can see the beauty I see, then they will work to save the animals and trees that give them food and shelter." Go to *www.janegoodallinstitute.org* for more information.

And I highly recommend reading Richard Louv's book, *Last Child in the Woods* – he hits on so many important reasons for getting our kids back outdoors.

MENTORING OUR CHILDREN

This book is based on over 30 years of teaching nature study and nature journaling. There is much I have left out and much I still have to learn. My mother didn't know the names of many birds, but she was outside gardening while we were playing in the sandbox. Growing up, I didn't consider I was outdoors; I just was.

I am a teacher of nature in large part because I had a science teacher who took us bird watching, mushroom hunting, and scrambling through the "wild" woods and fields surrounding our countryside school in Pennsylvania. She was so interested in everything we saw, we just had to be also!

Today, as an educator who supposedly knows about "local nature," I am aware that I am being watched to see how I respond, what interests me, and how engaged I am in spotting a crow, looking at dandelions, or admiring a spider web. To both parents and teachers, I say, "You are mentors to your children. If you are sincerely interested in bats and show your kids why and have them learning about bats, I guarantee they will join you. Why? Because they want to do things with you, if your interest is true. If you are afraid, they will be too."

Children need vivid, extensive, structured but open-ended immersions in nature all year round, not just during summer vacations. And they need parents willing to save the stones they find in their children's pockets.

— DAVID SOBEL, "A POCKETFUL OF STONES," ORION MAGAZINE, 1993

Safety in Nature

For centuries, kids played in the woods, fields, and streams around their homes. They had adventures, learned about their surroundings, and probably got into trouble of some sort or another, but survived to tell the tale and become a bit wiser. Today, we shelter our children so much that for many of them, nature has become either boring or scary or almost invisible.

I've worked with children who have told me that they are "allergic to nature." One student wore gloves to be outdoors and another said his parents were cutting down all the trees on their property as he was allergic to pollen. One girl had a letter from her parents requesting that she stay indoors. She decided to go outdoors with her class anyway and soon I was watching her bending and touching and smelling and quite forgetting she was "allergic." (I love to imagine that today that child could be a park ranger!)

When our children want to explore their neighborhood, wander into shadowy woods, or ride their bikes off to a local pond, what are we adults afraid of? What do we instill in our children when we say to them, "Don't go far," "Watch out for strangers wherever you go," "Don't touch that," "Come home right away," and "Don't be out after dark"?

For many adults, the fear of the unknown and the feeling of not being in control makes us want to corral our children into controlled places and not let them loose in nature. I have learned the hard way that if you are to keep your child from being frightened of the outdoors (or of anything for that matter), you must confront your own fears. Children pick up very quickly on our fears and hesitations. It is critical to know what is important to fear and what is not. Nature is not full of booby traps! (As a parent, I had to learn this too.)

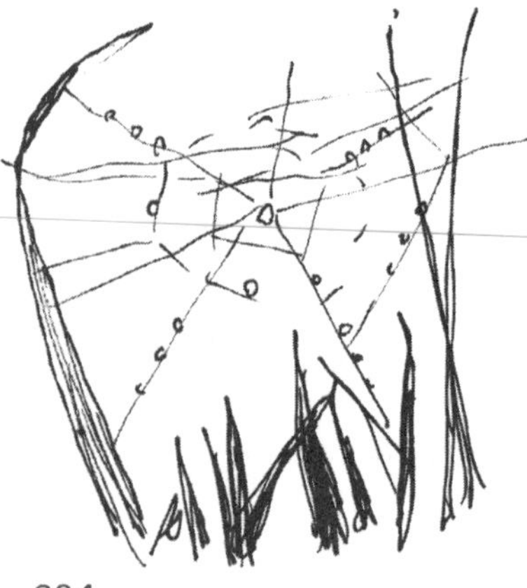

Here are a few simple tips for calming your own fears, as well as your child's, and making time outdoors enjoyable. These are ones I still use in my own teaching.

* **Go with your children the first few times;** on a nature hunt, hiking a nearby hill, or swimming in a pond. If they trip or fall or get a scratch, that's okay. Talk with them about their fears and sort out real from not real.
* **Tell them where they can and cannot play** and when you expect them to be home. Let them disappear into the yard, park, local woods to explore on their own and build the trust that they will come home. 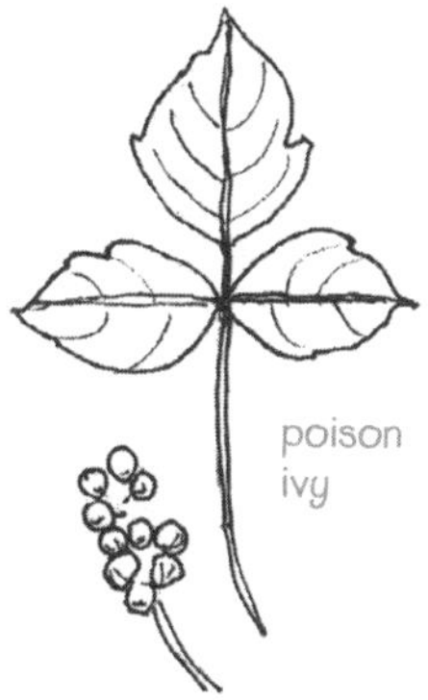
* **Learn with your child about poisonous plants, mushrooms, and berries** that grow in your area and how to identify and avoid them. Find out together by looking at guidebooks or online.

poison ivy

* **Talk to them about ticks** and, more important, do a tick check when they get home.
* **Teach them not to swat at bees or yellow jackets.** If you stand still, they will eventually go away. If they are allergic, learn what to do in case of a sting and carry the proper supplies with you. 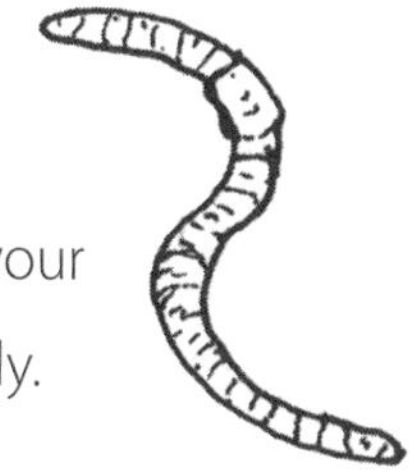
* **Gently pick up slugs, spiders, and worms to show that you're not afraid.** If you can't bring yourself to do that, at least don't discourage your child from touching, smelling, and experiencing nature more intimately.
* **Encourage curiosity with respect.** Some kids love to scatter ant nests or chase birds. They may need some extra help learning to sit and watch patiently.
* **Above all, have fun together outdoors** — even if you're just doing "nothing." And turn off your cell phones for just a little while!

How to Use Nature Journals in Your Teaching

Although I am primarily an artist, that is not my focus when I go into classrooms. My goal is to help kids (and teachers) observe, appreciate, and learn more about this beautiful world around them. The appeal of having your students keep nature journals is that it takes very little equipment to start and no specialized "nature knowledge" on your part. All you need is curiosity and the desire to go outdoors, explore the nature around you, and share your enthusiasm with your students. (For ways to fit nature study into your state curriculum standards, see pages 288–289.)

When I lead classes of any age, we first meet indoors and set up our notebooks with the date, time, place, weather, moon phase, and sunrise and sunset times. We share what we might see outside in this place, at this time of year. When we go outdoors, we have certain expectations — to start in silence and to walk for a little ways together just listening and watching. Then, the treasure hunt begins! What will we find just outside our door? When we find something, we record it.

A group may spend anywhere from 30 minutes to three days exploring — schoolyards, woodland edges, ponds, coastal beaches, mountain meadows, city lots. We draw simple images (I don't call them drawings), carefully documented, as on pages 44–45 and page 89. I draw with the group, drawing as they do, for no more than three minutes per image. We are looking for the whole picture, always asking, "What's happening in nature here and now?" and taking plenty of notes. We are scientists here, not artists!

Back indoors, drawing more carefully can take hours, depending on the group's age, interest, and intent. But I always recommend having on hand plenty of field guides and reference materials to foster continued interest and accurate learning.

FIELD TRIP TIPS

* **Keep it simple!** I recommend using whatever paper you have on hand — blank computer paper works fine — folded in half or into quarters. A piece of stiff cardboard or a clipboard supports the paper.

* **Use any type of pencils and make sure you have plenty** of sharpened extras.

* **Drawings should be done quickly and standing up so you can keep exploring.** Tell kids not to worry about making mistakes or erasing lines — just draw over or go on to the next thing.

* **Binoculars and magnifying glasses aren't necessary,** but can add to the experience if enough are available for the group to reasonably share. I often don't use them, as they can be distracting, especially with younger children.

  Consult page 9 for creating a complete nature adventure kit for longer outings.

IN THE CLASSROOM

* **Keep plenty of different writing and drawing supplies in the classroom** — sharp pencils (regular and colored), ballpoint and felt-tip pens, markers, crayons, watercolors. Many kids love to refine their sketches into finished drawings. I tell students not to worry about skill or talent. Like any skill, drawing well takes years of practice.

* **Keep the curiosity going** and you will have your class eager to go out with you season after season.

* **Create a library of good field guides to local birds, animals, trees, and plants.** Take one or two relevant ones along on your outing, but be aware that too many books can distract the class from just looking and seeing. There's plenty of time for further research once you're back in the classroom.

Using This Book to Meet State Curriculum Standards

We must draw our standards from our natural world . . .
We must honor with the humility of the wise
the bounds of that natural world
and the mystery which lies beyond them,
admitting that there is something in the order of being
which evidently exceeds all our competence.

— VACLAV HAVEL, *LIVING IN TRUTH*

With changes happening more and more rapidly to our global ecosystem, it is becoming increasingly vital that our children learn about nature right around them so that they can grow up to protect it responsibly and actively. Despite this urgent need, teachers and parents are also understandably concerned that subjects taught in school comply with state and federal testing standards. A study of the environment is critical to our children's education and can fit with any academic subject. Increasingly, state science standards are expanding to include local nature study. As one eleventh-grade student said to me, "We depend on nature, so we need to know something about it."

I have been using the methods gathered in this book for decades in my teaching, adapting both to meet the needs of different grade levels (from elementary through college), classroom settings, and curriculum requirements. This book is designed to be flexible and wide-ranging so that it can be used in a variety of ways while always keeping the focus on our connection to the wide world around us. State standards vary, of course, but here are some ways in which this book can address some widely accepted requirements for learning.

Earth Science

Pursuing scientific inquiry: asking how, what, why, and where
Doing scientific research: observing, recording, measuring
Learning about nature: sky, weather, seasons, trees and plants, animals, habitats and watersheds

Social Studies

Learning local history: explorers, pioneers, land use
Discussing environmental issues: local, national, global
Making maps and murals

Math

Applying concepts: maps, charts, graphs, listing
Quantifying information: measuring, comparing, counting

Language Arts

Writing: note taking, record keeping, telling stories, writing poems, plays, fiction and nonfiction
Reading: nature literature (fiction and nonfiction), oral reports
Communication: asking questions, formulating theories, gathering information, problem-solving
Learning to focus: paying attention, listening in a group

Art and Music

Observing: learning to see and record accurately
Drawing: fundamental drawing skills applied, students encouraged to work in own style using a variety of media, building confidence in skills, working together
Listening: learning to hear what is happening in nature, making sounds with natural objects, learning to be quiet

Physical Activity

Being outdoors: learning free play, becoming comfortable with nature and oneself
Getting exercise: walking, hiking, running, skipping, health and physical fitness

Bibliography and Suggested Reading

Many of these books may seem old, but they are still very useful. Of course, there are many other equally good and helpful books out there, depending on what you are looking for. I am giving you only the tip of my iceberg — my own glacial pile of resources — many of which I used in writing this book.

GENERAL REFERENCES

Christianson, Stephen G., ed. *The American Book of Days*. New York: H.W. Wilson, 2000.

Comstock, Anna B. *Handbook of Nature Study*. Ithaca, New York: Cornell University Press, 1986.

Durrell, Gerald and Lee Durrell. *The Amateur Naturalist.* New York: Knopf Doubleday, 1989.

Lagasse, Paul, ed. *The Columbia Encyclopedia*, 6th ed. New York: Columbia University Press, 2000.

National Geographic Society. *The Curious Naturalist*. Washington, DC: National Geographic Society, 1998.

The Old Farmer's Almanac. Dublin, New Hampshire: Yankee Publishing Inc., published yearly.

Editors of *Reader's Digest*. *Joy of Nature: How to Observe and Appreciate the Great Outdoors.* Pleasantville, New York: Reader's Digest Association, 1977.

Editors of *Reader's Digest*. *North American Wildlife: An Illustrated Guide to 2,000 Plants and Animals*. Pleasantville, New York: Reader's Digest Association, 1998.

Palmer, E. Laurence and Horatio Seymour Folwer. *The Fieldbook of Natural History*. New York: McGraw-Hill Company, 1978.

FIELD GUIDES

Alden, Peter. ***Peterson First Guide to Mammals of North America***. Boston: Houghton Mifflin. 1987. There are other books in this series, by other authors: ***Trees***, ***Insects***, ***Reptiles*** and ***Amphibians***, ***Fish***, etc.

The Audubon Society Nature Guides. New York: Knopf, dates vary. This is a series on different habitats: deserts, grasslands, Pacific Coast, Atlantic Coast, eastern forests, wetlands, etc.

Brown, Lauren. ***Weeds in Winter***. New York: W.W. Norton, 1986.

Burris, Judy and Wayne Richards. ***The Life Cycles of Butterflies***. North Adams: Storey Publishing. 2006.

The **Golden Guide** series. New York: St. Martin's Press, dates vary. This series of small nature books is inexpensive, full of useful information, nicely illustrated, good for classroom and day pack.

Ludlum, Donald M., Ronald L. Holle, and Richard A. Keen. ***National Audubon Society Pocket Guide to Clouds and Storms***. New York: Alfred A. Knopf, 1995. Look for other guides in this series: ***Familiar Mammals, North American Birds of Prey, Insects,*** and more.

Peterson, Roger Tory and Margaret McKenny. ***Peterson Field Guides to Wildflowers: Northeastern/North-central North America***. Boston: Houghton Mifflin, 1998.

Petrides, George A. and Janet Wehr. ***Peterson Field Guides to Eastern Trees.*** Boston: Houghton Mifflin, 1998.

Robbins, Chandler S., Bertel Bruun, and Herbert S. Zim. ***Birds of North America.*** New York: Golden Press, 1983.

Stokes, Donald W. ***A Guide to Nature in Winter.*** Boston: Little, Brown & Co., 1998.

Sibley, David. ***The Sibley Guide to Trees.*** New York: Alfred A. Knopf, 2009.

NATURE EDUCATION

Art, Henry W. and Michael W. Robbins. ***WoodsWalk.*** North Adams, Massachusetts: Storey Publishing, 2003.

Cornell, Joseph Bharat. ***Sharing Nature with Children.*** Nevada City, California: Dawn Publications, 1998.

Katz, Adrienne. ***Naturewatch.*** Reading, Massachusetts: Addison-Wesley, 1986.

Kirkland, Jane. ***Take A City Nature Walk.*** Lionville, Pennsylvania: Stillwater Publishing, 2005.

Kowalski, Kathiann M. ***The Everything Kids' Nature Book***. Holbrook, Massachusetts: Adams Media Corporation, 2000.

Louv, Richard. ***Last Child in the Woods.*** Chapel Hill, North Carolina: Algonquin, 2008.

Mitchell, John and The Massachusetts Audubon Society. ***The Curious Naturalist.*** Amherst, Massachusetts: University of Massachusetts Press, 1996.

Nabhan, Gary Paul and Stephen Trimble. ***The Geography of Childhood.*** Boston: Beacon Press, 1994.

Parrella, Deborah. ***Shelburne Farms: Project Seasons***. Shelburne, Vermont: Shelburne Farms, 1995.

Russell, Helen Ross. ***Ten Minute Field Trips.*** Arlington, Virginia: NSTA Press, 2001.

Sobel, David. ***Childhood and Nature.*** Portland, Maine: Stenhouse Publishers, 2008.

Ward, Jennifer. ***I Love Dirt.*** Boston: Trumpeter, 2008.

Young, Jon, Ellen Haas, and Evan McGown. ***Coyote's Guide to Connecting with Nature***. Shelton, Washington: OWLLink Media, 2008.

CLIMATE CHANGE

Calhoun, Yael. ***The Environment in the News***. New York: Chelsea House, 2007.

Dow, Kirsten and Thomas E. Downing. ***The Atlas of Climate Change***. Berkley, California: University of California Press, 2006.

Gore, Al. ***An Inconvenient Truth***. New York: Rodale, 2006.

Knauer, Kelly, ed. ***Global Warming.*** New York: Time, 2007.

Kolbert, Elizabeth. ***Field Notes from a Catastrophe: Man, Nature, and Climate Change.*** New York: Bloomsbury USA, 2006.

NATURE ARTISTS AND NATURALISTS

Barlowe, Dorothea and Sy Barlowe. ***Illustrating Nature***. New York: Portland House, 1987.

Borland, Hal. ***The History of Wildlife in America***. Washington, D.C.: National Wildlife Federation, 1975. Contains illustrations and paintings by Merriweather Lewis and William Clark, John James Audubon, Albert Bierstadt, Thomas Moran, Charlie Russell, and Thomas Cole.

Busby, John. ***Drawing Birds***. Bedfordshire, England: The Royal Society for the Protection of Birds, 1986.

Carson, Rachel. ***The Edge of the Sea***. Boston: Houghton Mifflin, 1998.

Davis, Harry. ***The Art of Tasha Tudor***. Boston: Little, Brown, and Co., 2000.

Hobbs, Anne Stevenson. ***Beatrix Potter's Art: Paintings and Drawings***. London: Frederick Warne, 2004.

Holden, Edith. ***The Nature Notes of an Edwardian Lady***. New York: Arcade Publishing, 1989.

McLuhan, T.C. ***Touch the Earth: A Self Portrait of Indian Existence***. New York: Outerbridge and Dienstfrey, 1971.

Nice, Claudia. ***How to Keep A Sketchbook Journal***. Cincinnati, Ohio: North Light Books, 2001.

Wilson. Edward O. ***Naturalist***. Washington, DC: Island Press, 1994.

Wright-Frierson, Virginia. ***A Desert Scrapbook***. New York: Simon & Schuster, 1996.

———. ***An Island Scrapbook***. New York: Simon & Schuster, 1998.

SEASONAL CELEBRATIONS

Barth, Edna. ***Holly, Reindeer, and Colored Lights***. New York: Clarion Books, 2000.

———. ***Lilies, Rabbits, and Painted Eggs.*** New York: Clarion Books, 2001.

———. ***Witches, Pumpkins, and Grinning Ghosts***. New York: Clarion Books, 2000.

Baylor, Byrd. ***I'm in Charge of Celebrations***. New York: Aladdin Paperbacks, 1995.

Carmichael, Alexander, ed. ***Carmina Gadelica: Hymns and Incantations***. Edinburgh: Floris Books, 1992.

Christianson, Stephen G., ed. ***The American Book of Days***. New York: H.W. Wilson, 2000.

Frasier, Debra. ***On The Day You Were Born.*** New York: Harcourt Brace, 1991.

SUGGESTED BOOKS FOR KIDS

Atkins, Jeannine: *Girls Who Looked Under Rocks*

Azarian, Mary: *When the Moon Is Full*

Bash, Barbara: *Urban Roosts*

Bruchac, Joseph: *The Thirteen Moons on Turtle's Back and Keeper of the Animals* (with Michael Caduto)

Burnett, Frances Hodgson: *The Secret Garden*

Calhoun, Mary: *Cross-Country Cat*

Cleary, Beverly: *The Mouse and the Motor-cycle*, *Runaway Ralph*, and *Ralph S. Mouse*

Conrad, Pam: *Pedro's Journal: A Voyage With Christopher Columbus*

Deedy, Carmen Agra: *Agatha's Feather Bed: Not Just another Wild Goose Chase*

De Gerez, Toni: *Louhi, Witch of North Farm*

George, Jean Craighead: *Dear Rebecca, Winter Is Here*; *Julie of the Wolves*; *My Side of the Mountain*; *Frightful's Mountain*; *The Talking Earth*

Grahame, Kenneth. *The Wind in the Willows*

Hannigan, Katherine: *Ida B. and Her Plans to Maximize Fun, Avoid Disaster and (Possibly) Save the World*

Jacques, Brian: *Redwall* series

Holling, Clancy: *Holling Paddle to the Sea* and *Seabird*

Lawson, Robert: *Rabbit Hill*

Maxwell, Gavin: *Ring of Bright Water*

Mazer, Anne: *The Salamander Room*

McLerran, Alice: *Roxaboxen*

Milne, A.A.: *Winnie the Pooh* and *The House at Pooh Corner*

Morrison, Gordon: *Nature In The Neighborhood*

Mowat, Farley: *Never Cry Wolf*

Paulsen, Gary: *Hatchet* and many others

Pearson, Susan: *My Favorite Time of Year*

Pollock, Penny: *When The Moon Is Full*

Pringle, Laurence: *An Extraordinary Life: The Story of a Monarch Butterfly*

Rowling, J. K.: *Harry Potter* series

Sams II, Carl and Jean Stoick: *Lost In The Woods*

Svedberg, Ulf: *Nicky The Nature Detective*

White, E.B.: *Charlotte's Web*, *The Trumpet of the Swan*, and *Stuart Little*

Wilder, Laura Ingalls: *The Little House* series

Wright-Frierson, Virginia: *An Island Scrapbook* and *A Desert Scrapbook*

Yolen, Jane: *Owl Moon*

FOR ADVANCED READERS

Carson, Rachel: *The Sense of Wonder*

Dillard, Annie: *Pilgrim at Tinker Creek*

Ehrlich, Gretel: *The Solace of Open Spaces*

Finch, Robert and John Elder: *Nature Writing: The Tradition in English*

Hay, John: *In Defense of Nature*

Lear, Linda: *Beatrix Potter: A Life in Nature*

Leopold, Aldo: *A Sand County Almanac*

Oliver, Mary: *New and Selected Poems*

Pyle, Robert M: *The Thunder Tree*

Roberts, Elizabeth and Elias Amidon: *Earth Prayers From Around the World*

Williams, Terry: *Tempest: Refuge*

Other Resources

NATIONAL AND STATE ORGANIZATIONS

Appalachian Mountain Club
800-372-1758
www.outdoors.org
Programs for families, teens, kids: Youth Opportunities Program, Family Adventure Camps, and Teen Wilderness Adventures.

Boy Scouts of America
www.scouting.org
They are doing a lot with kids to get them outdoors. A good resource.

Canadian Geographic
800-267-0824
www.canadiangeographic.ca
Publishes *Canadian Geographic,* an out-of-the USA perspective on the environment, from polar bears to urban green spaces.

Children, Nature and You
http://childrennatureandyou.org
Helping parents and educators foster a bond between children and nature; part of "Hooked on Nature," a network of individuals and organizations dedicated to instilling children with a love and respect for Earth.

Cornell Lab of Ornithology
800-843-2473
www.birds.cornell.edu
Publishes *Living Bird*, and the newsletter, *Birdscope,* and offers great programs for kids and adults.

Ducks Unlimited
800-453-8257
www.ducks.org
A venerable and respected conservation organization protecting thousands of acres of waterfowl and wildlife habitat around the country.

Environmental Defense Fund
800-684-3322
www.edf.org
Dedicated to protecting the environmental rights of all people, including future generations.

International Dark-Sky Association
520-293-3198
www.darksky.org
Preserving and protecting the nighttime environment through environmentally responsible outdoor lighting.

The Jane Goodall Institute
703-682-9220
www.janegoodall.org
A global nonprofit that builds on Dr. Goodall's scientific work and her humanitarian vision to empower people to make a difference for all living things.

National Audubon Society
212-979-3000
www.audubon.org
Publishes *Audubon*. Runs nature centers and natural history camps for all ages around the country.

National Ocean Service
National Oceanic and Atmospheric Administration
http://oceanservice.noaa.gov
The NOS education team supports teacher infusion of NOS content into local curricula through professional development opportunities at conferences and through Web-based avenues.

National Parks and Conservation Association
800-628-7275
www.npca.org
Publishes *National Parks* with information on our national parks, places you can visit, conservation organizations near you, and their programs.

National Weather Service
National Oceanic and Atmospheric Administration
www.nws.noaa.gov
Offers many educational resources on weather and climate.

National Wildlife Federation
800-822-9919
www.nwf.org
Publishes *National Wildlife* (excellent articles and photos for middle school and up), *Ranger Rick*, *Your Big Backyard* and *Wild Animal Baby*. Programs include Schoolyard Habitats, Campus Ecology, and the Great American Backyard Campout.

The Orion Society
413-528-4422
www.orionsociety.org
Publishes a magazine *Orion* which has essays by contemporary writers and artists on the environment.

Real School Gardens
817-348-8102
www.realschoolgardens.org
An organization based on getting ongoing gardens into elementary schools.

The Sierra Club
415-977-5500
www.sierraclub.org
Publishes the magazine *Sierra* which has interesting articles and guided trips throughout the United States and abroad. Some are for families.

Teton Science Schools
307-733-1313
www.tetonscience.org
Teaching about the natural world and the Greater Yellowstone Ecosystem since 1967 through a variety of programs for children, youth, and adults.

Project FeederWatch
Cornell Lab of Ornithology
800-843-2473
www.birds.cornell.edu/pfw
A winter-long survey of birds by people all over North America. The data help scientists track long-term trends in bird distribution and abundance.

Sharing Nature Worldwide
530-478-7650
www.sharingnature.com
Activities and ideas for teaching nature from Joseph Cornell, author of Sharing Nature with Children.

The Trust for Public Land
800-714-5263
www.tpl.org
Engages people of all ages in land conservation. Publishes *Land&People* which is full of hopeful stories.

U.S. Fish and Wildlife Service
www.fws.gov
There are different websites for each state.

Urban Ecology Institute
617-552-1247
www.urbaneco.org
Based out of Boston, Massachusetts; works to engage urban youth in learning about local birds and local ecology.

Valley Quest
802-291-9100
www.vitalcommunities.org/ValleyQuest
A place-based education model of creating and exchanging treasure hunts in order to collect and share your community's distinct natural and cultural heritage.

Wilderness Awareness School
425-788-1301
http://wildernessawareness.org
Offers wilderness education courses that combine ancient and modern ecological wisdom, and empower people of all ages to become stewards, mentors, and leaders.

World Meteorological Organization
www.wmo.int
Global organization with resources on weather, climate, and water.

ESPECIALLY FOR KIDS

Acorn Naturalists
800-422-8886
www.acornnaturalists.com
This is one of the best catalogues of books and activities for nature study, for all ages. A great resource!

The Center for Education, Imagination and the Natural World
www.beholdnature.org
Engages small children in wonder outdoors.

Children & Nature Network
www.childrenandnature.org
Inspired by Richard Louv's important book, *Last Child in the Woods*. This is an online resource site with lots of information about what is being done and where.

Cricket Magazine Group
www.cricketmag.com
Produces 14 different magazines for curious kids of all ages. All are free of advertising and several (*Ask*, *Muse*, and *Odyssey*) focus on science and exploration.

For Spacious Skies
www.forspaciousskies.com
A program aimed at educating children to look up and become aware of the sky.

Journey North
www.journeynorth.org
A fascinating site, devoted to monthly phenology observations for the classroom. Packed with information, maps, and photographs.

NASA Eclipse Web Site
http://eclipse.gsfc.nasa.gov

National Geographic Society
www.kids.nationalgeographic.com
Website has activities, games, stories, and other information. The Society publishes *National Geographic Kids* for ages 6-14.

Roger Tory Peterson Institute of Natural History
www.rtpi.org
Has classes in nature and literature for all ages.

World Wide Waldens
www.worldwidewaldens.org
Involves school kids in environmental projects having to do with where they live.

Index

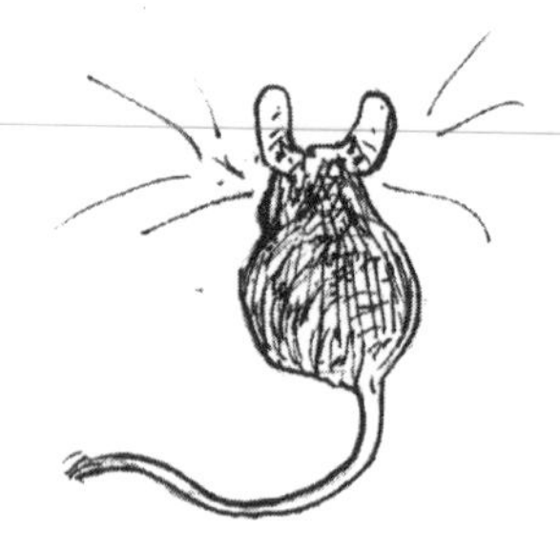

OTHER BOOKS BY CLARE WALKER LESLIE

The Ancient Celtic Festivals and How We Celebrate Them Today. Rochester, Vermont: Inner Traditions, 2000.

The Art of Field Sketching. Dubuque, Iowa: Kendall/Hunt Publishing, 1995.

Drawn to Nature Through the Journals of Clare Walker Leslie. North Adams, Massachusetts: Storey Publishing, 2005.

Keeping a Nature Journal. North Adams, Massachusetts: Storey Publishing, 2003.

Nature All Year Long. Dubuque, Iowa: Kendall/Hunt Publishing, 2002.

Nature Drawing: A Tool for Learning. Dubuque, Iowa: Kendall/Hunt Publishing, 1995.

Nature Journal: A Guided Journal. North Adams, Massachusetts: Storey Publishing, 2004.

Other Storey Titles You Will Enjoy

Catch the Wind, Harness the Sun, by Michael J. Caduto.
More than 20 exciting activities and experiments focused on renewable energy.
224 pages. Paper. ISBN 978-1-60342-794-4. Hardcover. 978-7-60342-971-9.

The Family Butterfly Book, by Rick Mikula.
Projects, activities, and profiles to celebrate 40 favorite North American species.
176 pages. Paper. ISBN 978-1-58017-292-9. Hardcover. ISBN 978-1-58017-335-3.

Keeping a Nature Journal, by Clare Walker Leslie & Charles E. Roth.
Simple methods for capturing the living beauty of each season.
224 pages. Paper with flaps. ISBN 978-1-58017-493-0.

The Life Cycles of Butterflies, by Judy Burris & Wayne Richards.
A visual guide, rich in photographs, showing 23 common backyard butterflies from egg to maturity. Winner of the 2007 Teachers' Choice Children's Book Award!
160 pages. Paper. ISBN 978-1-58017-617-0.
Hardcover with jacket. ISBN 978-1-58017-618-7.

Nature's Art Box, by Laura C. Martin.
Cool projects for crafty kids to make with natural materials.
224 pages. Paper. ISBN 978-1-58017-490-9.

The Secret Lives of Backyard Bugs,
by Judy Burris and Wayne Richards.
A one-of-a-kind look at amazing butterflies, moths, spiders, dragonflies, and other insects.
136 pages. Paper. ISBN 978-1-60342-563-6.

These and other books from Storey Publishing are available wherever quality books are sold or by calling 1-800-441-5700.
Visit us at *www.storey.com.*